STRATEGIC WATER

IRAQ AND SECURITY PLANNING IN THE EUPHRATES-TIGRIS BASIN

Frederick Lorenz and Edward J. Erickson

Marine Corps University Press
Quantico, Virginia

DISCLAIMER

The views expressed in this publication are solely those of the authors. They do not necessarily reflect the opinions of the organizations for which they work, Marine Corps University, the U.S. Marine Corps, the Department of the Navy, or the U.S. Government. The information and Web site addresses contained in this book were accurate at the time of printing.

Published by

Marine Corps University Press

3078 Upshur Avenue

Quantico, VA

22134

www.mcu.usmc.mil/mcu_press

1st Printing, 2014

PCN 10600009500

ISBN 978-0-9911588-0-5

Contents

FOREWORD

After the final phase of drawdown of U.S. troops in Iraq, it is important to do what we can to help maintain a level of stability and to look ahead to emerging security threats. *Strategic Water: Iraq and Security Planning in the Euphrates-Tigris Basin* by Frederick Lorenz and Edward J. Erickson makes an important contribution to this effort by taking a close look at a serious problem that is often neglected—the decline in freshwater availability and its impact on regional security. With convincing authority, the authors make it clear that the situation in Iraq is deteriorating much faster than expected, and in a few years much of Iraq's water supply will be undrinkable, largely due to high salinity levels. This book not only predicts a crisis, it provides some details on what that crisis might look like: an ugly mix of human suffering, governmental instability, population movement, and a rise in extremist violence. Despite the fact that the United States may have less influence in Iraq in the short term, we cannot deny that it remains a vital U.S. interest to keep the region secure. And there are things that can be done in the short term to help avoid the worst-case scenario.

Environmental security is an emerging mission for the U.S. military; for these nontraditional missions, we need problem solvers and innovators. We have to constantly look beyond the short-term problems and try to identify the security issues that will become critical in the years ahead. In the Euphrates-Tigris basin we have an extraordinary situation when the actions of our NATO ally, Turkey, might negatively impact the water supply in the country we have worked so hard to stabilize, Iraq. Ineffective water management from a lack of experience and a lack of modern technology is only part of the problem. Cultural barriers exist to efficient water use, and Islamic tradition tells us that water should not be sold or controlled. As we look to each new crisis, there seems to be an underlying element of water or resource scarcity that seems to make the problem unsolvable.

This book not only identifies a threat that is not often analyzed, it also makes detailed recommendations on how to deal with it effectively. In the final chapter, Lorenz and Erickson prioritize what needs to be done and describe the relative cost and probable chance of success for each option. For each alternative, they provide a definition of "success" and the probable impact if progress is made. Two key recommendations are emphasized: the need for better coordination of our efforts and more effective use of technology—the science and diplomacy linkage.

The U.S. military's budget is now in full retreat, and the amount of resources available for foreign aid will be in steady decline in the next few years. But the problems of water scarcity and the resulting instability in the Middle East will certainly be on the rise. Our nation will face some difficult choices in the years ahead, and this book contains the type of analysis that our leaders should embrace. It should be required reading for those who recognize the strategic importance of Iraq and want to understand the emerging water scarcity threat.

General Anthony C. Zinni, USMC (Ret.)

PREFACE

As we write this preface in the summer of 2013, the Arab world continues to be shaken by unrest and political instability, with no clear resolution in sight. In two countries critical to our study—Syria and Iraq—the changes are swift and present major challenges to U.S. foreign policy. The government of Syria has defied international efforts to help resolve an increasingly deadly conflict. Many predict the Syrian government will soon fall, but the Assad regime has shown surprising resiliency. In Iraq there are signs of economic development, but underlying divisions within the government, sectarian attacks, and corruption remain obstacles to progress.

This book is about water security in a broad context and is much more than a simple discussion of access to water. The National Intelligence Council recently issued a report noting that water challenges could trigger social disruption, and in some states where other stressors exist, state failure is possible. In the Middle East, water security is closely entwined with political stability, and it will become increasingly important to U.S. national interests. This work is designed to focus attention on Iraq and to make detailed recommendations on what can be done to assist.

Political instability in Syria and Iraq will undoubtedly complicate the picture described within these pages, and perhaps delay the time when the regimes can effectively deal with water issues. Yet the fundamental assumptions, analysis, and recommendations in this book remain un-changed, despite the fast-paced changes in the region. Water scarcity and insecurity will be driven by inevitable demographic and hydrolog-ical factors that can be predicted with some degree of certainty. Action needs to be taken soon, well before the regional political situation is fully resolved.

Acknowledgments

This project began in 1997 with funding from the U.S. Air Force Institute for National Security Studies while the authors were on active duty and Frederick Lorenz was on the faculty of the National Defense University. This initial grant was used for travel to the region and a research project that was published in 1999 by National Defense University Press as *The Euphrates Triangle: Security Implications of the Southeastern Anatolia Project.* In that publication, we benefited from the assistance of Brian R. Shaw, Aaron T. Wolf, and John F. Kolars, and we have tried to build on that foundation as we prepared this book.

In 2004 and 2005, we were again able to travel to the region with funding from the U.S. Department of Defense and the U.S. European Command. We would like to thank the staff of the U.S. embassies in Ankara, Turkey; Damascus, Syria; and Baghdad, Iraq, for their assistance in arranging travel and making contacts in the local area. We are indebted to Dr. J. A. "Tony" Allan, whose groundbreaking research and writing had a major influence on this book. Over the past four years, students in the Water and Security in the Middle East course and faculty at the Jackson School of International Studies at the University of Washington in Seattle made valuable comments on early drafts of this work.

We are also indebted to our editor, Shawn Vreeland, for his superb attention to detail and his suggestions on making this a better book. This book has been "a long time coming," and Shawn's continued support and stick-to-it attitude have been instrumental in seeing it through to publication. We also thank our graphic designer, Rob Kocher, for his creative layout and design suggestions.

INTRODUCTION
WATER AND THE FUTURE OF IRAQ

"And its water was dried up"

Although the title of this section comes from the book of Revelation 16:12 ("Then the sixth angel poured out his bowl on the great river Euphrates, and its water was dried up"), it is meant neither as a prediction nor as a prophecy. As a matter of course, in today's world a river does not have to actually "dry up" to affect people's lives. Water may be diverted for industrial, agricultural, or domestic needs. Rivers may be so polluted by human activities as to become nonpotable or clinically "dead." Aquifers may become depleted or unusable due to high salt or chemical levels. Excessive damming of rivers may lead to microclimate change, siltation, and habitat disturbances. In fact, it is rare for rivers to dry up, but some once-mighty rivers—such as the Jordan and the Colorado—have no discernible outflow at their terminus today and have effectively "dried up." Human interventions, usage, and diversions have already altered the flow of the earth's waters in significant ways, and the impact is not yet fully understood. We do know for a fact, however, that water scarcity, from whatever the cause, drives poverty, contributes to malnutrition, and lowers standards of living—all of which serve as sources of instability and insecurity.

Issues of water scarcity have always been of vital concern to humans, and water in the modern world is increasingly characterized as a strategic issue.[1] But water is unique and more than a strategic resource such as oil, gas, or mineral wealth; it is inherently unstable in quantity and quality. Throughout this book, the authors use the term *strategic water* to help refine our understanding of water as an unstable and critical element in the strategic context. Strategic water can be on the surface, in the ground, and even in the soil. It is variable from year to year, difficult to quantify, and often unpredictable. It may be measured in a variety of ways, including volume, quality, and accessibility. It is affected by both nature and by human use, and when it flows across national borders, each state will develop its own claims based on concepts of national sovereignty. Strategic water therefore presents major challenges at national and international levels. Thus, we might define *strategic water* as an unpredictable resource with profound effects on the human condition that is soon to become a problem of major concern.

This is not a book about predictions but rather an attempt to apply current research and knowledge of how water scarcity might cause instability in a volatile region of the world. It is written from the perspective of the year 2013 with the understanding that the human landscape and natural environment may change dramatically in the space of a few short years. The authors hope that the observations and recommendations in this book will serve as a platform for further work and analysis. Is it likely that the Euphrates-Tigris River system will dry up? Certainly not, but it seems certain that within the next 10 to 20 years that the water usage and demand by the riparian nations of Turkey, Syria, and Iraq will exceed the supplies. Increased levels of pollution will make the management of the limited supply of Euphrates-Tigris water even more difficult for the nations that rely on it. The riparian nation that will be most affected by the impending crisis is the one farthest downstream—Iraq.

---

[1] "Strategy" refers to a plan of action designed to achieve a particular goal; it is of military origin, deriving from the Greek word *strategos*.

The Future Security Environment

The problems of climate change and decreasing water resources have emerged in the twenty-first century as key issues in the future security environment. A recent intelligence estimate predicted that in the next 10 years "water problems will contribute to instability in states important to U.S. national security interests."[2] While there may be lingering debate regarding the question of "global warming," the Defense Department recognizes that climate change will affect U.S. security interests in several ways, one of which is that climate change will shape the operating environment, roles, and missions that the department undertakes. Of particular concern are physical changes such as "increases in heavy downpours, rising temperatures and sea level, rapidly retreating glaciers, thawing permafrost, lengthening growing seasons, lengthening ice-free seasons in the oceans and on lakes and rivers, earlier snowmelt, and *alterations in river flows*" (italics added).[3] These changes, in turn, must then drive assessments of the geopolitical impacts that climate change might have around the world, as these changes contribute to poverty, environmental degradation, and the further weakening of fragile governments. According to the Department of Defense, "Climate change will contribute to food and water scarcity, will increase the spread of disease, and may spur or exacerbate mass migration."[4] The report further noted that "while climate change alone does not cause conflict, it may act as an accelerant of instability or conflict."[5] In sum, according to the U.S. government, climate, water, and food production are interrelated issues of strategic concern.

---

[2] Office of the Director of National Intelligence, *Global Water Security* (2012), iii, http://www.dni.gov/files/documents/Special%20Report_ICA%20Global%20Water%20Security.pdf.

[3] U.S. Department of Defense, *Quadrennial Defense Review Report* (Washington, DC: U.S. Department of Defense, 2010), 84, http://www.defense.gov/qdr/images/QDR_as_of_12Feb10_1000.pdf.

[4] Ibid.

[5] See also Christine Parthemore and Will Rogers, *Promoting the Dialogue: Climate Change and the Quadrennial Defense Review*, working paper (Washington, DC: Center for New American Security, 2010).

The *Marine Corps Vision and Strategy 2025* refines this thinking and identifies water scarcity as a threat to the future security environment.[6] Moreover, this document notes that "by 2025, more than half the global population will live under water stressed or water scarce conditions." A recent article in the *Economist* illustrates this by pointing out that the 2000 world population of six billion has increased by almost a billion today and is predicted to peak around nine billion in 2050.[7] Unfortunately, the overall increase in population belies the real problem that the proportion of people living in countries chronically short of water will rise from 8 percent in 2000 to 45 percent in 2050. It is certain that one region of particular geostrategic interest that will experience increased water scarcity in the future is the Euphrates-Tigris River system, the basin of which overlays an area of preexisting instability and includes the countries of Iran, Iraq, Syria, and Turkey.

Of particular concern to the United States and the world community is Iraq, which has drawn the attention of the world since the first Gulf War in 1991. Since the 2003 invasion, the international community has devoted a tremendous amount of effort and resources to Iraq's reconstruction. With the primary emphasis on security and rebuilding infrastructure, the challenges have been formidable and well documented. The United States remains committed to the goal of a sovereign, stable, and self-reliant Iraq.[8] However, another threat has been often overlooked, one that will become increasingly important in the years ahead. Iraq heavily depends on the waters of the Euphrates and Tigris Rivers, the sources of which come primarily from outside its own borders. More recent American assessments

---

[6] U.S. Marine Corps, *Marine Corps Vision and Strategy 2025* (Washington, DC: Headquarters Marine Corps, [2008?]), 20, http://www.marines.mil/Portals/59/Publications /Vision%20Strat%20lo%20res.pdf.

[7] *Economist*, "For Want of a Drink: Special Report on Water," 22 May 2010, 3, http://www .economist.com/specialreports?page=2&year[value][year]=2010&category=All.

[8] President of the United States, *National Security Strategy* (Washington, DC: the White House, 2010), 25, http://www.whitehouse.gov/sites/default/files/rss_viewer/national _security_strategy.pdf.

reflect an increasing awareness of this issue.[9] Turkey continues to build a series of dams and agriculture infrastructure that will significantly affect water quantity and quality in both Syria and Iraq. Moreover, the semiautonomous Kurdish Regional Government in northern Iraq is determined to develop both oil and water resources free from the central government's control. Without a plan to preserve the long-term strategic water for Iraq, and without decisive action, any gains in the security or economic sphere in Iraq may be lost. A number of measures are possible to avert a crisis, including the formation of an international commission or regional initiative for the Euphrates-Tigris basin. The United States and the international community have the capacity to assist Iraq in terms of technology and training to manage its own water resources. A detailed examination of options will be made later in this book. With the right support, the people of the basin can begin to move towards cooperation rather than conflict with regard to their water resources, and this will ultimately help to preserve the fragile gains in Iraq that are so essential to regional stability. To this end, this book seeks to tie an assessment of the current state of hydropolitics in the Euphrates-Tigris basin into a framework for action that would reduce the risk of instability in the region.

Water as a Regional Issue

Water covers nearly three-quarters of the earth's surface, but less than one percent is "fresh," and that amount is unevenly distributed. It is abundant in humid regions, but arid and semiarid regions are afflicted with a chronic shortage. As the world's population rapidly expands, water deficiencies have become particularly noticeable in arid regions such as the Middle East. Dams and river diversions have provided irrigation and hydropower benefits, but at the price of dislocating native peoples and causing significant environmental damage. When rivers cross international boundaries the most difficult questions arise: who is entitled to the

---

[9] See, for example, the Director of National Intelligence's news release, "Assessment on Global Water Security," from 22 March 2012, which identifies the Euphrates-Tigris basin as a strategically important area threatened by water challenges. Available online at http://www .dni.gov/index.php/newsroom/press-releases/96-press-releases-2012/529-odni-releases -global-water-security-ica.

water, and how can downstream countries be protected? International law provides little guidance on these questions, for reasons that will be explained in chapter 6.

The available supply of global freshwater is certain to decrease as a growing population and new demands strain hydrologic systems. Concern has also risen as to the declining water quality caused by human impacts. But the question of whether there will be enough clean water to support the world's population in 20 years is controversial. In terms of U.S. security policy, the question of the potential for conflict over water has become increasingly important. For example, should the United States be prepared to defend its North Atlantic Treaty Organization (NATO) partner Turkey in a conflict over the waters of the Euphrates and Tigris?[10] If there is a potential for conflict, what can be done to reduce the threat?

Water and Security

The question of water and conflict is receiving increased attention from scholars and policy makers. Most agree that the last time two nations went to war exclusively over water was about 4,500 years ago, when the Sumerian city-states of Lagash and Umma fought a border dispute.[11] But there is a long history of water playing a role in conflict; the chronology written by Peter H. Gleick of the Pacific Institute is the most comprehensive listing.[12] The chronology is regularly updated, and the most recent events are generally attributed to terrorism, including the 2003 bombing of a water supply pipeline in Iraq. Although water has rarely been the primary factor in war, there is an emerging consensus that the likelihood of conflict over water will increase in the next 20 years "as countries press against the limits of available water."[13] The Pacific Institute developed a new format

---

[10] The NATO charter makes this a relevant concern, with article 5 binding the parties to collective defense.

[11] Aaron T. Wolf, "Conflict and Cooperation Along International Waterways," *Water Policy* 1, no. 2 (1998): 251–65.

[12] See Peter H. Gleick, "Water Conflict Chronology," Pacific Institute, http://worldwater.org/conflict.html (accessed 18 March 2011).

[13] See http://www.cia.gov/nic/speeches/index.htm.

in 2009 to better illustrate how conflict over water impacts history. The following are the current categories or types of conflict included by the institute:

Control of Water Resources (state and nonstate actors): where water supplies or access to water is at the root of tensions.

Military Tool (state actors): where water resources, or water systems themselves, are used by a nation or state as a weapon during a military action.

Political Tool (state and nonstate actors): where water resources, or water systems themselves, are used by a nation, state, or nonstate actor for a political goal.

Terrorism (nonstate actors): where water resources, or water systems, are either targets or tools of violence or coercion by nonstate actors.

Military Target (state actors): where water resource systems are targets of military actions by nations or states.

Development Disputes (state and nonstate actors): where water resources or water systems are a major source of contention and dispute in the context of economic and social development.[14]

These definitions are imprecise, but this is natural as history evolves and new factors become more important.

The world's water consumption has quadrupled during the last 50 years, and estimates regarding water availability in the future are uniformly bleak. For example, according to one source, "by the year 2025, thirty-seven countries are likely to be without enough water for household and agricultural needs, let alone water for industries, energy production, navi-

---

[14] See Gleick, "Water Conflict Chronology."

gation, recreation, and other societal needs."[15] A 2008 report by the National Intelligence Council warned that by 2025 nearly half the world's population—more than three billion people—will live in countries that are "water-stressed"—having less than 1,700 cubic meters of water per capita per year.[16] Using a different metric, other experts have noted that "76 percent of people live in water-stressed areas (less than 1,000 centimeters of rainfall per year), most in politically unstable regions."[17] Water shortages occurring in combination with other sources of tension—particularly in area of strategic interest such as in the Middle East—will be the most worrisome.

Water Scarcity and Water Stress

By 2010, a broad understanding by both government and industry regarding the effect that water scarcity and water stress might have on the future had evolved.[18] This is a result of not only decreasing water availability and increasing consumption but also of an intersection of water scarcity with an impending energy and food crisis. In truth, people will likely continue to have enough water to drink; however, food supplies are another matter as much of the world's water used by humans is dedicated to the production of food crops. One way to look at this is through the rough equation that it takes about one liter of water to produce one calorie from food crops. Meat, in turn, takes about 10 times that to produce one calorie of food.[19] Thus, "the average daily diet in California requires some 6,000 liters of water in agriculture, compared with 3,000 liters in countries such

---

[15] Arun P. Elhance, *Hydropolitics in the Third World: Conflict and Cooperation in International River Basins* (Washington, DC: United States Institute of Peace Press, 1999), 8–9.

[16] National Intelligence Council, *Global Trends 2025: A Transformed World* (Washington, DC: U.S. Government Printing Office, 2008). Also available at http://www.dni.gov/nic /PDF_2025/2025_Global_Trends_Final_Report.pdf.

[17] Jerome Delli Priscoli and Aaron T. Wolf, *Managing and Transforming Water Conflicts*, International Hydrology Series (Cambridge: Cambridge University Press, 2009), xxii.

[18] See, for example, Marc Grossman, *What Next for Energy and Environmental Diplomacy?* Policy Brief: Climate and Energy Program (Washington, DC: German Marshall Fund of the United States, 2010).

[19] Peter Brabeck-Letmathe, "A Water Warning," in *The World in 2009*, special issue, *Economist* (2008): 112.

as Tunisia and Egypt."[20] This calculation does not take into account the water that is used for hygiene, drinking, and manufacturing. According to Peter Brabeck-Letmathe, the chairman of Nestlé, which is the world's largest water bottler, "Under the present circumstances and the way water is being managed, we will run out of water long before we run out of fuel."[21]

Adding to this dilemma are increasing amounts of subsidies to grow crops for the production of biofuels (fuels such as ethanol that are produced from renewable biological resources). For example, it takes 9,100 liters of water to grow the soy for one liter of biodiesel and 4,000 liters of water to grow the corn needed to produce one liter of bioethanol. Because of this, the substitution of biofuels for fossil fuels may be a terribly misguided and inefficient trade-off, a fact that is being increasingly recognized by some governmental agencies. All of this water scarcity and stress, of course, may be accelerated by global warming trends that appear to be decreasing rainfall in many parts of the water-challenged world.

The Middle East

In the Middle East the water situation is increasingly problematic. In his article on "virtual water," Tony Allan of the School of Oriental and African Studies at the University of London states that "the Middle East as a region ran out of water in the 1970's."[22] Allan theorizes that the shortage has been made up by importing food, and the water is now "virtual" in that it is contained or "embedded" in the imported commodities. As an example, it takes 1,160 cubic meters of water to produce a ton of wheat.[23] Put another way, 40 liters of water are required to produce a slice of bread and 70 liters of water are needed to grow an apple. It can be said that all agricultural products have a "water footprint."

---

[20] Ibid.

[21] Ibid.

[22] [J. A.] Tony Allan, "'Virtual Water': A Long Term Solution for Water Short Middle Eastern Economies?" (paper presented at the 1997 British Association Festival of Science, Water and Development Session, University of Leeds, England, 9 September 1997). Available at http://www.soas.ac.uk/water/publications/papers/.file38347.pdf.

[23] World Water Council, ed., *E-Conference Synthesis: Virtual Water Trade—Conscious Choices* (2004), 4, http://www.waterfootprint.org/Reports/virtual_water_final_synthesis.pdf.

A nation that is water scarce can make up for its shortage by importing food. But this is not an answer for countries that do not have the economic resources, and in matters of food security a nation will rarely rely on the goodwill of neighboring states to make the food available. Virtual water trade is not new; it is as old as the basic exchange of food. In 2000 it was estimated that virtual "water food trade" amounted to one-fourth of the global virtual water budget.[24] Food and water are inextricably linked, another layer of complexity in making any security assessment related to freshwater availability.

There have long been dire predictions of water wars. In a 1988 article in *U.S. News and World Report*, for example, Richard Z. Chesnoff described the following scenario:

> November 12, 1993. War erupted throughout the Middle East today in a desperate struggle for dwindling water supplies. Iraqi forces, attempting to smash a Syrian blockade, launched massive attacks on the Euphrates River valley. Syria answered with missile attacks on Baghdad.[25]

The scenario depicted above has not yet occurred, more than 20 years after Chesnoff predicted it would. The water pessimists have been consistently proven wrong, but their alarm may not be misplaced. In this book it will become apparent that although there is not a clear and present danger of a water war in the Middle East, the next 20 years are likely to see more political instability and declining public health in the region. A crisis is likely, but not in the sense of a classic shooting war over water. Rather there seems to be new consensus that water will become an increasingly volatile strategic issue because of regional instability.[26] This is illustrated

---

[24] See Daniel Zimmer and Daniel Renault, "Virtual Water in Food Production and Global Trade Review of Methodological Issues and Preliminary Results," 13, http://www.fao.org/nr/water/docs/VirtualWater_article_DZDR.pdf.

[25] Richard Z. Chesnoff, "When Water Feeds Flames," *U.S. News and World Report*, 21 November 1988, 18.

[26] Jason J. Morrissette and Douglas A. Borer, "Where Oil and Water Do Mix: Environmental Scarcity and Future Conflict in the Middle East and North Africa," *Parameters* 34, no. 4 (Winter 2004–5): 86.

by the current crisis in the African Sahel, a broad band of arable land between the Sahara Desert to the north and the savannahs to the south that is rapidly becoming a desert. Unpredictable weather and hotter, drier conditions have destroyed sizable parts of the agrarian economy of Niger, Chad, and the Sudan, leading to significant instability and migration.[27] Some analysts believe the problem is not water stress per se (as with conditions within individual countries), but rather the unilateral attempts to develop an international river without an agreement with neighbors.[28]

The Euphrates-Tigris Region

In the past several years, the strategic landscape in the region of the Euphrates-Tigris Rivers has changed dramatically, and it is still unstable. Without increased international effort, a failure to deal with the problem is likely to deteriorate into a situation that will undermine other factors that might otherwise favor regional stability. Even though the situation in Iraq remains unsettled, the long-term consequences of a water crisis in the next 10 to 20 years cannot be ignored.

Both Iraq and Syria are heavily dependent on the flow of water from the Euphrates-Tigris and have historic claims to these "Rivers of Eden." Turkey controls the headwaters of the Euphrates and a major portion of the Tigris, and it intends to fully exploit these resources. The massive Southeastern Anatolia Project (Guneydogu Anadolu Projesi or "GAP" in Turkish) includes 22 dams and 19 hydropower projects that will eventually irrigate and transform an area about the size of the state of Kentucky. The Ataturk Dam alone can hold more than two years of the entire natural flow of the Euphrates River. Both Syria and Iraq have objected to Turkey's

---

[27] *Economist*, "Survival in the Sahel: It's Getting Harder All the Time," 2 December 2010, 62.

[28] Sandra L. Postel and Aaron T. Wolf, "Dehydrating Conflict," *Foreign Policy*, September–October 2001, 60–62. According to this article, "The overarching lesson to draw from the basins of the Jordan, the Nile, and the Tigris and Euphrates rivers and other regions of water dispute is not that worsening scarcity will lead inevitably to water wars. It is rather that unilateral actions to construct a dam or river diversion in the absence of a treaty or institutional mechanism that safeguards the interests of other countries in the basin is highly destabilizing to a region, often spurring decades of hostility before cooperation is pursued."

major diversion of water and have demanded increased water allocations. See the latter portion of chapter 5 ("Hydropolitics") for more detail on the claims of Syria and Iraq.

Multiple reports from the region have shown significant signs of this impending water crisis.[29] In one part of the Euphrates basin in northern Syria, only 60 of more than 200 traditional wells are still functioning, and local officials are pumping precious groundwater to fill dry riverbeds that lead to parched fields. Syria has a poorly designed and inefficient water infrastructure, and its government has ambitious plans to divert water from the Euphrates when water will simply not be available.[30]

The Focus on Iraq

In Iraq the decline in water quality and quantity is complicating the already difficult program of reconciliation and reconstruction. Under the leadership of Saddam Hussein, Iraq was uninterested and largely uncooperative in planning and coordinating water issues with Syria and Turkey. Water infrastructure in Iraq went into a steady and catastrophic state of decline. The Joint Technical Committee on Regional Waters—formed in 1980 between Turkey and Iraq (with Syria joining later)—did not meet for a decade. But after the initial invasion of Iraq in 2003, dialogue reopened when Turkey began to provide a limited amount of water flow data to the new Iraqi Ministry of Water Resources.[31] The Iraqi Ministry of Water Resources, reorganized and staffed with U.S. assistance, began a series of projects to reconstruct the country's shattered water infrastructure, and started 121 active water projects in Iraq.[32] It also began planning for a transboundary water commission in the hopes of meaningful coordina-

---

[29] Frederick M. Lorenz and Edward J. Erickson, *The Thread of Life: A Survey of Hydropolitics in the Tigris-Euphrates Basin* (2004), Lorenz trip reports, annex 12. On file with the authors.

[30] Syrian Arab Republic Ministry of Agriculture and Agrarian Reform, National Agricultural Policy Center. *National Programme for Food Security in the Syrian Arab Republic* (Damascus: National Agricultural Policy Center, 2010), ix.

[31] Waleed-Abdel Hammad (Iraqi Ministry of Water Resources), interview by Frederick Lorenz, 1 August 2004, Baghdad.

[32] Inter-Agency Information and Analysis Unit, *Water in Iraq Factsheet*, October 2010.

tion with Iraq's upstream neighbors.[33] In 2008, the three riparian nations restarted a Joint Trilateral Committee on water but "to date no meaningful discussion has taken place."[34]

In Turkey, meanwhile, the GAP is moving ahead, with most of the hydropower units completed.[35] Also, there have been significant signs of improvement in the regional economy in the southeast. But funding shortages have put the irrigation portions of the project years behind schedule, and only 15 percent of the GAP's available 1.8 million hectares were irrigated in 2004.[36] Turkish agriculture has not received the amount of water promised 10 years ago, and while this will delay a major impact in Syria and Iraq, it certainly will not prevent one. Even more important than water quantity is the question of water quality. As more land is brought into production in Turkey, agricultural return flows will surely reduce the quality of water received by the country's neighbors to the south.

Water War?

Will there be a water war in the Euphrates-Tigris basin in the next 10 to 20 years, when the major projects in Turkey reach the final stages of development? Rather than a classic shooting war, we are more likely to see increasing tensions, exacerbated relations, a rise in human suffering, and additional conflicting interests. With greater demands being made on the rivers by uncooperative parties, water quantity and quality are likely to be a central cause of regional instability, leading to a decline in economic and public health conditions. This decline will in turn make the region's peoples more susceptible to fundamentalism and extremism, thereby undermining American interests in the region.

---

[33] Lorenz and Erickson, *Thread of Life*, annex 7, document 3.

[34] Geopolicity, *Managing the Tigris Euphrates Watershed: The Challenge Facing Iraq* (Dubai: Geopolicity, 2010), 16, http://www.geopolicity.com/upload/content/pub_1293090043 _regular.pdf.

[35] Republic of Turkey, *Turkey Water Report 2009* (Ankara: General Directorate of State Hydraulic Works, 2009), 41, fig. 5.5.

[36] Republic of Turkey, *Turkey Water Report 2009*, 39.

Moreover, although the national security and military policies of the United States address climate change and water scarcity as strategic concerns, the American government is, at this time, poorly organized and underresourced to deal with these issues. For example, the management of a crisis affecting the Euphrates-Tigris basin cuts across American combatant commands' areas of responsibility (AORs), which are the cornerstone of American whole-of-government[37] regional response and action. Turkey falls under the AOR of the U.S. European Command, which is headquartered in Germany, while Iraq and Syria fall under the AOR of the U.S. Central Command, which is headquartered in Florida. During Operation Iraqi Freedom this particular combatant command boundary created serious coordination problems between European Command and Central Command when Kurdish insurgents conducted terrorist attacks from Iraq into Turkey.[38] The American response was slow and incomplete, and problems continue to be an issue today for the countries involved.[39] The U.S. State Department is also organized along lines that often do not reflect the need for regional coordination on transboundary rivers. For instance, the department's Bureau of Near Eastern Affairs includes Syria, Iraq, and Iran but not Turkey, which is within the boundaries of the Bureau of European and Eurasian Affairs. In the future, the State Department foresees a more nuanced approach employing the whole-of-government concept and the U.S. Agency for International Development to assist in solving similar problems. However, this idea lacks resources at present, and it is unlikely that America will be postured to deal more effectively with a regional crisis caused by water scarcity in the future than it is today.

---

[37] See President Barack Obama, 27 May 2010: "Our security also depends on diplomats who can act in every corner of the world, from grand capitals to dangerous outposts; development experts who can strengthen governance and support human dignity; and intelligence and law enforcement that can unravel plots, strengthen justice systems and work seamlessly with other countries." Jim Garamone, "New National Strategy Takes 'Whole-of-Government' Approach," http://www.defense.gov/news/newsarticle.aspx?id=59377.

[38] Steven A. Cook, lecture (Marine Corps University, Quantico, VA, 2 March 2011).

[39] Barçin Yinanç, "Turkish Ties with N Iraq to Continue despite Cable Revelations, Official Says," *Hürriyet Daily News* (Turkey), 9 December 2010.

A Plan of Action

What can be done? The final chapter of this book makes an attempt to provide some answers. There may be a historic opportunity for the creation of an effective transboundary water initiative for Turkey, Syria, and Iraq. There are a number of working models that can provide insight, such as the Mekong River Commission coordinating water management efforts in Southeast Asia. These and other models are discussed in more detail in chapter 6. The U.S. State Department recently identified a U.S.-based public-private partnership established to unite American expertise, knowledge, and resources, and mobilize those assets to address water challenges around the globe, especially in the developing world.[40] The international community and the World Bank can also provide assistance, making it a truly international endeavor. With the right support, the people of the Euphrates-Tigris basin can begin to move in the direction of cooperation rather than conflict with regard to their water resources. This book will thus attempt to answer the following questions:

1. How does history inform the study of water and security in the Euphrates-Tigris basin? See chapter 1.

2. How do political, economic, and military factors interact in the basin, and how is the strategic landscape changing with current developments in Iraq? See chapter 2.

3. What are the current and projected future demands for freshwater in the basin, and how will these demands impact regional security? What is the current status of major water and development projects in the region, including the GAP in Turkey? How will climate change impact these calculations? See chapter 3.

4. How will the autonomy or independence of Kurdistan affect the regional balance and the availability of freshwater? See chapter 4.

---

[40] The U.S. Water Partnership was announced 21 March 2012. Details can be found at http://uswaterpartnership.org/.

5. How do the countries of the basin view their own rights to water, and what is the intersection of water and politics in the region? Can Turkey use water as a strategic weapon? See chapter 5.

6. How does international law influence water rights between the parties? What technological and scientific initiatives might be leveraged to improve the transparency of information related to water? How can these initiatives be linked with diplomacy to improve the level of cooperation between the parties? See chapter 6.

7. Considering all the factors mentioned previously, what are the dangers and threats? What are the likely outcomes in terms of conflict and potential for violence and instability? If there is a "crisis" in the region, what will it look like? Are there any frameworks, rules, or models that can be used to reduce the risk of conflict? For each of the potential options, what is the probability of success? How can the international community support cooperation and stability in the region? See chapter 7.

In the coming century, we know that strategic water is projected to assume an importance equal to that of energy. We know today that the demand for water in the Euphrates-Tigris basin will exceed the availability of water supplies. We also know that the United States and the international community are poorly prepared and underresourced to deal effectively with a regional crisis caused by water scarcity. These are not predictions but unpleasant facts, and we hope that this book can lead to action to help deal with the problem.

CHAPTER 1
THE EUPHRATES-TIGRIS BASIN AND ITS HISTORY

This chapter outlines the impact of civilization on the Euphrates-Tigris basin and how people affect both the rivers and the surrounding areas. Early empires and later the Arabs and Ottomans built irrigation and water management systems that made the lower basin the breadbasket of the Middle East. It was, however, the collapse of empires after the First World War and the consequent establishment of artificially imposed political boundaries that created the basis for regional instability in the contemporary world.

Geography and Early History

The history of the Euphrates-Tigris basin has been shaped by its unique geography and, in particular, its access to water. The "Rivers of Eden" find their source in what is today modern Turkey, in the central highlands where rain and snow are plentiful. Turkey has been fortunate to have an environment that can optimally utilize the waters of these great rivers. Deep valleys, cooler temperatures, and fertile soil provide good conditions for catchment, diversions, and agriculture. In Syria and Iraq

---

Portions of this chapter are derived from the authors' earlier publication *The Thread of Life: A Survey of Hydropolitics in the Tigris-Euphrates Basin* (2004).

the rivers flow through mostly flat arid and semiarid land, creating more challenging conditions for utilization and higher rates of evaporation. The Euphrates flows through Syria and Iraq to the head of the Persian Gulf where it joins the Tigris as the Shatt al-Arab. The Tigris flows directly from Turkey to Iraq, where it obtains additional flows from the Zagros Mountains in Iran.

With a total length of 2,700 kilometers (km; approximately 1,678 miles), the Euphrates is the longest river in Southwest Asia: it forms a catchment basin of 82,330 square km (approximately 31,788 square miles). Virtually all the water of the Euphrates originates in Turkey, with a minor contribution from Syria and none from Iraq. The Tigris is the second longest river in Southwest Asia, and like the Euphrates it shows great variations in flow from winter to summer. About 45 percent of the Tigris River's water originates in Turkey; the remaining amount is contributed mostly by tributaries in Iraq and Iran. Since the Karun River of Iran enters the Shatt al-Arab close to the confluence with the Persian Gulf, Iran is rarely included in flow data for the riparian countries, or those countries that share a transboundary water source. Turkey makes the greatest contribution to the waters of the Euphrates-Tigris basin (map 1.1; more detail on the quantity is provided in chapter 3).

The Tigris and the Euphrates lie in a transition zone between maritime and desert climates. Like the Nile, they are "exotic rivers," deriving their waters from outside the region from which they flow. Much of the downstream region (modern southeastern Turkey, Syria, and Iraq) receives insufficient precipitation to sustain rain-fed agriculture, but the rivers convey enough surplus water to compensate for the deficit. Farming first developed in the more humid zones but then moved to river valleys in the arid zone where crops could be grown under cultivation with the aid of irrigation. Recent archeological evidence supports the theory that a small core area within this Fertile Crescent (map 1.2) provided the earliest example of domesticated crops, dating from between 8900 and 8600 BC.[1]

---

[1] Simcha Lev-Yadun, Avi Gopher, and Shahal Abbo, "The Cradle of Agriculture," *Science* 288, no. 5471 (2 June 2000): 1602. Previous studies indicated that crops were first domesticated in the Jordan Valley.

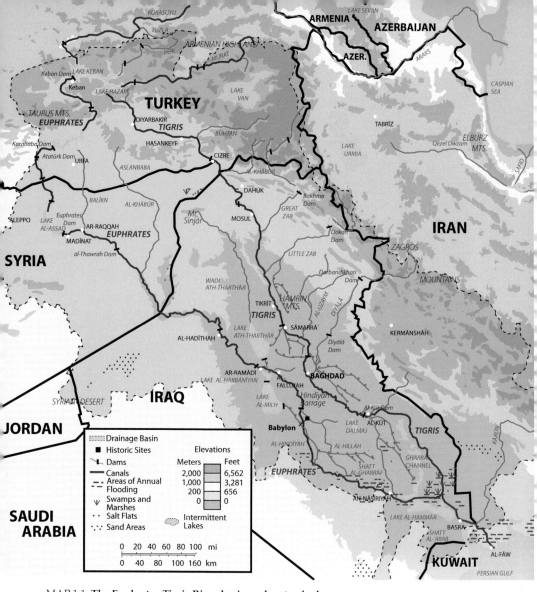

MAP 1.1. **The Euphrates-Tigris River basin and watershed.**

It is said that history began in the Euphrates-Tigris basin. Some believe it to be the location of the biblical Garden of Eden, and this region is often referred to as the "cradle of civilization." As early as the fourth millennium BC, agricultural settlements and basic irrigation networks were part of the Mesopotamian landscape.[2] The Sumerians and Babylonians used

[2] Daniel Hillel, *Rivers of Eden: The Struggle of Water and the Quest for Peace in the Middle East* (Oxford: Oxford University Press, 1994), 41.

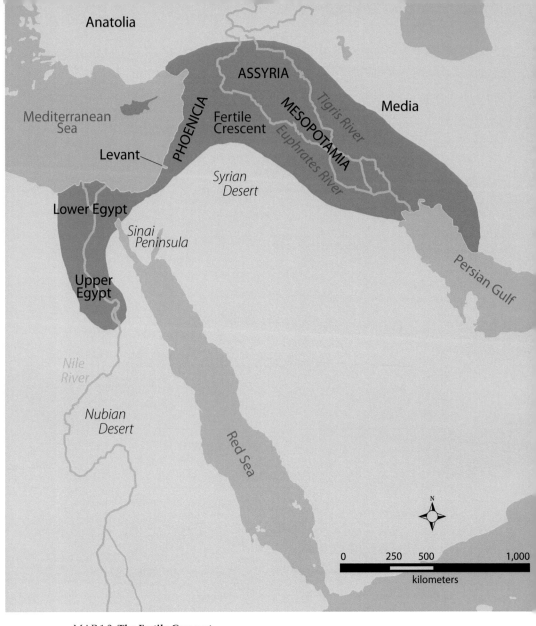

MAP 1.2. **The Fertile Crescent.**

the water of the Euphrates, and documents from the time of the Babylonian lawgiver Hammurabi (reigned circa 1792–1750 BC) refer to the maintenance of these irrigation systems. The Bible provides early references to conflicts over water as well. One of the first of these is in Genesis 21, with Abraham reproaching Abimelech for having his servants take over a well used by Abraham's servants. In the same passage, there is a description of the dispute over Isaac's wells, and indeed many of the biblical names of these and other wells in the region have been retained as place names today.

The early inhabitants of the region revered water. The springs of water seemed to be alive, and they inspired divine and animistic associations. The Mesopotamians had a creation myth based upon a battle of the gods to create a firmament from the sea. The primacy of water in the region is also reflected in the local languages. For instance, the word for "water" in classical Persian (and the first word in the Persian dictionary) is *ab*. From that word came the words *abad*, meaning "abode," and *abadan*, meaning "civilized."

Arab culture arose from this life in the desert, where competition over a limited resource was fundamental. Water is often associated with the Arab myth of the amniotic fluid that nurtures life. Water is also a major theme in the Koran, with numerous references to water, rivers, fountains, springs, and clouds throughout the text. The use of freshwater for ceremonial ablution and purification prior to prayer became essential to Muslim religious practice. Indeed, any visit to a mosque in the region today, even in the driest of areas, is preceded by the cleansing at a fountain containing multiple spigots for the faithful.

Scholars often attribute the decline of early civilizations to political, military, and economic factors, or even to moral decay. Historians today, however, are becoming increasingly aware that environmental degradation often was the key factor in the demise of early societies.[3] In the Euphrates-Tigris region, early exploitation of land and water resulted in the first documented environmental disaster—a consequence of salination

---

[3] Milt Freudenheim, "The Ancients Had Water Politics, Too," *New York Times*, 13 September 1981.

(also referred to as "salinization"), siltation, and waterlogging.[4] Agricultural success in the basin often created an insidious cycle in which inhabitants took infertile land, irrigated it, and initially produced high crop yields. But the continued irrigation required to maintain production eventually led to soil degradation, and ultimately resulted in infertile soils. This soil degradation was caused by the aforementioned salination, silting, and waterlogging, all inevitable products of this seductive cycle. This process was particularly apparent in southern Mesopotamia in the time of the ancient Sumerians and Babylonians, who faced declining amounts of arable land.[5] Soil degradation is still at work today—particularly in modern Syria and Iraq—and today's challenge is to learn from the past and avoid the mistakes that made life so difficult for the early inhabitants.

According to ancient Mesopotamian beliefs, the buildup of soil salinity (salination) was attributed to mysterious forces or a contest between Apsu, the god of freshwater from above, and Tiamat, the evil goddess of salt water from below.[6] By keeping the land fallow in alternating years, the ancients found that native plants would send down roots and draw away the saline water. This would delay but not prevent the inevitable consequence of the rising water and increasing salt levels. In modern times salination can be prevented or remedied by subsoil drainage when there are sufficient resources to build a drainage system. But as later chapters of this book will indicate, salinity is again a significant threat, particularly for Syria and Iraq.

The Sumerians were a great civilization—inventing writing, sailboats, and wheeled vehicles, among many other accomplishments. Despite their achievements, they unwittingly brought about their own decline by causing the degradation of their soils. Deforestation and overgrazing

---

[4] *Salination* or *salinization* refers to the process of increasing the salt content of soil, which renders it infertile. *Siltation* is the increased concentration of suspended sediments and the increased accumulation (temporary or permanent) of fine sediments on bottoms where they are undesirable. *Waterlogging* refers to the saturation of the soil by groundwater sufficient to prevent or hinder agriculture.

[5] Hillel, *Rivers of Eden.*

[6] Ibid., 57. The story of the contest between the good god Apsu and the evil goddess Tiamat is related in the *Enuma Elish*, the Babylonian equivalent of the book of Genesis.

caused increased runoff and soil erosion, resulting in unstable riverbeds and irrigation works clogged by siltation. As detailed above, a greater problem was salination, caused by the increased use of irrigation water and the accompanying return flows to groundwater. The result was an unnatural rising of the salt-laden water table that destroyed crops in poorly drained, waterlogged lands. The loss of agricultural lands ultimately contributed to population movement and a corresponding overall decline in Sumerian civilization. Traveling through the region today, it is difficult to imagine that thriving civilizations existed in places that are now barren, empty deserts.[7]

Mesopotamia enjoyed an agricultural revival when the Babylonians built an elaborate canal system in the sixth century BC, and they built the Nimrod Dam on the Tigris to divert water into the canal system.[8] Their Nahrawan Canal transferred water from the Tigris to the Diyala River plain, which was also dammed. The Babylonians also built a canal that transferred water between the Euphrates and Tigris Rivers; Nebuchadnezzar II (ruled 605–562 BC) built the famous Hanging Gardens of Babylon using intricate canals and hydrological engineering; and Cyrus the Great (ruled 559–530 BC) constructed 360 canals during his reign.[9]

Subsequent conquerors occupied the region, including Persians, Macedonian Greeks, and Romans. Central to all of these empires were the two rivers and the great cities that grew up along their banks. In the mid-seventh century AD, Muslim warriors extended their control over the region and a new civilization emerged under the Umayyad dynasty. Trade and culture flourished under the Umayyads, and Islam entered its first golden

---

[7] In his 1929 book, *Ur of the Chaldees*, C. Leonard Wooley wrote, "Only to those who have seen the Mesopotamian Desert will the evocation of the ancient world seem well-nigh incredible, so complete is the contrast between past and present. . . . It is yet more difficult to realize, that the blank waste ever blossomed, bore fruit for the sustenance of a busy world. Why, if Ur was an empire's capital, if Sumer was once a vast granary, has the population dwindled to nothing, the very soil lost its virtue?"

[8] Arnon Soffer, *Rivers of Fire: The Conflict over Water in the Middle East*, trans. Murray Rosovesky and Nina Kopaken (Lanham, MD: Rowman and Littlefield Publishers, Inc., 1999), 83.

[9] Mostafa Dolatyar and Tim S. Gray, *Water Politics in the Middle East: A Context for Conflict or Co-operation?* (London: Macmillan, 2000), 129.

The Hanging Gardens of Babylon, one of the Seven Wonders of the World.

Reprinted from J. A. Brendon, *The Ancient World from Early Egypt and Babylonia to the Decline of Rome* (London: Blackie and Son Limited, 1924)

age, extending from Spain to the Indus River. The empire encompassed the three early river valley civilization basins: the Nile, the Euphrates-Tigris, and the Indus.[10] But the Umayyads were soon overthrown and replaced by the Abbasids, who continued to preside over a flowering of civilization and culture. Important to this narrative was the establishment of the city of Baghdad by the caliph al-Mansur in 765 AD.[11] This was critical juncture in the history of Islam because the establishment of the Abbasid center of power in the Euphrates-Tigris valley moved the epicenter of Muslim power and wealth eastward from the Nile basin. Baghdad soon became the center of a renewed Islamic golden age that encouraged science, mathematics, architecture, medicine, and trade. To support the increases in population and trade, the caliphs restored many of the ancient irrigation systems. Within several hundred years, however, the empire and dynasty began to decline. A modern scholar has attributed this to the decline of the empire's agricultural base caused by man-made soil erosion and rising soil salinity. This decline, in turn, caused food shortages, leading to the importation of expensive grains and a parallel loss of tax revenue, which was based on land and agricultural production.[12] The loss of wealth and tax revenue led to loss of political control, which combined with a regionwide cycle of climate change involving substantially drier

---

[10] Tamim Ansaray, *Destiny Disrupted: A History of the World through Islamic Eyes* (New York: PublicAffairs, 2009), 67–78.

[11] Ibid., 86–87.

[12] Douglas E. Streusand, *Islamic Gunpowder Empires: Ottomans, Safavids, and Mughals* (Boulder, CO: Westview, 2010), 17.

conditions, caused the Abbasids to grow progressively weaker as they lost their grip on the both the farming and nomadic populations of the region.

Around 1050 the nomadic Seljuk Turks swept out of the Altai Mountains in central Asia through what is now Iran and began to assimilate the moribund Abbasids. The Seljuks established their own empire and restored some of the prosperity and civilization that had been lost. Then catastrophe struck in the form of invasions from the west and the east. European crusaders invaded the Holy Land in 1095 in a continuing series of resource-draining campaigns that lasted for nearly 200 years. However, a much more devastating invasion came from the east in the form of the Mongol horde. The final destruction of the Abbasids came in the late 1250s at the hands of the nomadic Mongol leader Halagu.[13] The fury of the Mongolian conquest was unmatched historically in the Euphrates-Tigris basin, and many cities were burned to the ground and destroyed as the Mongols swept into the area. Baghdad itself was sacked in 1258—its world-famous library was destroyed, and perhaps as many as a million inhabitants and refugees were put to the sword. Importantly, the complex system of irrigation canals and waterworks was intentionally destroyed as a military tactic to deny a livelihood to the local population. In the following years, the system was rendered useless by neglect and the breakdown of the central government administration. Large tracts of land that had been productive in antiquity returned to desert, and the land between the two rivers fell into a lethargy from which it did not recover until the twentieth century.

In the late thirteenth century, bands of Turkic warriors from central Asia under chieftains such as Bayazid I and Timur the Lame conquered and replaced the Mongols. Soon to be known as the Ottomans, these Turkic tribes established an empire that would eventually extend from North Africa to the gates of Vienna, forming a dynastic regime that ruled over more than 30 different religious and ethnic groups. During the long rule of the Ottoman Empire (1530–1918), the Euphrates-Tigris was essentially contained in the boundaries of a single political administra-

---

[13] Ibid., 21–22.

tion, and some effort was made to restore the irrigation systems. Over the centuries, however, the ever-growing subjects of Ottoman rule became increasingly despondent with the status quo, and by the early nineteenth century the empire began to disintegrate from within. Of note, Midhat Pasha, the famous Ottoman reformer, made strenuous efforts in the 1870s to restore the long-dysfunctional irrigation systems when he served as governor of Baghdad.[14] He also constructed dams and cleared sections of the Euphrates-Tigris Rivers in order to improve navigation; nevertheless, these projects were too poorly resourced to restore the lost prosperity of the river basin. The Ottomans renewed their efforts to reenergize the basin based on a report in 1911 from British hydrological engineer William Wilcocks, which suggested the construction of Euphrates dams.[15] Wilcocks's idea was to control water and provide it to a resurrected irrigation system. Based on this, the Ottoman government began construction of the Hindiyah Barrage (a barrage is an obstruction built to divert or alter the course of water flow), which was completed in 1913.[16] The outbreak of the First World War in 1914 ended all further Ottoman projects.

It is clear from the history of the region that the inhabitants of the Euphrates-Tigris basin were both enriched and impoverished by the waters on a periodic basis. Climate and human actions seem to be the main elements in this drama, especially in relation to the existence and operation of extensive irrigation systems. The location lent itself to this as well simply because Mesopotamia was sometimes a crossroads for invaders and sometimes an objective in and of itself, resulting in man-made destruction on a vast scale. It is fair to say that water scarcity and usage problems are not new issues for the riparian nations of the Euphrates-Tigris River system.

Modern History, Partition, and Water

This section briefly details the story of how the modern countries of Iraq, Syria, and Turkey came to govern the Euphrates-Tigris basin and outlines

---

[14] Stanford J. Shaw and Ezel K. Shaw, *History of the Ottoman Empire and Modern Turkey*, vol. 2, *Reform, Revolution and Republic: The Rise of Modern Turkey, 1808–1975* (Cambridge: Cambridge University Press, 1977), 67–68.

[15] Dolatyar and Gray, *Water Politics in the Middle East*, 132–33.

[16] Elhance, *Hydropolitics in the Third World*, 146.

Hindiyah Barrage, the first modern dam on the Tigris River (early twentieth century).
Photo by American Colony (Jerusalem). Library of Congress Prints and Photographs Division

current problems whose origins lie at the end of the First World War. In fact, many of the modern Middle East's problems stem directly from European interference in the dismemberment and partitioning of the Ottoman Empire at Versailles in 1919. Aptly called "a peace to end all peace" by historian David Fromkin, the Treaty of Versailles formalized national boundaries and established political relationships that have troubled and are still troubling the entire region.[17] While neither the boundaries nor water dominated the table at Versailles, other regional issues such as oil; European interests; independence for the Arabs and other national minorities, such as the Jews and Kurds; and the creation of a modern Turkish national state plagued the negotiations. The arbitrary division of the region into competing states by the post–World War I powers created new obstacles to the efficient use of the rivers' water. The new regional map was drawn

[17] David Fromkin, *A Peace to End All Peace: The Fall of the Ottoman Empire and the Creation of the Modern Middle East* (New York: Henry Holt, 1989).

by those who intended to serve their own colonial interests, ignoring the unique histories and cultures of the region. As the Ottoman Empire was systematically dismantled between 1918 and 1923, new states and national lines were formed that would have numerous and profound effects. One of these—a significant one for our purposes in this book—is that the Euphrates-Tigris basin was divided between three countries (and the Jordan River between four).

The Ottomans divided the lands of the Euphrates-Tigris basin into vilayets or provinces that were centered on major cities. These provincial divisions tended to be based on geographical and economic considerations rather than political or ethno-religious reasons. The Ottoman vilayets in the lower basin comprised Mosul, Baghdad, and Basra, and those of the upper basin consisted of Aleppo, Van, and Diyarbakir. While much of the area contained ancient and sophisticated civilizations, by 1900 the region had deteriorated into the backwater of the empire. It was not serviced by modern communications or railroads, and the Ottomans experienced continuing difficulties with the tribes that inhabited the Euphrates-Tigris basin. The outbreak of the First World War saw the Ottomans poorly positioned to defend the region, and in November 1914 the British occupied the Shatt al-Arab, or the outlet of the river system into the Persian Gulf.[18] British interests concerned maintaining access to the oil reserves of the Anglo-Persian Oil Company, upon which the Royal Navy was increasingly dependent.

In early 1915, the British had already started to actively consider the acquisition of the Euphrates-Tigris River basin, and according to Lord Horatio Kitchener, "If the Ottoman Empire is to be wholly or partially broken up, it is imperative that Mesopotamia should become British."[19] Kitchener's reasons included not only ensuring continued access to oil and keeping the Russians and French out of the area, but also "incorporating Mesopotamia

---

[18] Edward J. Erickson, *Ordered To Die: A History of the Ottoman Army in the First World War* (Westport, CT: Greenwood Press, 2001), 66–68.

[19] Memorandum by Lord Kitchener for the Committee of Imperial Defence, 16 March 1915, the National Archives, Kew, United Kingdom, Cabinet Records (CAB 24/1/12), 2.

into the Empire on the grounds of its potential agricultural resources."[20] Through the fall of 1915, the war in Mesopotamia went well for Britain as an expeditionary force reached the gates of Baghdad. However, the tiny army, commanded by Major General Charles V. F. Townshend, was encircled and forced to surrender at Kut al-Amara in April 1916. Subsequently, a greatly reinforced Anglo-Indian army, commanded by Lieutenant General Sir F. Stanley Maude, captured Baghdad in 1917. Maude died of cholera and the British offensive ground to a halt; nevertheless, his successor seized the oil-rich city of Mosul in November 1918.

Kitchener's machinations matured into a full-blown plan by the Allies to divide the Ottoman Empire at the end of the war. By 1918, a number of overlapping agreements and proclamations destroyed any logical or equitable solution to what was dubbed "the Eastern Question."[21] Among the most famous are Hussein-McMahon letters (1915–16) that pledged British support for Arab independence and the Balfour Declaration (November 1917) that promised support for the establishment of a Zionist state in Palestine. The Constantinople Agreement with Russia allocated the Turkish straits to the czar, while the Treaty of London gave Italy the Turkish city of Antalya and a number of islands. However, it was the Sykes-Picot Agreement of May 1916 that had the most direct bearing on the waters of the Euphrates-Tigris. British diplomat Sir Mark Sykes and his French counterpart Francois Georges-Picot famously sketched a hand-drawn map of how the victorious Allies would divide the Middle East.[22] According to the agreement, France would receive direct control over Syria and Lebanon, while Britain would control Mesopotamia. An international zone of control was envisioned for Palestine; however, in the wake of General Edmund Allenby's victories in 1917–18, Britain retained direct control over this area as well. The Mondros Armistice ended the fighting in the Middle East at the end of October 1918, and the Ottoman Empire lost control of not only

---

[20] Ibid., 2–4.

[21] Edward J. Erickson, *Defeat in Detail: The Ottoman Army in the Balkans, 1912–1913* (Westport, CT: Praeger, 2003), 37–38.

[22] Roger Ford, *Eden to Armageddon: World War I in the Middle East* (New York: Pegasus Books, 2010), 388, 397–400.

Arabia, Lebanon, Mesopotamia, Palestine, and Syria, but also of a large portion of Cilicia (southwest Anatolia), the Cilician Gate, Constantinople, and the Dardanelles in Turkey.[23]

The various peace treaties ending World War I then produced a profound effect on the region. The Treaty of Versailles in 1919 resulted in a new League of Nations, the covenant of which established the mandate system to oversee the former territories and colonies of the defeated Central Powers. In the Middle East, the mandate system formalized the Sykes-Picot Agreement (map 1.3). Versailles, however, did not close the book on the Allied war against the Ottoman Empire, and it was not until the Treaty of Sèvres in 1920 that hostilities formally ended.[24] Unfortunately, the Sèvres treaty was badly skewed in favor of the Allies, and it split major portions of the Turkish Anatolian heartland between Greece, which received western Anatolia; Italy, which received southern Anatolia; and France, which received most of southeast Anatolia. Sèvres also pledged the establishment of an independent Armenian state that would have included most of the headwaters of the Euphrates-Tigris Rivers. Competing for much of the same areas claimed by the Armenians were the Kurds, but the treaty merely promised them autonomy.[25]

Reaction to the harsh terms of the Sèvres treaty was immediate and in large measure served as the catalyst that created the Turkish nationalist movement led by Mustafa Kemal.[26] The Greeks, in particular, were eager to claim their share and launched an invasion from Smyrna (modern Izmir) into the Anatolian hinterlands that had almost reached Ankara by 1921. The Italians and French also sent troops into their areas, of which the French-constructed Armenian Legion wrought considerable havoc.

---

[23] James L. Gelvin, *The Modern Middle East: A History* (Oxford: Oxford University Press, 2008), 178–85.

[24] Michael G. Roskin and James J. Coyle, *Politics of the Middle East: Cultures and Conflicts*, 2d ed. (Upper Saddle River, NJ: Pearson / Prentice Hall, 2008), 151.

[25] For a comprehensive treatment of these events, Briton C. Busch's *Mudros to Lausanne: Britain's Frontier in West Asia, 1918–1923* (Albany: State University of New York Press, 1976) remains the definitive work.

[26] Margaret MacMillan, *Paris 1919: Six Months that Changed the World* (New York: Random House, 2003), 427–55.

MAP 1.3. The casually drawn map of the Sykes-Picot Agreement, in which Britain secured Iraq (in red) and Zone B while France secured Lebanon/Syria (in blue) and Zone A.

Concurrently with these incursions, the British continued their occupation of Constantinople and the Bosporus and Dardanelles straits, while Armenians and Kurds in the Caucasus bitterly contested the controls of an evolving Turkish state. In a remarkable turn of events, the Turks defeated the Greeks and forced the remaining Allies out of Anatolia. The destruction of the Anatolian population, economy, and infrastructure caused by nearly continuous wars between 1914 and 1922 was monumental. In the end, the war-weary Allies finally agreed to return to the conference table to revise the Sèvres treaty.

The Treaty of Lausanne in 1923 constructed the modern political boundaries that define the riparian states using the Euphrates-Tigris waters to this day. The treaty was unique because it was the only meeting where a defeated Central Power was treated on anything remotely resembling equal terms. Opening on 20 May, the Turkish delegation, led by Ismet Pasha, began to advance positions favorable to the new Turkish nation. There was much "horse trading" as the Turks agreed to demilitarize the Bosporus and Dardanelles in return for control of Thrace. The boundaries of the modern Turkish republic were finalized, with the exception of the provinces of Hatay and Mosul, which remained under French and British occupation, respectively.[27] Moreover, the Allies agreed to withdraw all of their forces from the parts of Turkey they still occupied, notably Constantinople and the straits. If Turkey emerged the winner from Lausanne, it was surely the Kurds who emerged as the loser.

The Armenians, led by Boghos Nubar, were well organized and represented themselves successfully at Versailles and Sèvres. This was in large part due to their rebellion and status as active opponents of the Turks. Unfortunately for the Armenians, by 1923 no Allied state, including America, was willing to support their aspirations of statehood beyond the tiny and isolated rump state high in the Caucasus. The Kurds, on the other hand, were Islamic and, as subjects of the Ottoman sultan, were classified with the Turks as an enemy. Consequently, the Kurds were the subject of much debate, not as an independent people in search of self-determination, but rather as a sort of bartering chip or deal breaker. Indeed the Kurdish puzzle seemed to defy a reasonable solution, and Lausanne ended badly for the Kurds.

The Kurdish problems began in March 1921 at a Cairo conference brokered by the British, who were tying to sort out their obligations and the promises they made to the Arabs during the First World War in return for support against the Turks. There were two main Arab tribal groups

---

[27] Andrew Mango, *Atatürk: The Biography of the Founder of Modern Turkey* (New York: Overlook Press, 1991), 373–87.

the British tried to placate by dividing up former Ottoman lands.[28] The British gave the house of Ibn Saud[29] control over the Hejaz (a western portion of modern day Saudi Arabia), including the holy cities of Mecca and Medina, while the Hashemite house of Hussein received lands the lands in between Arabia and the French mandate of Syria. There were two Hashemite princes who had participated in the Arab Revolt (1916–18) and to whom the British owed favors. Abdallah was offered the throne of Transjordan, and Faisal was offered the throne of Iraq. Thus, the British seemed to have solved their problem, but this solution led to other, more difficult questions. The newly crowned King Faisal of Iraq took up residence in his new capital of Baghdad. He soon inquired as to the status of the former Ottoman province of Mosul, which contained the predominantly Kurdish cities of Mosul, Erbil, Sulaymaniyah, and Kirkuk. As these areas were known to hold vast deposits of oil, the British were understandably reluctant to cede control to Faisal, who was left with the area between Baghdad and Basra. The issue surfaced at Lausanne and the British attempted to work a deal with the Turks, who claimed the former Ottoman vilayet for themselves.

In the end, the issue of Mosul and the Kurds was put on hold so as not to obstruct the final resolution of the treaty, which was signed on 24 July 1923. The status of the province as well as the final definition of the international boundary between Turkey and Iraq was turned over to the League of Nations for arbitration and future resolution. In 1925, the league ruled in favor of Britain and awarded Mosul and its hinterlands to Iraq, then still a British mandate. This was a critical decision because it automatically created a restive Kurdish minority within the predominately Arab Iraq. Alternatively, its acquisition by Turkey would have created an even larger Kurdish minority within Turkey, as well as endowing the Turks with substantial oil reserves. In either case the Kurds were destined to lose.

---

[28] Gelvin, *Modern Middle East*, 180–85.

[29] King Abdul-Aziz (1880–1953), the first monarch of Saudi Arabia who was commonly referred to as Ibn Saud, meaning "son of Saud."

In the following decades, Mustafa Kemal assumed the surname of Ataturk (father of the Turks) and became the first president of the infant Turkish republic. Continuing the domestic policies of the defunct Committee of Union and Progress, he embarked on a vigorous program of modernization and westernization that moved Turkey closer to Europe. Importantly,

Ataturk defined a new Turkish identity built on nationalism and secularism (sometimes known as Kemalism), which served to build a cohesive society but at the same time culturally excluded the Kurds.[30] Turkey maintained a carefully guarded neutrality during the Second World War, and in the 1950s it joined the new North Atlantic Treaty Organization (NATO) and participated in the Korean War. Although Ataturk himself was more or less a dictator, he successfully established a constitutional democracy that is his true legacy. Unfortunately, the Turkish experiment with democracy has been marred by a number of military coups, which in turn saw control returned to civilians. Throughout these periods of domestic turmoil, Turkey remained a staunch NATO partner and a strategically important component of the alliance. A particularly strong partnership developed between the United States and Turkey, which had been one of the first nations to receive military aid under the Truman Doctrine[31] in the late 1940s. This strong relationship was thrown off track in the mid-1970s by America's arms embargo over the Turkish invasion of Cyprus, a condition

Mustafa Kemal Ataturk, the father of modern Turkey, in 1918.
Courtesy of the Presidency of the Republic of Turkey

---

[30] Mango, *Atatürk*, 500, 537.

[31] On 12 March 1947, President Harry S. Truman gave a speech to Congress in which he recommended a policy of U.S. support for Turkey and Greece to prevent their falling under Soviet influence. This policy became known as the Truman Doctrine, and it is regarded by many historians as the beginning of the Cold War.

which lasted about 10 years. The 1991 Gulf War hurt Turkey economically by cutting off trade with Iraq, but increasingly robust trade with Europe more than compensated for this.

Syria and Iraq continued in their status as mandates of France and Britain, respectively, through the end of World War II. But while French-dominated Syria was relatively stable, British-dominated Iraq was a seething cauldron of bloody revolts and internecine massacres.[32] Famously, the Royal Air Force played a key role in the 1920s by maintaining a highly visible aerial presence over previously violent parts of Iraq. However, postwar decolonization saw the collapse of the rule of law in both countries and the rise of military dictatorships. In 1949, an army colonel seized control of Syria, and in 1958 Iraqi military officers assassinated the king (Abdullah, heir of the Hashemite Faisal). By the mid-1960s, coups led by ex-military officers had installed the Baath (Resurrection) Party, which was ideologically socialist and nationalist, in both Syria and Iraq. In the following years both nations would drift away from the West, mainly over the issue of Israel and the Palestinians. Syria briefly experimented with a political union with Egypt called the United Arab Republic, but this fell apart quickly. Confronted by a heavily armed Israel, Syria turned to the Union of Soviet Socialist Republics (USSR) for military assistance and by the 1970s had become something of a Soviet client state. Iraq fell into the hands of Saddam Hussein, who by 1980 had declared war on Iran and actively suppressed the Kurdish minority inside Iraq. In both cases, he used weapons of mass destruction, including chemical and biological munitions. His war against the Islamic Republic of Iran drew him into a de facto alliance with the West, particularly with the United States, whose President Ronald W. Reagan thought him to be the lesser of two evils and a valuable bulwark against the Iranian ayatollahs.

The end of the Cold War in 1991 brought an end to Soviet involvement in the Middle East and a corresponding American willingness to involve itself militarily in the region. The events of the 1991 Gulf War are well

---

[32] Jeremy Salt, *The Unmaking of the Middle East: A History of Western Disorder in Arab Lands* (Berkeley: University of California Press, 2008), 91–120.

known and resulted in a significant degradation of Saddam's power, as well as international embargos and sanctions designed to weaken his regime. At the same time Syria—oddly an active partner of the United States in the Gulf War—became progressively weaker as Soviet aid came to an end. The American invasion of Iraq in 2003 ended Saddam Hussein's and the Baath Party's rule but certainly led to a higher degree of regional instability caused by the U.S. failure to install or allow an effective Iraqi follow-on government to evolve. This subject will be examined in depth in the next chapter.

There are few real territorial issues today between the governments of Turkey, Iraq, and Syria. The issues of Hatay and Mosul have long been put to rest, and all three nations are satisfied with the current boundaries. Although there is a Turkmen minority in Iraq and an Arab minority in Turkey, there are few irredentist problems with these populations. However, one of the great tragedies of the mandate period was the betrayal of the Kurdish people who lived in the region of modern western Iran, northern Iraq, eastern Syria, and southeastern Turkey. Though they were promised their own political sovereignty, the Kurds were never given the possibility to form their own state; indeed, they became aware too late of the terms of the Sykes-Picot Agreement in which the postwar powers secretly divided the area among several powerful nation-states. The failure by the Kurds to produce credible leadership compounded the problem, and hopes for independence or some degree of political autonomy were dashed when the League of Nations agreed on the region's final political boundaries in 1926, dividing it between five countries.[33] This issue continues to affect regional stability and will be addressed in detail later in this book.

Use of the waters of the Euphrates-Tigris Rivers was not a controversial issue during the Ottoman period, but immediately after the First World War, issues dealing with water rights began to emerge. During the mandate period, the Allies were concerned about water use but not enough to raise the potential for conflict. In 1920, the French and British signed a conven-

---

[33] David McDowall, *A Modern History of the Kurds* (London: I.B. Tauris, 1997), 146.

tion establishing consultative committees over the use of the two rivers.[34] This was at the request of the French, who envisioned diverting the Tigris to irrigate vast areas of Syria. France remained concerned about this as the Republican Turks fought for independence, so the French negotiated a bilateral treaty with the Turks on 20 October 1921, which concerned downstream riparian rights and tapping the Euphrates for use by the city of Aleppo.[35] The Treaty of Lausanne signed between the Allies and the new nation of Turkey on 24 July 1923 included the following provisions in article 109 regarding the uses of international water.

> In default of any provisions to the contrary, when as the result of the fixing of a new frontier the hydraulic system (canalisation, inundation, irrigation, drainage or similar matters) in a State is dependent on works executed within the territory of another State, or when use is made on the territory of a State, in virtue of pre-war usage, of water or hydraulic power, the source of which is on the territory of another State, an agreement shall be made between the States concerned to safeguard the interests and rights acquired by each of them. Failing an agreement, the matter shall be regulated by arbitration.[36]

This article has been interpreted by some authors as "an explicit appreciation of the rights of the downstream parties."[37] Other specialists have construed it to mean that "Turkey should confer with Iraq before beginning any activities that may alter the flow of the Euphrates."[38] In any event, the French renegotiated a second treaty—titled the Convention of Friendship and Good Neighbourly Relations—on 30 May 1926, ratifying the previous agreement. A third Franco-Turkish protocol was signed on 3 May 1930 that committed the two nations to coordinating any plans to use the waters of

---

[34] Dolatyar and Gray, *Water Politics in the Middle East*, 133.

[35] Ibid.

[36] Carnegie Endowment for International Peace, *The Treaties of Peace 1919–1923*, vol. 2 (New York: Carnegie Endowment for International Peace, 1924), article 109.

[37] Dolatyar and Gray, *Water Politics in the Middle East*, 133.

[38] Yahia Bakour and John Kolars, "The Arab Mashrek: Hydrologic History, Problems and Perspectives," in *Water in the Arab World: Perspectives and Progress*, ed. Peter Rogers and Peter Lydon (Cambridge, MA: Harvard University Press, 1994), 139.

the Euphrates. The outbreak of World War II ended further conversations about water in the Euphrates-Tigris basin.

Two treaties were signed between Iraq and Turkey: one in 1930, when Iraq was still under the British mandate, and another in March 1946, after Iraqi independence, that was titled the Treaty of Friendship and Good Neighbourly Relations.[39] In these treaties, Turkey consented to Iraq's construction of dams in Turkey to regulate the flow of the rivers into Iraq. Though the dams were never built, Iraq might argue today that the effect of these treaties was Turkish acceptance of Iraq's vested right to receive the amount of water established in the 1930 treaty. Moreover, Turkey obligated itself to begin monitoring data for the rivers and sharing it with Iraq. Iraq then became the first of the three riparian countries to seek full development of the potential of the rivers' waters. Although a number of barrages were constructed to divert waters for irrigation—on the Diyala in 1927–28 and at Kut in 1934–43 (as well as for the construction of the Habbaniyah and Abu Dibis lakes, which were created by filling depressions with water)—the Iraqis built no actual dams. More barrages were built on the Euphrates at Ramadi in 1954 and on the Tigris at Samara in 1957, and dams were constructed on the Little Zab and Diyala in 1959 and 1961.[40] The first Syrian effort began in 1965 and was finished in 1973 as the Tabaqah Dam.

Turkey initiated investigations of water resources in southeastern Turkey following the establishment of hydrometric stations on the Euphrates River in 1936 and the Tigris in 1947. In subsequent years, topographical and hydrologic surveys were conducted. Reconnaissance studies were completed in 1958, and initial plans were developed for three dams on the lower Euphrates and five dams on the Tigris, producing a total irrigation area of 20,000 hectares. The Directorate of State Hydraulic Works (DSI) prepared studies to assess the energy potential in 1963, and the first major dam at Keban entered into operation in 1974. This was the beginning of a program that would come to be called the Southeastern Anato-

---

[39] Dolatyar and Gray, *Water Politics in the Middle East*, 134.

[40] Soffer, *Rivers of Fire*, 85–87.

lia Project (often known by its Turkish initials, "GAP"; it will be referred to as the GAP in this book). The Turks completed their second Euphrates dam, the Karakaya, in 1988 and finished their iconic signature of the GAP, the Ataturk Dam, in 1990. The subsequent filling of the mammoth Ataturk Dam caused such disruption in the flow of the Euphrates River that Turkey and Iraq had previously negotiated a boundary water agreement on 26 December 1975 to formally allocate water to the downstream nation.[41] Even so, the Turks unilaterally released large amounts of additional water to make up the shortfall. These treaties have little relevance today, and the current state of international law in the region is covered in chapter 6.

In recent years, conflict surrounding access to oil in the Middle East has largely obscured a much older and more acute problem of resource scarcity, of which the rise of the Iraqi, Syrian, and Turkish dams are only one example. Although some countries in the Middle East are oil-rich, all are water poor—and getting poorer. Water scarcity is compounded by serious environmental problems that have grown out of the ancient cycle of deforestation, desertification, soil erosion, salination, and the contamination of water supplies. Increased water demands for hydropower and irrigation in the years ahead may reach crisis proportions without an allocation agreement between riparian nations. This is particularly true in the Euphrates-Tigris basin, where population growth and projected demands on the rivers will eventually exceed the dwindling supply of water. Future solutions will depend on the cooperation of riparian nations and, potentially, a fourth riparian actor in the form of an autonomous or independent Kurdistan.

---

[41] Delli Priscoli and Wolf, *Managing and Transforming Water Conflicts*, appendix G (treaties that delineate water allocations).

CHAPTER 2
GEOPOLITICS
IN THE EUPHRATES-TIGRIS BASIN

This chapter examines the geopolitical situation as it affects the riparian nations of the Euphrates-Tigris basin. It very briefly outlines the domestic, foreign, and national security (military) policies of Turkey, Syria, and Iraq with particular attention on how these policies create a framework that impacts the overall stability of the region. The chapter also covers other factors that have an effect on the regional security environment in the river basin area in 2013 (Israel and Iran, in particular) as these factors intersect with American foreign and security policies, which affect the policies of the riparian nations. Finally, it presents an appreciation of how the intersecting policies and interests of Turkey, Syria, Iraq, and the United States compete with, complement, and conflict with one another. Unfortunately, these intersecting policies and interests have contributed to a decline in U.S. influence and led to a consequent erosion of America's ability to act in the region.

Domestic Politics and Agendas

This section outlines the political processes that stand behind the governments of Turkey, Syria, and Iraq and the associated domestic policies, primarily economic, that affect the management and usage of the Euphrates-Tigris waters. Iran is a riparian nation of the Tigris River; its water consumption at present is minimal but is expected to increase significantly in the next 10 years. A series of proposed new dams in Iran

MAP 2.1. **Relief map of Turkey.** *Central Intelligence Agency*

Turkey

The Justice and Development Party (AKP) achieved a dominant position in Turkish politics in the July 2007 general election when it increased its share of the national vote to 47 percent from 34 percent in the 2002 election. This enabled the AKP, led by Prime Minister Recep Tayyip Erdogan, to obtain an absolute majority in parliament (340 out of 550 seats). The AKP was further strengthened when Abdullah Gul, the former foreign minister, was elected to the presidency in August 2007. The AKP has its roots in the now-banned Islamist Welfare Party, but it enjoys broad support from a wide spectrum of secular Turkish constituencies, including Alevis, Kurds, and Armenians. The AKP's victories are, in many ways, a reaction to the poor performance and corrupt practices of the previous administration (the CHP or Republican People's Party) rather than a reflection of an emerging Islamist movement in Turkey.

Prime Minister Erdogan presents himself as a moderate determined to maintain the secular Ataturkism of the modern Turkish state. However, his assurances that he will defend the secular principles of the Turkish constitution are clouded by his support to ease the ban on women wearing Islamic-style headscarves in universities as well as his advocacy to revamp the 1982 constitution. Moreover, over the past five years the AKP government has packed many government agencies (notably the Ministry of Education) with AKP members, who appear to advocate a return to traditional Islamic ways of life. There is deep-rooted suspicion on the part of the Turkish military and the hard-line secularist elite toward Erdogan and President Gul that is the source of much tension in both the Turkish government and Turkish society. The AKP itself narrowly avoided being banned by the constitutional court in 2008 (over its supposed deviation from the secular tenants of the republic), which served as a sort of wake-up call, causing Erdogan to pull back from some of his proposed reforms.[1] However, his constitutional reform package, designed to increase civilian oversight over the military and the judiciary, passed overwhelmingly in a national referendum on 12 September 2010.[2]

The AKP government appears firmly entrenched in power and is increasing civilian oversight over the military and the judiciary. Its election agenda calls for increased democratization and a new constitution to replace the 1982 constitution that was imposed by the military. However, freedom of expression issues plague Turkey as the Erdogan government has come under close international scrutiny because numbers of journalists have been imprisoned for being critical of the government. Moreover, a large number of senior military officers—both active and retired and including a former chief of the general staff—are also in jail facing conspiracy and terrorism charges.

---

[1] *Economist*, "The Worrying Tayyip Erdogan," 5 December 2008, 54.

[2] Economist Intelligence Unit, *Country Report—Turkey* (London: Economist Intelligence Unit, 2011), 4.

The Turkish economy is a robust, world-class economy, especially in comparison to its Caucasian, Iranian, and Arab neighbors. With 73 million people and a young and well-educated workforce, Turkey has the world's sixteenth largest economy.[3] The economy is well balanced between agricultural commodities and industrial production (employment is structured in 2009 with 30 percent of workers in agriculture, 25 percent in industry, and 45 percent in services). Turkish government economic policies are designed to maintain macroeconomic stability, enhance competitiveness, and further attract direct foreign investment.[4]

Despite a contraction during the financial crisis of 2008–9, the Turkish economy has recovered strongly with a 6.5 percent gross domestic product (GDP) growth in 2010. Turkish fiscal policy is sound with the government maintaining a sharp watch on currency and on public debt, which is expected to fall to 4 percent of the GDP. The AKP government remains committed to European Union (EU) accession and to maintaining a healthy economy marked by controllable inflation and lower levels of unemployment in order to please its domestic constituencies. The government is seen as likely to continue pursuing privatization as well as continuing to encourage the extension of credit by banks to businesses and industry.[5] Although GDP growth has dropped to around 4–5.5 percent (well below its annual 2003–7 average of 7 percent), it will remain several percentage points above the United States and the EU average.[6]

Of importance to this study is a review of the Turkish agricultural industry, which accounts for 10.2 percent of all exports and 7.5 percent of all imports (according to 2009 data).[7] Turkey is a net exporter of food and aims to increase this in the future. In 2009, 62 percent of Turkey's total irrigable land was under cultivation, and completion of the GAP (Southeastern

---

[3] *Invest in Turkey* (Ankara: Republic of Turkey Prime Ministry Investment Support and Promotion Agency, 2011).

[4] Economist Intelligence Unit, *Country Report—Turkey*, 7–9.

[5] Ibid., 16–18.

[6] Ibid., 5–9.

[7] Ibid., 25.

Anatolia Project) will raise that figure to an astonishing 91 percent.[8] Commodities data from 2009 show that many of Turkey's products—cow's milk, wheat, tomatoes, watermelons, and potatoes, for example—require water intensive agricultural methods.[9] In addition to raising production, current Turkish agricultural policy is intended to bring Turkey in line with the EU, and new legislation is under consideration to accomplish this.[10] However, there is some concern on the part of Europeans that Turkey has "taken a step backwards"[11] by continuing to raise price supports. In 2009, price supports rose to 34 percent, well above the European average, which is seen as undermining ongoing reform efforts.

Syria

Backed by an effective system of security services and the ruling Baath Party, President Bashar al-Assad continues to maintain a strong grip on Syria.[12] Assad is a member of the minority Alawi[13] sect as are many members of his core elite, many of whom he has appointed to key posts. This has given him increased control over state institutions but has narrowed his power base. Assad, fluent in English and educated in the United Kingdom, projects a friendly and articulate presence to the West, and he appeared to advocate political and economic reform when he took power. However, he has proven to be repressive and slow to take steps that would diminish the power of his party. Assad has pledged reforms, including such measures as enacting a political parties law designed to increase political participation, creating a second chamber of parliament, creating an advisory council to expand the decision-making circle and further the legislative process, and formulating local administration laws to bring about

---

[8] Republic of Turkey, *Turkey Water Report 2009*, 39.

[9] Food and Agriculture Organization of the United Nations Corporate Statistical Database (FAOSTAT), "Preliminary 2009 Data, Top Agricultural Production—Turkey," http://faostat .fao.org/site/339/default.aspx.

[10] OECD (Organisation for Economic Co-operation and Development), "Turkey," in *Agricultural Policies in OECD Countries: At a Glance 2010* (Paris: OECD, 2010), 66.

[11] Ibid.

[12] Economist Intelligence Unit, *Country Report—Syria* (London: Economist Intelligence Unit, 2011), 4–5. Assad was reelected to a second seven-year term in 2007.

[13] The Alawis are a mystical offshoot of Shia Islam concentrated in Syria.

MAP 2.2. **Relief map of Syria.** *Central Intelligence Agency*

greater decentralization. All of these measures would serve to weaken the grip that the president has on power, and he has made minimal progress in implementing his promises.

In truth, Syria remains a country that represses dissent and discourages efforts aimed at furthering democratization. Activists such as those associated with the Damascus Declaration (a proclamation advocating democratic reform) have been rapidly rounded up and arrested. Likewise, new demonstrations in the spring of 2011 were suppressed. Assad's intelligence services and security forces are highly effective and deeply embedded in every sphere of Syrian society. Consequently, opposition to the regime, in all forms, remains dangerous and problematic.

In April 2011, the regime was facing its greatest challenges in 30 years in the form of street demonstrations and local riots. By the spring of 2012, these demonstrations had turned into a full-blown civil war in which thousands of Syrians have been killed and thousands of refugees have fled into neighboring Turkey. The Assad regime faces international sanctions and intense scrutiny for human rights abuses related to this civil war. However, predictions regarding Syria's future are mixed, and the chances of the Assad regime's survival are mixed as well. The consequences of regime change at this writing are unknown, but they could be profound for the region.

Syria has a population of about 18 million people and, defeating predictions, the GDP grew by 4 percent in 2010.[14] The Syrian economy is largely based on agriculture, but it does export oil in small amounts. The past 40 years saw substantial investment in irrigation and agriculture, but the clumsy and inefficient planning produced poor results.[15] Syria has an old-style centrally planned economy, which is gradually being discarded in favor of a mixed economy linked to Western systems. That said, the government launched its latest five-year plan (2011–15), which is directed toward improvements in the country's infrastructure.[16] The economy is currently characterized by government subsidies, wage and price controls, government purchase of crops, and restrictions on foreign currency transactions. Much of the economy is centered on state-owned enterprises that the government would like to transform into private ownership. To enable this, the government was attempting to diversify the economy away from state-owned enterprises such as oil by encouraging investments. Reinforcing this, Syria was receiving grants from the Gulf states as a reward for

---

[14] Economist Intelligence Unit, *Country Report—Syria*, 6.

[15] Elie Elhadj, "Dry Aquifers in Arab Countries and the Looming Food Crisis," *Middle East Review of International Affairs* 12, no. 4 (December 2008): 5–7.

[16] Economist Intelligence Unit, *Country Report—Syria*, 11–13.

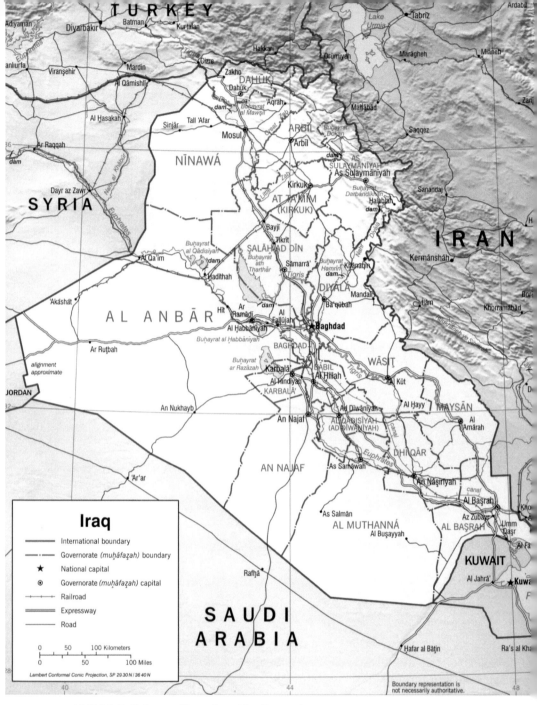

MAP 2.3. **Relief map of Iraq.** *Central Intelligence Agency*

its support of the Doha Agreement and had recently opened the Damascus Stock Exchange. Fiscal policy was moving toward measures designed to facilitate foreign investments and modernize the banking sector. The economic challenges that Syria faces are considerable and include low growth, inflation, declining oil production, and decreasing agricultural production.[17] However, the ongoing civil war has all but crippled these initiatives, and it is hard to see how the country will move forward.

With regards to water, agriculture is the main source of revenue for 47 percent of Syrians, and it generates 20–25 percent of the country's GDP.[18] Food security is a government priority, and Syria is committed to achieving it by introducing a market-oriented approach to agricultural reform.[19] Water shortages continue to remain a "risk" that plague the agricultural sector, so Syria is constructing 10 additional dams and irrigation projects to alleviate this.[20] Major agricultural commodities include such thirsty crops as wheat, tomatoes, and cow's milk.[21]

Iraq

Elections in 2005 produced a permanent constitution in Iraq, and the Shia-dominated coalition government is led by Prime Minister Nuri al-Maliki. The political situation remains unstable but not as dangerous as it was in 2006–7. In the wake of national elections held in March 2010, Maliki not only failed to win a majority sufficient to form a government but took fewer seats than his secular rival Ayad Allawi. Nevertheless, he remained in power as a caretaker while a political impasse developed when the parliament was suspended. There were several false starts to form a government of national unity and reconciliation, but the fragmented parties refused to countenance compromise and power sharing. At various times, Allawi, the Sunnis, and the Kurds walked out of parliament. Although

---

[17] Ibid., 6–8.

[18] Syrian Ministry of Agriculture and Agrarian Reform, National Agricultural Policy Center, *National Programme for Food Security*, xi.

[19] Ibid., xii.

[20] Ibid., xi; and Economist Intelligence Unit, *Country Report—Syria*, 7.

[21] FAOSTAT, "Preliminary 2009 Data, Top Agricultural Production—Syria," http://faostat.fao.org/site/339/default.aspx.

Allawi's bloc and the Kurds have agreed to form a coalition government in return for key portfolios in the cabinet of February 2011, this has not yet coalesced. It is likely that Alawi himself will assume the newly created position of national security advisor. The new cabinet will surely be a fragile body embedded in a fragile federal state because the government is saddled with a compromised constitution that guarantees minority representation in both the Council of Representatives (the Iraqi parliament) and within the executive branch itself. For example, the major sects of Iraq must be represented in the presidency council, the cabinet, and the major branches of government. This has led to incessant political maneuvering by the major political parties, which tend to represent religious and ethnic constituencies. However problematic governing Iraq will prove to be, Maliki has proven himself to be adept at putting together and leading coalition governments, and his current government includes Shiites, Sunnis, and Kurds.

The sectarian and religious divides in a population of approximately 26 million cause major fractures in Iraqi politics.[22] The major political parties are numerous, and no single party has claims to anywhere near a majority share of the population. Maliki leads a moderate Islamist party, and he now also leads the State of Law Coalition that includes the largely Shia Iraqi National Alliance; the Kurdistan Alliance; and the Iraqi National Movement, which is led by former Prime Minister Allawi. Both Malaki and Allawi are considered to be nationalists, and Maliki increasingly seems to be leaning toward secularization.

Over the past several years, Maliki has distanced himself from the Supreme Iraqi Islamic Council (SIIC; sometimes called the Sadr movement), which is led by Muqtada al-Sadr. The SIIC maintains close ties with Iran and is often accused of receiving money from Iranian sources. SIIC supports the idea of Iran's first Supreme Leader, Ayatollah Ruhollah Khomeini, that an Islamic government must be controlled by Islamic scholars. The Sadr movement was formerly aligned with Maliki's party, but has withdrawn

---

[22] Xan Smiley, "Iraq Wants Its Sovereignty Back," in "The World in 2009," special issue, *Economist*, 19 November 2008, 120. Iraqi population estimates vary from 25 to 29 million, and there may be as many as 1–2 million Iraqis living in neighboring countries.

from both the ruling coalition and the government. The Sadr movement controls a military wing that retains considerable combat capability. Of note, the Shia bloc is heavily influenced by the Grand Ayatollah Ali Sistani, who is the top-ranking cleric among the Iraqi Shias. Sistani abstains from broad political activity due to his philosophy of faith but generally supports the government. Sistani normally does not engage in politics except to discourage violence.

Other political Iraqi blocs include the Kurds, Sunnis, and secularist groups. Of these, the Kurdish Alliance is the largest and most significant. It is composed of the Kurdistan Democratic Party (KDP) led by Massoud Barzani, who currently serves as the President of the Kurdistan Regional Government (KRG), and the Patriotic Union of Kurdistan (PUK) led by Iraqi national President Jalal Talabani. Although the KDP and PUK jointly administer the KRG, Barzani's party advocates independence and actively promotes autonomy (chapter 4 addresses the KRG and Kurdish politics).

While fragmented, the Maliki government has proven itself surprisingly resilient and agile in balancing the competing demands of the power blocs in Iraq with the constraints and conditions imposed by the United States. The government is crippled by its inability to pass critical legislation and controversial amendments to an admittedly flawed constitution. These issues include partial rescission of the de-Baathification laws (a key demand of the Sunni community); a national hydrocarbons law that equitably shares energy and oil revenues; right of return laws to rectify the demographic engineering of the former regime; reconciliation structures to retard sectarian partitioning and violence; anticorruption laws; and very importantly, security protocols with the Unites States regarding the status of American forces. Although the Maliki cabinet has suffered periodic withdrawals of Sunni and Shia members, it has maintained control over the component architecture of the Iraqi state. Recently, however, cracks have appeared as Sunni Vice President Tariq al-Hashimi faces criminal charges involving ordering death squads to conduct massacres. Al-Hashimi has subsequently fled to the area controlled by the KRG, which provides him with sanctuary and protection. This issue has driven a wedge between the Maliki government and both Sunnis and Kurds.

The most stable region of Iraq is the KRG, which declared itself a federated region (allowed under the 2005 Iraqi constitution) and which remains largely autonomous. It has remained almost entirely free of the violence that afflicted Iraq in the 2005–8 time frame and is seen as a model for the remainder of the country. The Shia south has stabilized to large degree, as have the central Sunni provinces. Levels of violence have dropped dramatically and center on Baghdad and the surrounding neighboring cities. While much of the credit for this may be attributed to the revised American military strategies of General David H. Petraeus, the Maliki government must also receive credit for its support of the Sunni Awakening Councils, which have been a major force in stabilizing the formerly uncontrollable Sunni provinces. At present, a formal or de facto partition of Iraq based on religious or ethnic lines appears unlikely as the rule of law is extended throughout the country.

The Iraqi economy is almost entirely based on oil revenues, and, notably, the Iraqi government enjoyed a monetary surplus at the end of 2008. Its GDP growth in 2010 was estimated at 5.5 percent.[23] As oil production increases in 2011–12, GDP growth is expected to rise by several percentage points. Government and coalition efforts aimed at introducing a capitalist consumer-based market economy have been only marginally successful, although there is a small Baghdad Stock Exchange. Most workers in Iraq work directly or indirectly for the government, and beyond the shopkeeper level, capitalism as practiced in the West is almost nonexistent. Banking, investment, and finance are in their infancy as the country struggles to find both capable people and viable enterprises. The formerly robust agricultural industry (Iraq was once a major exporter of wheat and rice throughout the region) is recovering slowly. The overall outlook for the Iraqi economy depends on the security situation but is seen as generally positive. Oil revenues are likely to increase as production, distribution, and exportation rise. The main aims of Iraqi economic policy appear to center on microeconomic components of the economy and are designed

---

[23] Economist Intelligence Unit, *Country Report—Iraq* (London: Economist Intelligence Unit, 2011), 7.

to improve project implementation, in part by encouraging greater local participation and cutting bureaucratic constraints.[24]

Iraqi agricultural policy is poorly defined at the current time and remains heavily dependent on U.S. and international advice and assistance. Nevertheless, agriculture is the second largest employer in Iraq (15 percent of its people) and is seen as "the engine of development."[25] This is tied to a 2008 U.S. Department of Agriculture Strategic Framework Agreement for Iraq that is designed to generate higher incomes with the basic idea that agriculture is an economic multiplier that speeds growth.[26] To accomplish this, Iraqi agricultural policy is aimed at reforming the inefficient system of subsidies by increasing production via irrigation technology and soil management, as well as improving animal health practices and the processing of food products.[27] Currently, agriculture accounts for 92 percent of freshwater withdrawals in Iraq (used mostly for irrigation and food production).[28]

Foreign Policies

This section outlines the foreign policies of Turkey, Syria, and Iraq that might affect their ability to negotiate and work together as cooperative riparian partners in the Euphrates-Tigris basin. Of note, all three countries have secular governments that appear committed to westernization and integration into the world economic community, and all three are emerging as independent actors in regional affairs. In 2011, a series of high-level cooperation meetings between Turkey, Syria, and Iraq indicated a trend toward increasing levels of cooperation in the fields of politics, the economy, energy, water, culture, and security. Events since that time have resulted in a less-promising picture.

---

[24] Ibid., 5.

[25] United States Agency for International Development, *The Role of Agriculture in Achieving Strategic Development Objectives in Iraq*, Agricultural Policy Dialogue Series #1 (2010), 1–5.

[26] Ibid., 6.

[27] U.S. Department of Agriculture (USDA), *USDA at Work for Agriculture in Iraq*, fact sheet, November 2009.

[28] Inter-Agency Information and Analysis Unit, *Water in Iraq Factsheet*, 1, http://www.iauiraq.org/documents/1138/Water%20in%20Iraq%20Factsheet-Final.pdf.

Turkey

The Republic of Turkey is a modern secular democracy that is fully integrated into international, European, and regional security and cooperation institutions. It is a member of the United Nations (UN), the Council of Europe, the North Atlantic Treaty Organization (NATO), the Organization for Security and Cooperation in Europe, the Organization for Economic Cooperation and Development, the World Trade Organization (WTO), the Organization of the Islamic Conference (OIC), the Black Sea Economic Cooperation Organization, the Economic Cooperation Organization, the Developing 8 (D-8), and the Conference on Interaction and Confidence Building Measures in Asia. Turkey is also well along the road toward accession in the EU.

The primary objective of Turkish foreign policy is to help secure a peaceful, stable, prosperous, and cooperative regional and international environment that is conducive to human development at home, as well as in neighboring countries and beyond.[29] This objective originated in the early Republican era and is somewhat of a legacy of Kemal Ataturk's famous dictum "Peace at home, peace abroad." In truth, Turkish foreign policy is a pragmatic approach to the problems of living in a region saddled with instability and conflict. A resurgent Russia lies across the Black Sea; to the northeast, the Caucasus region presents ethnic tensions and civil wars; to the east lies a rapidly nuclearizing Iran; in the south, Iraq struggles with the establishment of government and the rule of law while Syria struggles to reconcile residual Baathism with the realities of the twenty-first century; and in the west, the Balkans and Greece (as well as the island of Cyprus) also pose significant challenges. Turkey lies both at a crossroads of cultures and also at the epicenter of a ring of violence and strife. As a consequence of their geography and history, the Turks view themselves as honest brokers and their country as a multidimensional bridge for interaction and dialogue between East and West, Christianity and Islam, modernity and tradition, and democracy and totalitarianism. The huge scale of

---

[29] Turkish Embassy, *Foreign Policy—Synopsis* (Washington, DC: Turkish Embassy, 2011), 1, http://www.washington.emb.mfa.gov.tr/MFA.aspx.

Turkey's involvement in international and regional structures showcases this view.

In 2013, there are two major foreign policy objectives that define the Turkish vision for the future. Both spring from the ruling AKP and present Turkey as a much more assertive actor in regional affairs. The first is to achieve accession and become an integral part of the EU. Accession negotiations began on 3 October 2005 and hinge on the successful completion of the Copenhagen criteria (the rules that determine a country's eligibility to join the EU). Some feel that this goal is stumbling in the face of Islamophobic European opposition, yet the Turkish government remains committed to its success.[30] The second is to help create an environment of security, stability, prosperity, friendship, and cooperation around itself "at the natural convergence point of Europe, the Balkans, the Caucasus, the Black Sea, the Middle East, the Mediterranean and Central Asia."[31] The key to success in the first case, however, revolves mostly around changes to such domestic issues as civilian control of the military, minority rights, and freedom of expression (such as the wearing of headscarves in government buildings). The second case is much more newsworthy in the West and has brought Turkey onto the center of the world stage. This is the work of the AKP's charismatic, inventive, and aggressive foreign minister, Ahmet Davutoğlu, whose phrase "zero problems with neighbors" has come to personify Turkish foreign policy.[32]

Under Prime Minister Erdogan, Turkey has become a very active player in regional affairs. Of note are the efforts to help broker an Israeli-Palestinian settlement; resolve the Cyprus and Armenian normalization issues; and, along with the Brazilians, negotiate a solution to Iran's enrichment of nuclear materials. Unfortunately, none of these initiatives has been successful and "it is not a surprise that the Turks are not

---

[30] *Economist*, "A Fading European Dream," in "Anchors Aweigh: A Special Report on Turkey," 23 October 2010, 8–10.

[31] Turkish Embassy, *Foreign Policy—Synopsis*, 2.

[32] *Economist*, "The Davutoglu Effect," in "Anchors Aweigh: A Special Report on Turkey," 23 October 2010, 6–8.

doing well at this."[33] The basic problem with the "zero problems" foreign policy is that it breaks down under pressure. For example, Turkey's negotiations with Syria between Hizballah and Israel collapsed under the weight of the *Mavi Marmara* Gaza flotilla incident, in which five Turks and a Turkish-American were killed by Israeli commandos, turning Turkish public opinion against Israel.[34] Similarly, normalization agreements with Christian Armenia have foundered on Turkish support of Islamic Azerbaijan.[35] Moreover, sometimes Turkish policy has taken the government into direct confrontations with allies, as recently happened when the abortive Turkish-Brazilian initiative to negotiate the processing and storage of enriched Iranian uranium was crushed in the UN by the United States.[36] When asked directly about the question of Turkish recognition of southern Cyprus, Davutoğlu evaded the question and opined that Turkish interests would prevail in all cases.[37]

Some observers see a resurrected neo-Ottomanism in contemporary Turkish foreign policy—an idea based on the concept that the areas of concern to Turkey today geographically seem to overlap the former Ottoman Empire's farthest boundaries.[38] This is a seductive idea, but it disguises the fact that Turkey is simply dealing with neighboring states and ignores the fact that Ottoman foreign policy was basically reactive and defensive for the last 300 years of its history. Although the Turks regard their current foreign policy as coherent and complementary to a strategic partnership with the United States, it is becoming increasingly clear that there are cracks in the relationship.[39] In fact, the "zero problems" policy

[33] George Friedman, "Geopolitical Journey, Part 5: Turkey," Stratfor, 23 November 2010, http://www.stratfor.com/weekly/20101122_geopolitical_journey_part_5_turkey.

[34] James Traub, "Turkey's Rules," *New York Times Magazine*, 23 January 2011, 35–36.

[35] International Institute for Strategic Studies, "Dashed Hopes for Turkish-Armenian Rapprochement," *Strategic Comments* 16, no. 43 (November 2010): 1–3.

[36] International Institute for Strategic Studies, "Turkey's Bid to Raise Influence in Middle East," *Strategic Comments* 16, no. 38 (October 2010), 1–3.

[37] Ahmet Davutoğlu, "The Turkish-American Relationship" (lecture, Georgetown University, Washington, DC, 16 November 2010).

[38] See, for example, Traub, *Turkey's Rules*; and Friedman, "Geopolitical Journey."

[39] Steven A. Cook, "How Do You Say 'Frenemy' in Turkish? Meet America's New Rival in the Middle East," *Foreign Policy*, 1 June 2010, 1.

may well prove to be unworkable in a practical sense simply because it is a hostage to both Turkish national interests and Turkish political populism, as well as to the whims of the Turkish public. Moreover, because the "zero problems" policy seemingly offers blind support for its Islamic neighbors, it has driven a wedge between Turkey and its formerly close partners, the United States and Israel. In fact, the American interpretation of recent Turkish diplomacy is that Turkey has taken a pronounced "turn to the east," which has come to suggest that the AKP values close ties to its Islamic neighbors more than its ties to the United States.

Problems erupted in late 2011 that will force Turkey to make hard choices and threaten to derail the government's "zero problems" policy. These include a de facto civil war in Syria that has pushed thousands of refugees into southern Turkey and caused resulting international pressure on Turkey to somehow intervene in Syria. There has been a resurgence of terrorism associated with the Kurdistan Workers Party (PKK) in the southeast and the continuing cross-border Turkish bombing of northern Iraq. Territorial and continental shelf issues regarding seabed minerals, including important natural gas deposits, off the coast of divided Cyprus are impeding the dialogue over that island. In Europe, recent French legislative initiatives by the Nicolas Sarkozy government to formally recognize the sad events of 1915 as an Armenian genocide brought the Turkish ambassador home from France. These are not simple problems that can be wished away with diplomatic rhetoric and catchy phrases.

The foreign policy mechanisms by which the Turks are interacting with their southern neighbors, Syria and Iraq, come in the form of High-Level Strategic Cooperation Councils. The first of these was established between Turkey and Iraq in July 2008 and is composed mostly of the members of the respective cabinets, including the foreign ministries as well as the ministries of energy, trade, agriculture, and environment.[40] Problems with the status of the Kurds and the PKK interfered with this committee early on, but the relationship has recently become more workable as Turkey is

---

[40] Ayşegül Kībaroğlu, *Recent Developments and Prospects for Cooperation in the Euphrates Tigris Basin* (Ankara: Middle East Technical University, 2011), 2–3.

working more constructively with the KRG.[41] Turkey established a similar joint high-level committee with Syria in September 2009. At present, both of these initiatives are bilateral between the Turks and their two neighbors and serve mainly as a starting point for serious conversations about issues of mutual concern. Whether these High-Level Strategic Cooperation Councils mature into functioning institutions remains uncertain.

Finally, it must be noted that the Turks have a tradition of being very tough negotiators who do not give up anything without concessions in return.[42] Historically, Turkey has a record of refusal to negotiate in any way regarding issues of national sovereignty. Examples of this are numerous and include both bilateral partners as well as international partners. The Cyprus intervention in 1974 and Turkey's refusal to withdraw from the island resulted in a three-year U.S. arms embargo. Likewise, Turkey refuses to come to any agreement with Greece over long-standing issues regarding the status of the island of Limnos, Aegean air traffic control, territorial waters, and the ownership of Aegean islets. Since the mid-1990s, there have been serious disagreements between Turkey and neighboring Armenia over the status of Azerbaijan, which resulted in Turkey's refusal to establish a normal diplomatic and economic relationship with Armenia. Recently, Turkey has cancelled military agreements with Israel over the issue of Palestine. Similar patterns are present in NATO, particularly regarding Greece and the Aegean Sea as well as the allocation of top flag officer billets in NATO's command structure. In 1991 and 2003, Turkey refused to cooperate with UN-sponsored coalitions and American-sponsored coalitions, respectively. There is nothing to suggest that this pattern of extremely tough and nonnegotiable positions regarding issues of Turkish national sovereignty will not continue in the future.

---

[41] Ibid.

[42] While on active duty with the U.S. Army, one of the coauthors—then-LtCol Edward Erickson—served as the Special Assistant to the Commander-in-Chief (AFSOUTH) for the eastern Mediterranean. In this position, he served as a negotiator and political advisor to the NATO command in southern Europe. The paragraph above reflects his experiences in working with the Turks.

Syria

The Syrian Arab Republic is officially a parliamentary republic, but in truth it remains a secular Baathist dictatorship ruled by Bashar al-Assad. Assad is the son of Hafez al-Assad and is supported by key elements in the security services and the Baath Party leadership. Although Syria remains isolated, it maintains membership in the UN, International Monetary Fund (IMF), OIC, Arab League, and a number of Arab economic and development councils.

Syrian foreign policy appears oriented toward emerging from international isolation caused by its occupation of Lebanon, supporting terrorist organizations aimed at Israel, fostering a friendship with Iran, and developing suspected weapons of mass destruction projects. Under Bashar al-Assad, Syria has withdrawn its military forces from Lebanon and demonstrated a willingness to engage in diplomatic discussions aimed at normalizing its relations with its neighbors, particularly Lebanon and Israel.[43] Recent developments include support for the May 2008 Doha Agreement between opposing forces in Lebanon and its agreement to normalize diplomatic relations with Lebanon. Syria also appears ready to move toward rapprochement with the United States and toward restoring good relations with Egypt and Saudi Arabia. However, Assad's unpredictability makes this problematic as he continues a close relationship with Tehran and Hizballah.[44] In March 2011, the Syrians voted in the Arab League to censure Colonel Muammar Qaddafi of Libya and to support a UN Security Council resolution authorizing the use of force against Libya. However, the full force of the Arab Spring[45] demonstrations hit Syria shortly thereafter, and al-Assad responded with full-scale military interventions. The violence and corresponding government crackdowns worsened, but the government remains in firm control of the major cities. By early summer 2011, Syria had come under heavy UN criticism for human rights viola-

---

[43] Economist Intelligence Unit, *Country Report—Syria*, 2.

[44] Eyal Zisser, "Where Is Bashar al-Assad Heading?" *Middle East Quarterly* 15, no. 1 (Winter 2008): 35.

[45] The Arab Spring, or Arab Awakening, is a series of demonstrations and revolutions in the Middle East and North Africa that began in December 2010.

tions. Within months the demonstrations metastasized into a full-blown civil war in the cities of Daraa and Homs. However, given continuing Russian and Chinese support for Syria in the UN Security Council, an effective response by the international community has not been forthcoming. Moreover, it is unlikely that Syria will face punishing international military operations (as was the case in Libya) either. Not only does the Assad regime enjoy continued support, it maintains a large and sophisticated, albeit aging, air defense system. There is cause to reflect that in 1984, Syria shot down an American A-6 Intruder aircraft and held pilot Robert O. "Bobby" Goodman until the American civil rights advocate Jesse L. Jackson managed to negotiate his release.

Iraq

The Republic of Iraq is a secular democracy that has a weak and dysfunctional coalition-based central government. Although it remains a member of many international organizations, the collapse of the Baathist regime of Saddam Hussein left the country isolated from participation in regional and international structures. Iraq has seats in the following organizations: the UN, OIC, Group of 77, IMF, WTO, World Bank, and Organization of the Petroleum Exporting Countries (OPEC). Importantly, Iraq has regained its seat in the Arab League from which it had withheld dues since 1980. The continuing violence in Baghdad makes the opening of embassies and international offices problematic. Moreover, the collapse of the Baathist regime has left the government with few professional diplomats or qualified internationalists.

The primary pillar of Iraqi foreign policy is the restoration of its standing in the international community after the disastrous foreign policies of Saddam Hussein. There are a number of ongoing initiatives and objectives designed to overcome the legacy of the Baathist regime. These objectives are to protect Iraq's security, stabilize the country, and preserve territorial integrity; restore international diplomatic bilateral relations and reengage the international community in Iraq's reconstruction and development; reconstruct the economy and infrastructure to raise the standard of living of the Iraqi people; reactivate Iraq's diplomatic missions and promote Iraqi interests in all political cultural, economic, social, and cultural fields; rejoin, and engage in, all multilateral bodies; reform the Ministry of Foreign Affairs and its activities based on new values and principles; and pursue the chosen path of democratization within the framework of sovereignty, unity, and equal partnership.[46] In addition, the current government of Iraq seeks to maintain a strong political and security relationship with the United States. This is necessary for reasons of internal stability and rule of law and also for reasons of securing national sovereignty against neighboring countries such as Turkey, Iran, and Saudi Arabia.

National Security Policies and Strategies

This section outlines the national security policies and strategies of Turkey, Syria, and Iraq that affect outlook and behavior of the three riparian nations. Of note is Turkey's increasingly independent position as a military power, which may lead to it becoming a regionally hegemonic nation. Moreover, the Iraqi national security strategy explicitly identifies the upstream riparians as threats to Iraqi national security.

Turkey

As the end of the Cold War decisively altered both NATO and American security policies, so too did the collapse of the USSR alter Turkish national security policy. Until the mid-1990s, Turkish national security policy focused on the land defense of the Turkish straits and Caucasia. This was partly a function of NATO's intent to deny the Soviets the use of the Bosporus and Dardanelles and partly a function of the state of the Turkish army, which was armed with older, second-rate American weapons. In the late 1990s, a growing Turkish economy and a revised vision of the security challenges facing the country enabled the Turkish general staff to undertake a massive recasting of Turkey's national security policy.[47]

---

[46] Iraqi Ministry of Foreign Affairs, *Foreign Policy* (Baghdad: Iraqi Ministry of Foreign Affairs, 2011), 1–2, http://www.mofa.gov.iq/english/foreignpolicy/.

[47] For a summary of evolving Turkish defense policies, see Edward J. Erickson, "Turkey as Regional Hegemon—2014: Strategic Implications for the United States," *Turkish Studies* 5, no. 3 (Autumn 2004), 25–45.

In 1998, the Turks released their *White Paper — Defence 1998*,[48] which represented a major shift in how the Turks thought about their military role in a dangerous region as the world moved into the twenty-first century. The new policy was, in many ways, an extension of the changing NATO strategy and new vocabulary and articulated a policy of "forward engagement" and "crisis management."[49] These policies moved Turkey away from defensively oriented postures toward the idea of power projection and cross-border operations. The paper also outlined the hardware acquisition packages that Turkey would need to execute such a strategy. Two years later, the Turks published a second white paper on defense that added definition to the previous work and outlined Turkey's national security goals as deterrence, military contributions to crisis management and intervention, forward defense, and collective security. This paper went on to outline how Turkey would restructure its military and acquisition programs in order to develop deterrent military forces; enhanced command and control systems; advanced technology weapons and systems; superior operational capability; antimissile and nuclear, chemical, and biological defense capability against weapons of mass destruction; enhanced capability to mobilize rapidly to conduct operations other than war; and the capability to conduct joint and combined warfare. Importantly, the land forces were tasked with the mission to "transfer operations across borders when necessary."[50] This document set the course for the execution of Turkish national security policy for the next decade.

The Turks have not published subsequent defense white papers, and in general terms the 1998 paper still serves as the way ahead. However, under the AKP, the Turkish defense industry has made remarkable progress in the production of state-of-the-art military equipment and related technologies.[51] Turkey's defense industry is seen as shifting toward the

---

[48] Republic of Turkey Ministry of National Defence, *White Paper—Defence 1998* (Ankara: Ministry of National Defence, 1998).

[49] Republic of Turkey Ministry of National Defence, *Turkey's National Defense Policy Part Four*, white paper (Ankara: Ministry of National Defence, 1998).

[50] Republic of Turkey Ministry of National Defence, *Turkey's National Defense Policy, Part Four, Section One*, white paper (Ankara: Ministry of National Defence, 2000).

[51] Robert K. Ackerman, "Turkey's Defense Industry Matures," *Signal*, September 2010, 27–29.

production of top-end electronics, software, and sophisticated communications gear. This suite of capabilities complements the robust existing military industrial base that currently manufactures tanks, artillery, and fighter aircraft. Notably, there are reports that the Turkish National Security Council has revised its list of potential threats to include Israel while dropping Iran and Syria.[52]

Syria

Because of the secretive nature of the Syrian Baathist regime, public disclosure of national security and military policies remains obscure. The Syrian military has never recovered from the demise of its generous strategic partner, the Soviet Union, which provided it with a comprehensive arsenal of modern weapons. Generally speaking, the Syrian weapons inventory is 20 years or more out of date. Such money as has been available has gone into maintaining a few purchases for the air force and for missiles. In 2008, the Israelis bombed what they described as a suspected nuclear site in northern Syria; however, this is unconfirmed by other sources. The Syrian military today has absolutely no capacity for cross-border operations, and moreover it has no capacity to defend itself from either Israel or Turkey. Today, there is almost no money available for modernization or comprehensive acquisition programs, nor is there much money for training or operations. In truth, the Syrian armed forces are little more than aging caretakers of an increasingly obsolete force structure.

The primary focus of the Syrian armed forces in the past decade has been the retention of its occupation forces in Lebanon, which amounted to about two divisions. However, the 2007 Syrian withdrawal from Lebanon ended that, but it is thought that both the Syrian military and Syrian intelligence would like to reintroduce a Syrian presence in Lebanon.

Iraq

The most recent Iraqi national security strategy, titled *Iraq First*, was published in October 2007. In the absence of a published national security

---

[52] Haaretz Service, "Turkey Policy Paper: Israel's Actions Threaten Mideast," *Haaretz* (Israel), 1 November 2010, 1.

policy, *Iraq First* must serve in this role. The document provides guidance for a three-year period (2007–10) and presents a consensus from the office of the prime minister and all government ministries. *Iraq First's* authors were representative of the major sects and groups in Iraq.[53] The strategy focuses on the people of Iraq; links the country to the international community; is based on national reconciliation; and provides a broad definition of national security as security, political, economic, and informational interests.

Iraq First identifies threats to Iraq—for example, terrorism, insurgency, corruption, crime, armed groups and militias, foreign interference, ethnic and sectarian violence, the dictatorial mentality of the past, and serious societal ills. The strategy also defines four strategic components for using Iraq's resources to overcome threats and realize its interests:

a. Security component that includes sovereignty, territorial integrity, and the use of security forces.

b. Political component that includes national reconciliation, good governance, regional cooperation, and international agreements, that includes promoting human rights, compensating victims, attacking unemployment and poverty, and providing for amnesty.

c. Economic component that includes reformed societal institutions, combating corruption, and promoting economic growth.

d. Informational component that provides legal sanctions for free and responsible journalism and confronts incitements to violence and terrorism.[54]

Importantly for this formerly militaristic nation, the new national security strategy does not lean heavily on military power but rather on economic power and social well-being as the primary pillar of national security.

---

[53] Republic of Iraq Cabinet and National Security Council, *Iraq First: Iraqi National Security Strategy, 2007–2010* (Baghdad: Republic of Iraq, 2007). This document has not been superseded, and it is likely that the subsequent document will bear a close resemblance to this one.
[54] Ibid., 9–49.

One aspect of *Iraq First* bears significance relative to this study as it relates to the Euphrates-Tigris basin and the Syrian and Turkish dams. In listing significant threats to the nation, the government of Iraq notes the following.

<u>Ecological interdependence</u>

The problem of decreasing water levels in the Tigris and Euphrates Rivers is a dangerous phenomenon that directly threatens environmental and nutritional security. It affects the climate and wetlands, increases desertification, and even decreases the availability of potable water in the middle and southern regions. This problem stems essentially from the fact that there are large dams in Turkey and Syria for storing the water of the two rivers that do not take into consideration the rights of Iraq to water resources and the longer stretch of these rivers on its territory. Therefore, leaving this problem as it is due to the failure of joint committees formed to resolve it leaves Iraq subject to a catastrophe that threatens its current and future national security.[55]

The Iraqi national defense policy and military strategy complement the new national security strategy and run concurrently from 2008–11. The Iraqi Ministry of Defense (MoD) policy requires the creation of capable headquarters to handle tasks related to the organization, training, preparation, and continued use of Iraqi armed forces according to the constitution and the national security strategy and other government policies and directions. Through 2012, the MoD and joint staff are focused on force generation within a democratic context while maintaining and improving internal security. After that point the Iraqis plan to create a modern army of about 18 NATO-style divisions supported by tanks, artillery, and jets.

The United States in the Region

The United States continues to play a pivotal role in the politics of the modern Middle East. While American strategic interests in the region since 1991 have remained remarkably constant, there have been dramatic turnabouts in American foreign and military policy that have made it dif-

---

[55] Ibid., 16.

ficult for the United States to influence the governments and the people of the Middle East. In particular, the pendulum-like changes in American national security strategy have created a climate of mistrust that the current administration is working hard to dismantle. Likewise, the legacies of changing and conflicted American actions in the region have created few new friends while at the same time led to an increasing number of disenchanted old friends.

U.S. Foreign and National Security Policy

William J. "Bill" Clinton's presidency became the first post–Cold War administration that was forced to redefine American foreign and national security policy in a world that was no longer bipolar. The America of the late 1990s was often described as a "hyperpower" with immense resources and seemingly positioned to change the world for the better. Much of what Clinton achieved reflected his beliefs in globalization and multilateralism. Clinton's foreign policy focused on opportunity rather than a defined long-term policy or end state, unlike the "containment" that it replaced. American national security policy shifted toward a new reliance on alliance partners and active cooperation with the UN. However, cuts in the military structure soured many in the American defense establishment as the Clinton administration sought to balance the federal budget. Nevertheless, Clinton built up a reservoir of international friends and goodwill, leaving the United States well positioned to enter the twenty-first century.

His successor, George W. Bush, campaigned on unilateralism and moving America away from nation building. The 9/11 attacks clarified and strengthened Bush's determination to set America on a new foreign policy pathway. The "Global War on Terror" became the vehicle by which the Bush administration implemented its agenda in American foreign policy. In brief, the new American foreign policy under President Bush rested on three principles: a right to take unilateral and preemptive action (including military strikes), when necessary; American dominance in international affairs and forums; and the aggressive promotion of American-style democracy around the world. In essence, it was reactive and a return to the "Ugly American" attitudes of the 1950s and 1960s, by which Americans insisted on making key decisions and treated non-Americans in a paternalistic fashion.[56] The centerpiece of this policy was the famous 2002 State of the Union speech in which Bush identified Iraq, Iran, and North Korea as "the axis of evil."

The corresponding national security and military policies envisioned short, low-cost wars won by airpower supported by minimal commitment of American ground forces. Bush's Secretary of Defense Donald H. Rumsfeld began an immediate "transformation" of the American defense establishment aimed largely at deconstructing the Cold War–based armor- and artillery-heavy defense establishment. The surprisingly rapid and easy conquest of Afghanistan in 2001 appeared to vindicate these ideas. The term "shock and awe" entered the American lexicon when Bush authorized the invasion of Iraq in March 2003, and once again the administration's agenda seemed sound. However, the seductively easy victory over Saddam Hussein disguised the reality of occupying a country with too few soldiers, an inadequate understanding of the human terrain in Iraq, and no definable end state or exit strategy. The events that followed are well known and need not be repeated here.

The legacies of the Bush administration's foreign and military policies are legion and include a dangerously overstretched army, a zooming national debt, the alienation of many formerly staunch allies, seemingly endless wars in Iraq and Afghanistan, deteriorating relations with Russia, an inability to secure support in international forums, a rapidly nuclearizing Iran, and the loss of American prestige and influence throughout the world. This placed the incoming president, Barack H. Obama, in a difficult position, which, combined with a worldwide financial crisis in the fall of 2008, resulted in a major recasting of American policies.

---

[56] Widely read in the 1960s, *The Ugly American* (1958) by Eugene L. Burdick and William J. Lederer presents the idea that Americans insist on forcing the American way of politics, economics, and social structures on other peoples in the world in the name of democracy and human rights. In the story, the poorly informed antihero is actually out to further American interests at the expense of native peoples while cloaking his work in American ideals and virtues.

Under President Obama, U.S. foreign policy returned to Clinton-style realism and multilateralism that seeks to engage the world as an equal partner. The Obama administration recommitted the United States to working through and with international organizations, particularly the UN. There have been serious efforts to engage Middle Eastern nations directly and to dismantle the legacy of the "axis of evil" label, as well as attempts to restore good relations with Russia. In 2011, American combat forces departed Iraq and some shifted to Afghanistan, but by 2014 they will withdraw from there as well. Obama has tried to reconcile Israel with its neighbors, but these efforts have been ineffective. Unfortunately, the Obama administration has been unable to return America to the position of honest broker rather than the pro-Israeli backer that it is today. The idealistic American experiment to plant democracy and Western ideas about human rights in Iraq and Afghanistan will likely lead to an incomplete result when, after American withdrawal, those societies return to deeply embedded traditional cultural values.

As of 2013, American national security and military policy under Obama is undergoing brutal revisions as the full effect of the financial crisis of 2008 is felt. Inevitably, the huge U.S. defense budget will be slashed by cost cutters looking to balance the budget. Modernization and acquisition programs will be cancelled or pushed into an uncertain future, and there will be force reductions in the ground, air, and naval forces as well. Aside from the deleterious physical effects of the Bush years on the American military, there is a strong sense that America's ground forces, both active and reserve, are mentally and emotionally exhausted by 10 years of nearly continuous deployment cycles to warzones. This sense of war-weariness mandates something akin to a post-Vietnam style rebuilding period in which the ground forces reinvent themselves physically, intellectually, and spiritually.

In a 2011 report, the Congressional Research Service analyzed four possible U.S. policy approaches toward Turkey.[57] These are a status quo ap-

---

[57] Jim Zanotti, *Turkey-U.S. Defense Cooperation: Prospects and Challenges* (Washington, DC: Congressional Research Service, 2011), 23–25.

proach, an accommodative approach (accommodating a nation's expressions of national interest), a linkage approach (linking cooperation of a state to nonstate actors on issues of American national security interest), and a case-by-case approach. Such a menu of approaches may be indicative of America's drift toward pragmatic foreign policy solutions that closely examine ends, ways, and means.

In the spring of 2011, demonstrations and revolts swept through North Africa and the Middle East in what became known as the Arab Spring or Arab Awakening. The Obama administration proceeded cautiously at this time and applied diplomatic pressure through nontraditional means. American policy toward Egypt stands out in this regard when its diplomacy manifested itself effectively through the military-to-military contacts built up since 1979. In March 2011, the administration orchestrated a coalition of European and Arab partners to implement UN Security Council Resolution 1973 against Libya. By the end of April, the mission deteriorated into a stalemate that was undermining international law, threatening the integrity of NATO, and demonstrating incoherent U.S. foreign policy. However, this cloaked the orchestration of a NATO response that imposed a no-fly zone over the country in support of the rebels. By August 2011, with covert assistance from the West, the rebels defeated the Qaddafi regime and gained complete control of the country. In October, Qaddafi himself was captured and killed. What has become known as the Arab Spring continues, and America's response will have to be fully evaluated well after this book goes to press.

American Strategic Interests and Partnerships

American strategic interests in the Euphrates-Tigris basin reflect America's larger strategic interests in the region and the Middle East. These interests date from the ending of the Second World War when America ceased to be an oil exporter and became an importer of Middle Eastern oil. Throughout the Cold War, the United States sought to contain the USSR and to maintain a balance of power in the region, while safeguarding a supply of oil from friendly states. The Iranian Revolution in 1979, the collapse of the Soviet Union in 1991, the failure to resolve the Palestinian question, and the War on Terror in the twenty-first century irrevocably altered these policies. The Middle East has dropped from supplying one-third of America's oil in 1973 to one-fifth in 2008[58] and down to about 17 percent in 2011.[59] Despite these continuing reductions, oil remains central in all ways to American strategic interests in the Middle East.

Even though the United States imports significantly smaller amounts of oil from the Middle East, its strategic interests remain tied to the region. This is because the centralized pricing and management of the world's supply of oil make its actual point of origin increasingly irrelevant. This situation is likely to continue for the next decade. The keystone of American interests in the Middle East is therefore one of maintaining regional stability and guaranteeing peaceful relations among its community of nations. In the near term, the stabilization of Iraq and Afghanistan are central to these issues. Failure in either case is seen to lead to failed-state scenarios wherein these nations become a haven for terrorist networks and a launching pad for forces seeking to destabilize the region. Conversely, if Iraq and Afghanistan emerge as stable countries, they will have an overall positive effect on the region. In addition to the ongoing military campaigns, serious American efforts are underway to improve the political, economic, and social stability of both countries.

In the spring of 2011, when popular demonstrations broke out in Tunisia, Egypt, and a number of other Middle Eastern nations, the worldwide price of oil increased rapidly. In March 2011, a popular revolution aimed at overthrowing the Qaddafi regime disrupted the supply of oil from Libya. Although the OPEC oil cartel immediately made up the difference in overall supply, the price of oil skyrocketed, causing the United States to consider releasing its strategic petroleum reserves.[60]

---

[58] Gelvin, *Modern Middle East*, 258–61.

[59] U.S. Energy Information Administration, "How Dependent Are We on Foreign Oil?" U.S. Energy Information Administration, http://tonto.eia.doe.gov/energy_in_brief/foreign _oil_dependence.cfm, (accessed 2012).

[60] *Economist*, "The Battle for Libya: The Colonel Fights Back," 10 March 2011, 53–54.

There are other factors that affect American strategic interests as well, especially those dealing with bilateral relationships with large Middle Eastern states. Iran's support for dissident groups in Iraq and its ongoing nuclearization program are destabilizing elements in the region, which America must attend to. American foreign policy toward Iran, characterized by U.S. refusal to engage in direct dialogue, has proven to be perilously ineffective. At the same time, American foreign policy toward Pakistan has not been particularly effective, and although Pakistan supports the America-led War on Terror, the Pakistani government has been unable to secure the northwest frontier adjacent to Afghanistan. In both cases, American diplomacy resembles a patchwork solution. Relations with Turkey have been very rocky since the 2003 invasion of Iraq, and recent American support for Israel over Gaza and the West Bank have further weakened this historically strong relationship.[61] Taken altogether, the United States must, at the very least, attempt to restore working diplomatic relations with Iran while improving its damaged relationships with Pakistan and Turkey.

Recent defense policy changes, however, have somewhat clarified American strategic interests in the Middle East. In a significant shift of thinking, the Obama administration is "rebalancing toward the Asia-Pacific region."[62] That said, American strategic policy in the Middle East will "continue to place a premium on U.S. and allied military presence in—and support of—partner nations in and around the region."[63] This position effectively ties the United States to multilateral and collective solutions to regional problems. Supporting this policy, an associated budget document expressed returning to a posture of maintaining persistent presence

---

[61] See, for example, German Marshall Fund of the United States and Compagnia di San Paolo, "Turkey and the West—Drifting Away," in *Transatlantic Trends: Key Findings 2010* ([Washington, DC?]: German Marshall Fund of the United States and Compagnia di San Paolo, 2010), 23–28; and "Turks See US as Biggest External Threat, Poll Results," *Hürriyet Daily News* (Turkey), 5 January 2011, 1–2.

[62] U.S. Department of Defense, *Sustaining Global Leadership: Priorities for 21st Century Defense* (Washington, DC: U.S. Department of Defense, 2012), 2.

[63] Ibid.

in the region.[64] In the Middle East, the United States intends to "gradually transition security in Afghanistan and reestablish peacetime ground force presence" while "this region will also become increasingly maritime."[65] These policies do not mean that the United States is withdrawing from the Middle East, but rather they add clarity to the official U.S. national military strategy, which stressed security cooperation and partnering with allies in the "broader Middle East."[66]

The principal shortcoming in defining American strategic interests in the Middle East involves U.S. policy toward Israel. Since 2001 the U.S. government has moved to a position guaranteeing the territorial integrity and continued survival of the state of Israel. Indeed, in 2008, President George Bush, presidential candidates Barack Obama and John S. McCain, and vice presidential candidates Joseph R. "Joe" Biden Jr. and Sarah L. Palin repeatedly used the term "America's ally" to describe the relationship between America and Israel. While America has no actual formal alliance with Israel, there is certainly a strong, preexisting bipartisan de facto security pledge to Israel. This complicates America's Middle East policy as U.S. support for Israel's retention of the West Bank and Golan Heights, cross-border operations in Lebanon and the Gaza Strip, and the provision of American weapons and technology to Israel alienates the broader Muslim community in the region. Political scientists John J. Mearsheimer and Stephen M. Walt make a case that, in fact, the United States has no strategic interest in Israel and that support for Israel is counterproductive to America's real strategic interests in the region.[67] Moreover, Mearsheimer and Walt maintain that U.S. support for Israel is the product of a Jewish American pro-Israeli lobby. Regardless of the cause, the linkage of American strategic interests to Israeli national security acts

---

[64] U.S. Department of Defense, *Defense Budget Priorities and Choices* (Washington, DC: U.S. Department of Defense, 2012), 5.

[65] Ibid.

[66] U.S. Department of Defense, *The National Military Strategy of the United States of America 2011: Redefining America's Military Leadership* (Washington, DC: U.S. Department of Defense, 2011), 11–12.

[67] John J. Mearsheimer and Stephen M. Walt, *The Israel Lobby and U.S. Foreign Policy* (New York: Farrar, Straus and Giroux, 2007).

as an albatross on America's ability to build a coherent and consistent Middle Eastern policy.[68]

Finally, American awareness of water as a significant challenge affecting regional stability appears to be increasing. Despite this, opinion in the U.S. government regarding where and under what circumstances water issues might cause instability is mixed. For example, the U.S. Marine Corps Center for Emerging Threats and Opportunities' recent *2011 Edition of Flashpoints* posits water as one of 10 factors used to predict instability and catalysts for conflict.[69] According to the Marine report, Afghanistan is the country most at risk for conflict based on water issues, while Iraq appears far down on the list of potential water-related flashpoints.[70] This interpretation competes with a recent assessment from the Office of the Director of National Intelligence that lists the Euphrates-Tigris system as a potential region of concern (over the next 30 years) but does not mention the issue of Afghanistan-Iran hydropolitics.[71]

The Regional Security Environment

A number of factors affect the regional security environment of the Euphrates-Tigris basin; chief among these is stability in Iraq, but they also include terrorism, Iran's nuclear program, and the effect that the American relationship with Israel has on its relations with the riparian states. These factors are fluid, and their constantly changing nature lends unpredictability to the security posture of the riparian states.

Stability in Iraq

By almost any measurement, the U.S.-led Coalition appears to have been successful in stabilizing Iraq. Recent security gains have all but ended the

---

[68] In addition to Mearsheimer and Walt, a 2008 book by Australian Jeremy Salt traces the historical development of American policies in the Middle East and reaches similar conclusions. See Salt's *The Unmaking of the Middle East: A History of Western Disorder in Arab Lands.*

[69] Center for Emerging Threats and Opportunities, *2011 Edition of Flashpoints* (Quantico, VA: Center for Emerging Threats and Opportunities, 2011), 1.

[70] Ibid., 23, 60.

[71] Office of the Director of National Intelligence, "Assessment on Global Water Security," news release, 22 March 2012.

extreme levels of violence that occurred in Iraq's central provinces in 2006, although isolated and sporadic incidents of terrorism, kidnapping, and suicide and car bombings continue on an episodic basis. As Iraq enters the second decade of the twenty-first century, assessments of the combat effectiveness of the Iraqi army in independent operations are optimistic. Assuming that problems with reliability and professionalism can be straightened out, the Iraqi MoD has ambitious plans for upgrading the size and capabilities of the Iraqi armed forces. By 2012, the MoD planned to have 15 divisions trained and equipped, one of which would be mechanized. By that date the internal civil war and associated terrorism problem should have been eliminated, and thereafter the Iraqi armed forced should begin to shift from internal security roles to the defense of Iraqi territory. By 2020, an additional two armored, two mechanized, and three home defense divisions will be added to the Iraqi order of battle. The ground forces will be supported by an air force of about 100 helicopters in 2012 and several hundred attack helicopters and multi-role jet aircraft by 2020. The navy is projected to remain small but will include frigates and some landing ships by 2020 as well. The forces are programmed to be supported by a robust infrastructure, training bases, and acquisition programs. Whether the optimistic Iraqi plans will ever reach fruition depends on a number of internal and external dynamics, of which the most important may be Iraq's relationship with the United States. It is uncertain how much American support and training assistance will remain in Iraq in the period through 2020. However, it is problematic in that without substantial U.S. involvement the entire plan is in jeopardy and risks failure.

A report in the *New York Times* on 15 April 2011 may be emblematic of things to come. A Turkish company was dismantling U.S. fortifications in the Green Zone in Baghdad, and Iraq was hosting the annual meeting of the Arab League. If long-term stability is to be assured, it will have to be to the parties' economic and political advantage. And the United States will be playing a less influential role.

The Kurdistan Workers Party and the Kurds

A resurgence of the separatist PKK has presented difficulties to the United States, Turkey, and Iraq. The PKK consists of Turkish ethnic Kurds who aspire to independence and self-determination for the southeastern provinces of Turkey. Thought to have been crushed when its leader Abdullah Ocalan was captured by Turkish commandos in 1999, the PKK has enjoyed a rebirth in the mountains along the northern Iraqi border with Turkey. There were a number of PKK terrorist attacks in southeastern Turkey in 2007 and 2008 that resulted in the death and wounding of a number of Turkish soldiers. In response, the Turkish general staff conducted a number of cross-border operations, with special forces, commandos, attack helicopters, artillery, and jet aircraft. Public opinion in Turkey strongly supports both retaliatory and preemptive cross-border operations, and the Turkish parliament voted in October 2008 to extend the law authorizing such operations. Turkey blames the KRG and the Iraqi government for failing to stop the PKK attacks and for providing sanctuary and base areas for the terrorists. Secondarily, Turkey blames the United States for failing to recognize the seriousness of the PKK attacks by not influencing the Iraqi and KRG governments to take a more active posture against the PKK. In truth, as the Pakistani problem with its northwest frontier shows, it is very difficult in such harsh mountainous terrain to entirely prevent the movement of people across poorly defined and poorly guarded borders.

A crisis developed in the fall of 2007 when the Turks moved significant combat forces to the Iraqi border and threatened invasion because of PKK raids. While the Turks were careful to note that they had limited objectives and that they would withdraw as quickly as possible, both the United States and Iraq perceived the threats as destabilizing. Not only did the Maliki government appear weak, but America appeared powerless to influence its NATO ally and long-time Turkish security partner. The crisis was resolved by the shuttle diplomacy of General Petraeus, who brokered a deal between the Coalition forces in Iraq, the Maliki government, the

KRG, and the Turks. In return for preoperations notification by the Turks of cross-border incursions, the United States has provided real-time intelligence on PKK base camps and movements in northern Iraq. The Iraqi and the KRG governments were cut out of the Turkish-U.S. cycle by an American promise to share warnings that would keep Iraqi Kurds and Americans out of the way of the Turks. Thus far, the Petraeus solution has proven durable in keeping the main Turkish army out of Iraq.

The PKK problem continues, and the Turkish government holds the KRG responsible as the primary culprit because it appears to offer protection to its fellow Kurds, who want nothing less than independence and, perhaps, the opportunity to merge with the KRG. Barzani is seen by the Turks as supporting the PKK, and the continued KRG refusal to condemn the PKK as a terrorist organization, as well as its refusal to actively hunt down the PKK itself, appear to corroborate Turkish concerns. At present the Iraqi government and military remain cut out of the loop by the bilateral Turkish-American agreements and protocols.

Iran and Nuclear Weapons

Iran continues to contribute to regional instability by promoting violence through its support of terrorism and its alleged pursuit of nuclear weapons. The extent of the actual linkage of the official Iranian government to violence in Iraq remains cloudy and largely unproven. Likewise, the extent of Iran's nuclear program remains obscure, and its true purpose largely unproven. Officially, the Iranian nuclear program has a peaceful intent, but the public proclamations by Iranian president Mahmoud Ahmedinejad to eradicate Israel lend credence to another conclusion. That Iran continues to run its ever-increasing number of centrifuges is beyond doubt; nevertheless, whether the government will seek to create nuclear weapons is uncertain. Significantly, the Ahmedinejad government has removed many moderates and Western-leaning diplomats who oppose nuclearization from Iranian embassies and the foreign ministry.[72]

---

[72] *Economist*, "Iran's Battered Opposition: A Leadership Neutered," 10 March 2011.

While Iranian acquisition of nuclear weapons has little to do directly with the waters of the Euphrates-Tigris basin, the impasse with the West does have relevance. The present UN approach of gradualism in enacting sanctions and embargos does not appear to deter the Iranian program. Previously classified Central Intelligence Agency assessments, released in 2007, indicated that there was little authentic proof that Iran was weaponizing its nuclear program, further weakening international resolve. Moreover, the United States created almost impossible negotiating conditions by its refusal to open dialogue without preconditions (meaning that Iran must stop its centrifuges before starting negotiations), which served to self-remove the most powerful nation in the world from directly dealing with the issues. The American diplomatic efforts are described as "diplomacy by proxy" as the United States attempts to deal with Iran through intermediary nations. In essence, the Western response to the Iranian centrifuges has been notably ineffective and, in some ways, a victory for Ahmedinejad's reckless ambitions.

There are many possible outcomes of the continuance of the Iranian nuclear program. These range from preemptive Israeli and/or American air strikes to halt the program to monetary and economic incentives to deconstruct the Iranian nuclear facility (as has been used episodically in the case of North Korea). In the meantime, the number of operational Iranian centrifuges grows almost daily. In the worst case, a nuclear armed Iran will destabilize the balance of power in the region and possibly threaten Israel with annihilation. Moreover, a nuclear Iran will surely impact both Turkey and Iraq, who fear Iranian hegemony and would probably respond by increasing the size and scale of their military establishments. There is a further complication for Turkey—its increasing reliance on Iranian natural gas, which renders it somewhat of an energy hostage to Iran.

Iranian behavior with regard to the Euphrates-Tigris basin is difficult to assess because there are few precedents and no agreements to construct a framework of understanding. The Iranian government continues to demonstrate intransigence and an unwillingness to negotiate or resolve its difficulties in the international arena.[73] Iran is unlikely to cooperate in multinational water management efforts, especially if these might involve the United States or the West. However, this does not negate the possibility of bilateral cooperation between Iran and Iraq regarding the usage of Tigris waters.

Terrorism and External Actors

The presence of al-Qaeda and associated terrorist organizations remains a force for instability throughout the Middle East. It is difficult today to separate actual al-Qaeda operations from those that are sectarian, nationalist, separatist, ethnic, or religious. And while terrorism is certainly not a new force in the region, it receives media coverage disproportionate to its actual size, scale, and impact because of the global media networks. Every country in the Middle East has an internal terrorist problem to some degree. Many are the target of external actors as well, with Israel being the most visible in this regard. In addition to al-Qaeda, Hamas, Hizballah, the Muslim Brotherhood, and the PKK are some of the most wellknown terrorist organizations in the region. Currently Iraq is experiencing both domestic and imported external groups that are conducting sporadic operations; however, incidents are decreasing dramatically as the Maliki government increasingly asserts the rule of law.

Israel

The simple existence of the state of Israel is a source of dismay for much of the Arab and Muslim world and is a destabilizing force in the Middle East. The plight of the Palestinians and the refusal of the Israelis to deal constructively with the issue of Gaza, the West Bank settlements, and the Golan Heights occupation continue to act as a focal point for violence. Heightening this problem is the inability of the UN to engage Israel constructively and effectively because of continuing American vetoes in the UN Security Council.

---

[73] Economist Intelligence Unit, *Country Report—Iran* (London: Economist Intelligence Unit, 2011).

The rings of Israeli settlements around Jerusalem and the construction of a wall partitioning the West Bank indicate a solid Israeli commitment to retaining substantial portions of Palestine into the future. In effect, the Israelis have created the conditions for a never-ending security dilemma by refusing to return territory seized in the 1967 Six Day War. Making this worse, the election of a Hamas government in Gaza through a legitimate democratic process created an intractable adversary. Adding fuel to the fire, the endorsement by the United States of both the Palestinian and Lebanese elections (in which Hamas and Hizballah, respectively, emerged as viable political entities) has compounded the problem by legitimizing terrorist organizations in the parliaments of these states. Successive Israeli governments have been unable to deal effectively with the issue of the return of lands seized in violation of UN agreements and international law in 1967.

The Israeli invasion of southern Lebanon in 2006 was a foreign policy disaster in which thousands of innocent civilians were killed in indiscriminate Israeli air and artillery strikes. Moreover, the Israeli withdrawal and its seeming inability to bring Hizballah to its knees have been seen by the Arab world as a long overdue victory over Israel and the West. An important outcome of the inept execution of the 2006 invasion has been the degradation of the Israeli reputation for military invincibility. This has encouraged the opponents of Israel, and violent battles subsequently broke out in the Gaza Strip. In late December 2008, Israel began a vigorous retaliatory air campaign against Hamas in the city of Gaza, which was followed by a ground invasion to throttle Hamas rocket sites (known altogether as Operation Cast Lead). Although acclaimed by Israel as a military and political success, an immediate result was condemnation by the world community, followed by a UN report that pointedly accused Israel of violating international law and conventions.

Tensions between Syria and Israel have hardened as the Turks withdrew from trying to manage Syrian-Israeli negotiations in the wake of the Gaza campaign. The current civil war in Syria has brought Turkish and Israeli interests closer together as regional stability continues to deteriorate. Israel's relations with Egypt and Jordan continue to be amiable, while Saudi Arabia grows increasingly frustrated by Israeli intransigence over the West Bank and Gaza. Making things more difficult for the Israelis, the Arab Spring brought the Muslim Brotherhood to power in Egypt, potentially threatening the strategic equilibrium that has characterized a relationship that dates back to 1977. As a result of all of this, Israel's relationships with its neighbors have eroded badly in the past few years, and unfortunately this erosion has proven to have had a corresponding net negative effect on American influence in the region.

Intersecting Policies and Interests

How do the policies and interests of Syria, Iraq, and Turkey, as well as those of neighboring states such as Israel and Iran, intersect with those of the United States? This section presents an assessment of those policies and interests that compete with one another, those that conflict, and those that are complementary. The section concludes with a summary of how these competing, conflicting, and complementary policies and interests might be integrated into a generalized appreciation of their effect on regional hydropolitics.

Competing Policies and Interests

Agriculture. The agricultural policies of the three riparian states must be seen as competitive policies as all are designed to achieve self-sufficiency in terms of food as well as designed to improve the economy via the creation of employment. Most of the crops currently grown in the Euphrates-Tigris basin are water intensive, and it is hard to see how this might change. These expansionist agricultural policies are directly linked to a supply of water, which is predicted to decrease in the timespan of this study.

The Kurds. Kurdish demographics challenge all three governments as well—Kurds comprise 17 percent of Turkey, 9 percent of Syria, and about 15–20 percent of Iraq. All of these Kurdish populations exhibit some degree of restive behavior, although at the moment the vast majority of Kurds in each country appear reasonably content with the political currents of the times. However, the Kurds have a compelling cultural and linguistic identity that draws many to the idea of autonomy and independence. The Kurdish constituencies represent interests that compete with the concept of multiethnic nation states, and thus all three nations share a need to address this issue (this subject will be further addressed in chapter 4).

Conflicting Policies and Interests

National security. By listing the Turkish and Syrian dams as a significant threat to Iraqi national security, the Iraqis are clearly making an aggressive statement toward both countries. Importantly, the Iraqi national security strategy is a consensus document with a broad base of support among the parties involved in the governing of Iraq, and these dams are perceived as a serious threat by nearly every Iraqi citizen. Turkey, especially, is identified as an abusive neighbor when discussing riparian rights. This resonates loudly in Iraq and is likely to continue. But hydropolitics will play out at many levels (see chapter 5 for further discussion).

Foreign and domestic policies. There are vastly different patterns of international and domestic behavior exhibited by the three riparian nations. In the past, Syria often demonstrated a willingness to act outside the international system, and its tendency toward rogue-state behavior is increasing. Turkey, on the other hand, has in almost every case turned to international institutions and organizations for support and assistance in solving problems. However, this approach is often cosmetic, and when its interests are directly threatened, the Turks act unilaterally and in a hegemonic manner. Iraq continues to evolve, but at the present time its foreign and domestic policies are in a state of disarray and uncertainty.

The PKK. The continuing unofficial support of the PKK by the KRG and some Iraqi politicians continues to affect relations between Turkey and Iraq. Continuing raids by the PKK inside Turkey that kill Turkish soldiers and civilians receive high visibility in the Turkish press and enrage the public. As a result, the populist Turkish government and general staff often find themselves in a reactive posture, forcing direct or indirect military action. The PKK understands this dynamic and uses it strategically.

The United States. Relationships with the United States bring the three nations into conflict. Turkey has long-standing alliance and security partnerships with America, but this has deteriorated badly of late. Nevertheless, Turkey remains a NATO member and structurally aligned with the United States. In contrast, Syria has an anti-American posture and continues to maintain ties to Iran and Russia. The future of the relationship between Iraq and the United States is uncertain and hinges on the levels of support that the Americans provide in the future. Problems in Iraq, regardless of cause, will surely be blamed on America. Moreover, U.S. support for Israel serves to alienate the Muslim populations of all three riparian states.

Complementary Policies and Interests

Models of government. At the moment there are three secular models of government in the Euphrates-Tigris basin that may be seen as complementary. Turkey has a fully functioning and firmly entrenched parliamentary democracy in place. While most of the citizens of the Turkish republic are ethnic Turks, 17 percent are Kurds who are increasingly integrated and included in the political structure and the fabric of the Turkish economy. The Turkish government may be characterized as strong and able to affect the future of the country in real terms. Syria, on the other hand, has a secular Baathist dictatorship that remains in tenuous control as of the summer of 2012. Many in Syria (including the Christian minority) fear that the downfall of Assad will bring insecurity and Islamist control of government. Iraq also has a parliamentary government based on Western secular ideas. Unfortunately, the political fragmentation of Iraq based on sectarian and ethnic lines preordains a coalition government, which although it has proven to be weak in the past, is likely to continue.

International engagement. It is memberships in international structures and shared policies that will potentially bring Turkey, Iraq, and Syria closest together in the next decade. All three nations have strong motivations to increase their engagement in the world community of international institutions and organizations. Indeed, increased commitments to international structures are now declared policy objectives of all three nations. Iraq, a pariah state under Saddam Hussein, seeks to reconnect itself to regional and international structures. Despite international sanctions caused by the ongoing civil war, Syria—long isolated by Baathist nationalism—seeks in the long run to end its diplomatic and economic isolation by rebuilding international linkages. Turkey has a strong record of working within and through international institutions and is seeking accession into the EU and will surely continue its policies in this regard.

Economic systems. Two of the nations have state-managed economic systems, and to some extent Turkey is still saddled with the effects of a state-managed system as well. Although in differing stages of development and for different purposes, Turkey and Iraq seek privatization and foreign investments in their economies and infrastructure. Syria seeks the same ends, despite clinging to an old-style centrally managed economy. Both Syria and Iraq would like more balanced economies that are less dependent on oil exports, while Turkey would like to increase trade with both countries. There are very strong economic links between Turkey and Iraq. Turkey exports goods into Iraq and also provides significant amounts of industrial and entrepreneurial expertise. This is particularly important for economically challenged southeastern Turkey. Reciprocally, a large share of Iraq's oil flows out to the world through Turkish pipelines. Trade between Turkey and Syria is increasing annually as is a small but growing trade between Iraq and Syria. All three countries are strongly committed to continuing and increasing their trade with their water basin neighbors.

Integrating Policies and Interests

Taking the material in this chapter into consideration, the following statements may be made regarding the overlapping policies and interests of Turkey, Syria, and Iraq:

- As a matter of policy, all three riparian nations have strategic interests in increasing their levels of participation in international structures.

- All three riparian nations have complementary economic interests and a shared interest in continuing to develop strong trade relationships.

- All three nations have governments based on secular ideas and are moving, albeit at differing rates, toward modernity and westernization.

- All three riparian nations face domestic security difficulties caused by terrorism, insurgency, and mass violence. Moreover, all three have an interest in decreasing the levels of Kurdish nationalism prevalent in the Euphrates-Tigris basin.

However, there are a number of serious conflicting and competing problems as well, including the issues below:

- Iraq has serious concerns about the Turkish and Syrian dams as these affect the future national security of Iraq and its people.

- There is an increasing Turkish trend toward hegemonic behavior and an associated trend to place Turkish interests above that of its allies and neighbors.

- There are expansive water-dependent agricultural policies by all three countries in a water-challenged area that will lead to confrontations in the future.

- American presence, prestige, and influence have decreased in the region and will likely continue to decrease in the future. This affects the ability of the United States to assist the riparian states in regional affairs. Partnering with America may even be seen as counterproductive to the national interests of the water basin states.

An Uncertain Future

This leads to a series of questions regarding the future of the Euphrates-Tigris basin. Are the political entities durable and strong enough to cope with the problems of a regional water shortage? What about increasing salinity levels caused by the GAP in Turkey? What mechanisms, practices, and technologies exist that might assist these states in solving problems related to water? How will the United States and the international community be able to assist in fostering stability in a region that is of great strategic concern for Americans?

The geopolitical landscape in the Euphrates-Tigris basin is fragile but promising. The political entities of the riparian nations have much in common politically, economically, and socially. For now they share secular governments, in contrast to theocratic Iran and monarchist Jordan and Saudi Arabia (which is strongly fundamentalist as well). They share economies that aspire to more privatization, growth, and foreign investment. They share a common desire for increased integration with, and participation in, international institutions and organizations. None of the countries want confrontation with the West or cultural isolation from Western ideas. Nor do they want a nuclear armed Iran or a neighbor exporting Islamic fundamentalism. In essence, they have more in common with each other than with many of their other neighbors.

Yet the Euphrates-Tigris River basin also draws them together in negative ways that the Turks, Syrians, and Iraqis cannot ignore. The basin itself essentially overlays what might be called "Greater Kurdistan," itself a problem dating back to the 1920s and one that begs for reconciliation and solution. There are compelling and immediate problems with the decreasing flow of water that increased irrigation and agricultural production will worsen. Turkey, the upstream riparian state, articulates a foreign policy of cooperation while demonstrating an increasing willingness toward hegemonic behavior. Moreover, it is problematic to assume that the United States will be in a position to assist the riparians with financial support or that it might find itself serving as a neutral party to assist in negotiations.

This chapter and, in particular, the problems listed in the preceding paragraph provide the background for the development of the remainder of the book. The following chapters review the nature of the threat, address the Kurdish challenge, describe hydropolitics in the region, and provide a proposed framework for action.

CHAPTER 3
PROJECTED WATER DEMAND AND THE IMPACT OF CLIMATE CHANGE

This chapter will attempt to answer a preliminary question mentioned in the introduction as well as several other related questions. The preliminary question is, what are the current and projected future demands for freshwater in the Euphrates-Tigris basin? The related questions are the following: Will there be a freshwater deficit in the basin and, if so, how can this be measured? What will be the impact of major water and development projects, including the GAP (Southeastern Anatolia Project) in Turkey? In particular, how will Iraq, as the downstream riparian, be affected by these projects? (The situation in Syria is particularly relevant to Iraq since the entire flow of the Euphrates passes through Syria before it reaches Iraq.) Finally, how will climate change impact the situation in the next 10 to 20 years?

It should be stated at the outset that water demand is a subjective concept, based on uncertain statistics such as increasing populations and changing patterns of agriculture. Simply stated, *water deficit* is the difference between water supply and water demand. But in the Middle East, nothing is as simple as it seems. First of all, who are the "riparians" who geographically share the waters of the basin? The twin rivers of the Euphrates and Tigris originate in Turkey and pass through Syria and Iraq on their way to the Persian Gulf (map 3.1). The Euphrates (Firat in Turkish) is the domi-

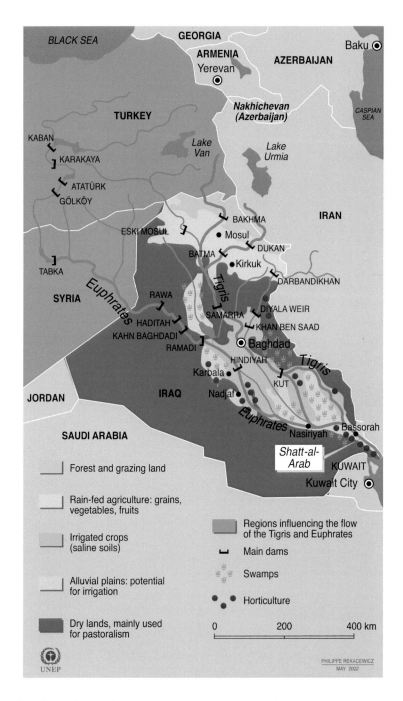

MAP 3.1. **The Euphrates-Tigris River basin, including main dams and land use.**
Map by Philippe Rekacewicz, UNEP/GRID-Arendal

nant river in terms of volume to Syria, while the Tigris (Dicle in Turkish) provides a greater portion of Iraq's water needs. Iran is a major regional player in terms of politics, economics, and military affairs, but it makes a relatively minor contribution to the water balance in the basin, contributing only 20–30 percent of the flow of the Tigris to Iraq. Nevertheless, increased dam building in Iran in the next 10 years will have an impact that needs to be assessed. Its contribution will be discussed later in the chapter. Although Saudi Arabia is technically a part of the Euphrates-Tigris basin, its water contributions to and withdrawals from the basin are insignificant. Thus, the term "riparian" is used in this book to describe the three principal countries in which the Twin Rivers flow: Turkey, Syria, and Iraq.

Water Quantity and Water Quality

Large volumes of water flowing in rivers are not easy to calculate and compare. To facilitate this, water quantity in this section will be given in billion cubic meters (BCM) and flow rates in cubic meters per second (CMS). There is room for confusion because water volume is sometimes given in cubic kilometers, and one cubic kilometer happens to be the same volume as one BCM. To compound this potential for confusion, it is more common in the United States to describe volumes of water in acre-feet. One acre-foot is the volume of water it would take to cover one acre to a depth of one foot. This term is common in many U.S. water management agreements; the Colorado River Compact, for instance, divides 15 million acre-feet (MAF) of water per year among seven western states. As a point of comparison, 1 MAF is the equivalent of 1.235 BCM, and a flow rate of 1 CMS equals 3.53 cubic feet per second (CFS), the common U.S. measurement for the rate of flow. In this chapter, in addition to BCM and CMS, we will also be using hectares, a unit of land measurement common in the Middle East; 1 hectare (10,000 square meters) equals approximately 2.47 acres.

Water quality is a factor that is often overlooked in water basin research, but the impact of declining quality in the Euphrates-Tigris basin will be greater, and more immediate, than declining water quantity. Rivers will not literally "dry up," but water quality will reach a point where agriculture becomes impossible and human health is seriously affected. Statistics for water quality are even more difficult to research than for water quantity. For large agricultural projects such as the GAP in Turkey, irrigation water will inevitably return as groundwater or to the river itself as return flow. The water quality prognosis for the Euphrates-Tigris basin is precarious and will be covered in greater depth later in the chapter.

Groundwater

Groundwater is generally overlooked in the analysis of river basins, not merely because it is less evident, but because the data on it is less available. The measurement and monitoring of groundwater use is particularly difficult in the Euphrates-Tigris basin. In agriculture, water is a low-cost resource, and most regional farmers are using primitive methods of extracting groundwater. In Turkey, more progress has been made in measuring groundwater, but that has largely been focused on measuring the declining water tables and not on measuring each farmer's extraction. Turkey claims to have exploitable groundwater resources of 14 BCM per year, of which 90 percent is used and allocated.[1] Turkey also claims that "there is no contamination in private areas and no over pumping," but this is contradicted by a number of global reports and one of the coauthors' travels through the GAP region.[2]

It is widely accepted that 90 percent of the surface flow of the Euphrates originates in Turkey.[3] But a basic understanding of hydrology and the water cycle reveals that surface waters regularly interchange with groundwater, and this exchange includes contaminants. The aquifers feeding the Balikh River and the Khabur River in northern Syria are charged by rainfall in Turkey, leading to the conclusion that more than 96 to 98 percent of

---

[1] Republic of Turkey, *Turkey Water Report 2009*, 5.

[2] Yoshihide Wada and others, "Global Depletion of Groundwater Resources," *Geophysical Research Letters* 37, L20402 (2010), doi:10.1029/2010GL044571.

[3] See Food and Agriculture Organization of the United Nations (FAO) Aquastat Database, "Turkey," http://www.fao.org/nr/water/aquastat/countries/turkey/index.stm.

the flow of the Euphrates can be seen as under Turkish control.[4] Turkish pumping of groundwater just north of the Syrian border has significantly reduced the flow to Syrian springs.[5] Further reducing the potential, the return flows from the region in the Harran Plain, just north of the Syrian border, have the potential to pollute groundwater and the river south of the border.[6] Although general water resource statistics are available through agencies such as the Food and Agriculture Organization (FAO), it is another matter for outsiders to obtain useful specific data concerning water flow, water demand, and water deficit.

Water Information as a State Secret

One of the challenges of research on this subject is the widely varying and inconsistent figures available. Turkey, Syria, and Iraq all carefully monitor the flow of water at key points, particularly where the Euphrates and Tigris leave Turkey and enter Syria and Iraq. Turkey has a sophisticated and comprehensive monitoring system tied to the operation of its dam system that is centralized in Ankara at the Directorate of State Hydraulic Works (DSI). Although some improvements in data sharing have been noted over the past several years, release of data is selective and still viewed as a matter of state security. This can be compared to the cooperative water management systems in Europe and North America, which have relatively plentiful water, transparent data mechanisms, strong economies, and a fairly high level of cooperation between riparian states. And when there is a water dispute in the United States or Europe, there are judicial mechanisms available to resolve the issue. This is not true for the international waters of the Euphrates-Tigris basin.

Each riparian state that has control of water statistics knows the political significance of the numbers, and the figures may differ by a factor of five to one. This is a phenomenon common in the Middle East wherein

---

[4] John Kolars, "Defining the Political/Ecological Threshold for the Euphrates and Tigris Rivers," *Arab Studies Quarterly* 22, no. 2 (Spring 2000): 104.

[5] Coauthor Lorenz visited the Khabur River region of Syria in summer 2004 and interviewed local water officials. Names of local officials are withheld by mutual agreement.

[6] Kolars, "Defining the Political/Ecological Threshold," 104.

each state tends to release numbers that will support its own position. For instance, the upstream riparian tends to underestimate the amount of water available for release downstream. The downstream state may over-estimate the amount available upstream and underestimate the amount available within its own borders. Upstream states are reluctant to reveal water quality measurements that might show pollution levels released downstream. Downstream states, in turn, will try to avoid data that shows the inefficient and wasteful use of its own precious water supply. In con-trast to all of this maneuvering, the new technology described in chapter 6 may be able to provide at least a partial solution to revealing and sharing water data.

Water Optimists and Water Pessimists

Secrecy issues are further complicated when the "outsiders" attempt to evaluate the conditions in a particular basin. Outsiders might be grouped into two widely divergent camps—water pessimists and water optimists. How can we reconcile the view of doom and gloom with a more benign perspective? One scholar in the field describes the issue this way:

> It is a paradox that the water pessimists are wrong but their pessimism is a very useful political tool which can help the innovator to shift the eternally interdependent belief systems of the public and their politicians. The water optimists are right but their optimism is dangerous because the notion enables politicians to treat water as a low policy priority and thereby please those who are prospering under the old order.[7]

Even if there were some agreement on the amount of water available, there are so many factors affecting demand, including predictions of pop-ulation increases and efficiency of use, that the determination of a possible water deficit becomes more a matter of art than science. The imprecision of current estimates is immense, and population predictions are specula-tive for most water basins in the next 20 years. What should be a reason-able per capita estimate of water usage in the dynamic political economies

---

[7] J. A. [Tony] Allan, *The Middle East Water Question: Hydropolitics and the Global Economy* (London: I.B. Tauris, 2002), 3.

of the future? There are wide variations when considering water demand for food, domestic, drinking, municipal, industrial, and leisure purposes. Should we consider "virtual" water, the amount of water embedded in imported food that will naturally replace water that is evident and drawn locally as surface or groundwater?[8]

In this chapter we will attempt to arrive at some conclusions, using data from the countries concerned and from experts who monitor the situation. Most experts consider countries with a per capita water availability below 1,000 cubic meters (CM) per year to be in water deficit.[9] Although the underlying figures are controversial, this measure provides some basis for comparison.

Turkey: The Dominant Riparian

Background

Turkey stands on the dividing line between Europe and Asia and has tremendous diversity in terms of its population, geography, and climate. The major cities are Istanbul (located at the key junction of the Bosporus) and the capital Ankara, which is about a five-hour drive southeast from Istanbul. Based on the 2008 census, the population of Turkey is approximately 72 million, with 65 percent of its inhabitants living in urban areas.[10] The poorest and least developed region of Turkey is the Southeastern Anatolia region, which has been subject to a long-standing conflict between the government and Kurdish separatists. The heart of Southeastern Anatolia is a uniformly stark and mostly arid landscape, within which are nestled the crowded provincial cities of Diyarbakir, Urfa, Gaziantep, and Mardin. Except for the western part of the region, history and progress seem to have bypassed both the inhabitants and the land.

The Ottoman Turks were not noted for their economic abilities, and Ataturk's early constitutional republic, founded in 1923, was saddled

---

[8] Ibid., 13.

[9] Ibid., 6. Countries below 1,000 CM per capita per year are said to be in a state of water scarcity according to the UN. See http://www.un.org/waterforlifedecade/scarcity.shtml.

[10] Republic of Turkey, *Turkey Water Report 2009*, 5.

with crippling debt and failed economic policies. Much like their Soviet Communist neighbors to the north, the early Turkish republicans chose to develop their country in economic and social terms through structured government programs. The first Turkish five-year plan in 1934 was designed to set up light industry near the base areas of native raw materials. The second plan, in 1939, focused on heavy industry. In the 1950s, the government's economic policies attempted to revive agriculture by bringing mechanization to Turkey. The results of these policies were generally successful in moving the primitive Turkish economy into the twentieth century. In practical terms, however, these economic and agricultural plans tended to develop only the western areas of the country. Thus, while Thrace, the Aegean areas, and the Anatolian heartland of Turkey gained much, the Southeastern Anatolian region fell further behind, as did the expectations and the hopes of the local populace.

The Turkish government in Ankara was aware of conditions in the rural southeast and the limited opportunities facing its inhabitants. The solution was the long-held dream—dating back to the Ottoman Empire—of building dams to benefit the region. In the 1930s, Ataturk proposed the construction of a series of dams with the idea of harnessing the mighty Euphrates and Tigris Rivers. Both rivers originate in the rugged mountains overshadowing Southeastern Anatolia, and at the time millions of gallons of cold, clean water poured through the basin. However, a lack of money combined with the rigid structure of the existing five-year plans made such a project seem impossible. Politicians periodically attempted to secure funds for development but failed in the face of more pressing economic priorities. It was not until the 1960s that the idea of developing the Twin Rivers became politically viable.

By the second half of the twentieth century, Turkey was searching for sources of electrical power at the same time as it was beginning to reach the limits of agricultural development. The time had finally come to convert the Ottoman dream into a viable concept for development. The concept was realized by a longtime member of the intellectual elite of Turkey, Suleyman Demirel. Demirel was a university graduate who was trained as an engineer and who had worked on Turkey's hydroelectric dams in his early years. After entering politics, he maintained an active interest in Turkey's water projects. A born survivor, Demirel was perennially in the government, either as prime minister or as president, for more than 40 years.

The vision for the taming of the Euphrates and Tigris was uncomplicated and predicated on a series of dams to produce hydroelectric power and unlimited water for irrigation. For 50 years, these dams were the central and immutable intellectual bedrock of the vision. Under Demirel's leadership, however, the transition from a hydroelectric project of limited scope to a unified, multiagency plan for regional and national development achieved its own identity. The modern vision, now inseparable from the name of Demirel, is more than just dams and irrigation ditches—it is the vast project known as the GAP.

The GAP

The development of the GAP represents the single issue that carries universal political appeal throughout Turkey. The GAP represents a source of great national pride; it is financed without the benefit of international financial organizations or the World Bank. This self-sufficiency has created a heightened sense of national pride, a focus on the industrialization of the nation, significant influence in the region, and a great degree of independence of action and control over the project. The GAP is intended to bring industrialization and growth to a poor region of the country. It sends electricity to population centers and adds to the agricultural export base of Turkey. No less important, it provides hope for the large Kurdish minority in region. There is something in this vision for almost every citizen of Turkey. Thus, the GAP is a tremendous source of pride at almost every level of Turkish society. During one of the coauthors' travels to Ankara and across Southeastern Anatolia in July 1997, and again in 2003 and 2004, there were few negative comments about the project. The attitude is best summarized by Ataturk's words emblazoned across the Ataturk Dam curtain in huge letters: "Ne Mutlu Turkum Diyene" (Lucky is the one who says he is a Turk).

The GAP is a large-scale and multisector regional development project with major implications for the region. It is one of the major river basin

Ataturk Dam, Turkey. *USDA Foreign Agricultural Service*

development projects in the world and the largest and most comprehensive project ever carried out in Turkey (map 3.2). The project is located in southeastern Turkey and involves eight provinces covering a vast area that includes Turkey's most desolate and poorest regions.

The region encompassed by the GAP is inhabited by 10 percent of Turkey's total population and covers about 10 percent of its surface area.[11] The project area includes 41 percent of the total watershed of the Tigris and Euphrates Rivers within Turkey, and when fully developed it will provide irrigation for 1.7 million hectares (nearly 4 million acres), or 20 percent of Turkey's irrigable land. The GAP Master Plan map provided by the GAP administration indicates the locations of dams and areas currently under development. The GAP includes 13 major irrigation and hydropower schemes that involve the construction of 22 dams and 19 hydroelectric power plants on the Euphrates and Tigris. The GAP will eventually double Turkey's hydroelectric capacity from 1984 levels and is expected

---

[11] Ibid., 105.

to generate 22 billion kilowatt hours (kWh) per year, a substantial portion of Turkey's electric power needs. Current generation levels indicate that GAP dams are already producing a significant part of the country's economically viable hydropower of 188 billion kWh.[12]

The original GAP Master Plan called for full development by 2010. In 2009 the GAP's hydroelectric production was estimated to be at approximately 96 percent of capacity, but the irrigation infrastructure was estimated to be only 30 percent complete, far behind the objectives described in the original master plan.[13] The regional economic growth also failed to match the predicted development indicated in the plan. A 6.8-percent increase was predicted, but the economy grew only 4.8 percent between 1990 and 1998. Turkey's historic economic performance, discussed more fully in earlier chapters, has been the primary factor in slowing completion of the GAP. Although Turkish economic performance has been strong recently, it has not been enough to transform the massive irrigation system, which has been behind schedule for so many years.

Because the GAP is internally financed, limits on financial aid for the irrigation projects required a scaling back of plans and the 2010 completion date was too optimistic. Financial delays translated into delays in irrigation expansion, as only 12 percent of expenditures were on irrigation, while approximately 75 percent of GAP's funding (9.6 billion U.S. dollars) went toward building dams.[14] But now with a stronger economy and dynamic political leadership, we can expect to see the original GAP Master Plan irrigation plans fulfilled in the next 10 years. Hydropower is more advanced because it presents a different and higher priority for Turkey. The immediate economic benefit of power generation was itself a strong motivation to keep those aspects of the project on track. As a result, resources were devoted immediately to the hydropower facilities.

---

[12] U.S. Energy Information Administration, *Turkey Country Analysis*, February 2011, http://205.254.135.7/EMEU/cabs/Turkey/pdf.pdf.

[13] See Republic of Turkey, *Turkey Water Report 2009*, 40.

[14] U.S. Department of Agriculture, Foreign Agriculture Service, "Southern Anatolia Becomes a Major Cotton Producing Region for Turkey" (2001), http://www.fas.usda.gov/pecad2/highlights/2001/08/turkey_gap/pictures/turkey_gap.htm.

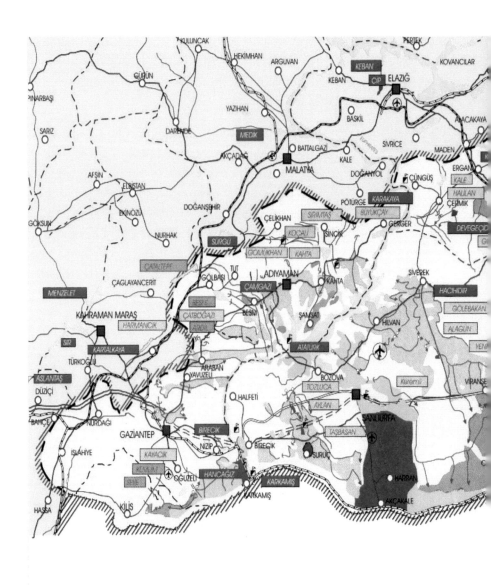

MAP 3.2. **GAP water resource project.** *Courtesy of the Directorate of State Hydraulic Works (Turkey)*

Turkey has an exemplary record of telling the story of the GAP and presenting the project in the best light. Visitors to Turkey are now offered tours of the GAP and the Ataturk Dam, which were previously off-limits to outsiders.[15] This transparency can be contrasted with Syria, where it is difficult to find any information on water issues, positive or negative, or to determine the official Syrian position. Over the past five years, the DSI has taken a more visible role in planning and implementation of Turkish water policy.[16] The English version of its Web site makes an important point:

> The State Institute of Statistics (DİE) has estimated Turkey's population as 100 million by 2030. So, the annual available amount of water per capita will be about 1,000 m³ [cubic meters] by 2030. The current population and economic growth rate will alter water consumption patterns.[17]

Turkey has long maintained that it is not water rich and will need to fully develop its own water resources to provide for a growing population.

Although the DSI maintains detailed information on water quantity and quality throughout Turkey, useful data for an outside researcher is not easy to obtain. For example, map 3.3 shows a number of monitoring stations just north of the point where the Euphrates River enters Syria. In April 2011 the authors enlisted the help of a civil engineer at an American university who was fluent in Turkish to assist in trying to locate relevant data on those stations. After a number of documents were analyzed, some provided by a coauthor of this book, it was apparent that any useful data relevant to flow of the Euphrates as it leaves Turkey was "classified."

Turkey is determined to fully exploit its water resources; in 2009 Turkey claimed that it had only developed 41 percent of the country's total water potential. Turkey hopes to "fully develop" its water potential by 2023,

---

[15] See a sample of a 2012 travel brochure offering such a tour at http://www.ezoptravel.com/html/tour_detail.asp?tour_no=174.

[16] See General Directorate of State Hydraulic Works, "Land and Water Resources," http://www2.dsi.gov.tr/english/topraksue.htm#.

[17] Ibid., under the heading "Water Resources versus Water Consumption Needs of Population."

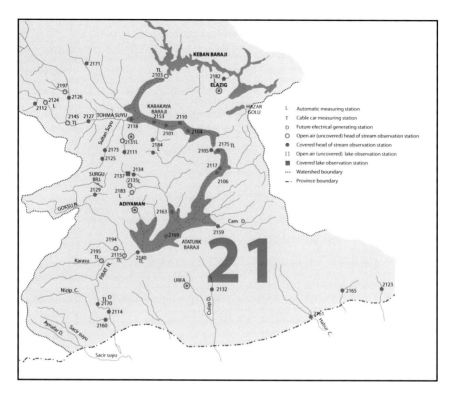

MAP 3.3 **The GAP project in the upper Euphrates-Tigris region.** *Courtesy of the Directorate of State Hydraulic Works (Turkey)*

which happens to be the one-hundredth anniversary of the Republic of Turkey.[18] Turkey today travels down essentially the same path as the United States in the 1930s, its hydrologic imperative based on a strong sense of national destiny.[19] Perhaps that is one reason why Turks bridle at the notion of Americans (and Europeans) lecturing them about the use of their own natural resources.

Slow progress on the irrigation infrastructure of the GAP indirectly benefits the downstream countries by delaying the inevitable impact on water resources. As noted above, although the total irrigation diversions are still behind schedule, nearly all the hydropower projects are finished. Once

[18] Republic of Turkey, *Turkey Water Report 2009*, 16, figure 3.2.

[19] See David P. Billington and Donald C. Jackson, *Big Dams of the New Deal Era: A Confluence of Engineering and Politics* (Norman: University of Oklahoma Press, 2006).

constructed, dams devoted exclusively to hydropower do not significant-ly reduce the flow of rivers and might be considered a "nonconsumptive use." But dams do change the flow rates in rivers and often bring about unintended environmental consequences. Economic and political factors may have slowed the pace of the GAP's completion, but its full develop-ment seems inevitable and the major impact downstream is certain to be felt in the next 10 to 15 years. The real problem will come as the infra-structure is finished, and the GAP takes its full toll on the waters of the Twin Rivers.

In a 2005 technical report for the Centre for Environmental Studies and Resource Management in Norway (CESAR), independent water quantity and quality data for the Euphrates River was publicly released for the first time.[20] The dynamic model in this report used input data obtained in part from publicly available data and in part from "grab samples" taken from the river by those preparing the study. The study also included an analy-sis of power production in the GAP region and how it would be affected by changing water flow levels. The study concluded that maintaining a minimum flow level of 500 CMS at the Turkey-Syria border would only slightly reduce energy generation within Turkey. A reduction in irrigation volume from 10 BCM/year (the target volume) to 5.5 BCM/year would actually increase energy generation by about 9 percent, however.[21] The report indicates the dynamic relationship between power generation and water flow, a subject that must be carefully calculated by Turkey but is still closely held as a national security matter.

The CESAR report and its related model calculate flow at the point the Euphrates enters Syria from Turkey and the point it enters Iraq from Syria. The study presents at a number of scenarios with different levels of power production and diversion for irrigation (see table 3.1). The most probable scenario, with full irrigation of the GAP region in the next 10 to 15 years, indicates that the flow of the Euphrates as it enters Syria will be less than

---

[20] See CESAR, *The Euphrates River and the Tigris River Water Resources Management: Water Resources Analysis Methodology*, 2006. Second reference document in Jon Martin Trondalen, *Water and Peace for the People: Possible Solutions to Water Disputes in the Middle East* (Paris: United Nations Educational, Scientific, and Cultural Organization [UNESCO], 2008).

[21] Ibid., 64.

TABLE 3.1 **Example of modeled statistics on Turkish-Syrian border**

Variable	Scenarios										
	E1	E2	E3	E4	E5	E6	E7	E8	E9	E10	E11
Irrigation:	No			Full¹				Reduced¹			
Min. flow requirement	—	—	—	300	400	450	500	300	400	450	500
Energy (terawatt hours)	0	28.0	23.43	23.23	22.8	22.97	22.89	25.34	25.12	25.10	25.09
Volume (10^9m³/year)²	31.3	30.3	20.4	20.4	20.5	20.6	20.7	24.7	25.0	25.0	25.1
Average (m³/sec)	994	962	648	648	649	654	655	782	794	794	795
SD³ (m³/sec)	838	688	755	672	433	429	377	714	512	510	508
Minimum (m³/sec)	182	0	0	300	400	450	-⁴	300	400	450	500
Consecutive weeks below 500 m³/sec	34	3	46	78	126	271	22	25	69	71	0
Percentage of weeks below 500 m³/sec	34	12	67	71	55	59	1	63	19	22	0

Notes:
1. Irrigation water is assumed diverted during three crop seasons, each eight weeks, and with intermittent periods of two weeks when no water is diverted.
2. 1 billion m³ = 1 gigam³
3. SD = Standard Deviation
4. A minimum value of 3 m³/sec was calculated for a short period of time, and it is possible to maintain 500 m³/sec for more than 99% of the 40 year period.

Adapted from CESAR, *The Euphrates River and the Tigris River Water Resources Management: Water Resources Analysis Methodology*, 2006, table 7-4. Second reference document in Jon Martin Trondalen, *Water and Peace for the People: Possible Solutions to Water Disputes in the Middle East.*

500 CMS and the flow into Iraq will be under 400 CMS, a dramatic reduction from current levels. This seems to confirm the data in the chart published by Kolars and Mitchell in 1991 and reproduced later in this chapter as figure 3.4. The CESAR report also reveals that agricultural return flow and high salt levels will be the most dangerous consequence of GAP development, another factor discussed later in this chapter.

Syria: Midstream and Vulnerable

Background

The Syrian Arab Republic consists primarily of semiarid and desert plateaus with a narrow coastal plain and mountains in west. Syria shares water basins with Turkey, Lebanon, Jordan, and Israel. These basins include the Tigris, Euphrates, Orontes, Tafiagh, Queiq, Afrin, the Northern Great, and the Yarmouk Rivers. The Syrian population is about 22 million, with an annual growth rate of 0.913 percent.[22] Syria is relatively poor in water resources, and the permanent water flow is low in comparison with the country's requirements. Based on the estimate of available arable land, Syria requires not less than 6 BCM of irrigation water annually.[23] Its permanent or semipermanent resources, including rivers (around 4 BCM) and springs (around 3 BCM), contribute only about 20 percent of the total

water resources. However, adding Syria's water allowance from the Euphrates to its permanent and semipermanent resources, the country's total surface water is around 36.8 BCM, of which the Euphrates water contributes about 80 percent.

Inefficient groundwater pumping to fields near Quamshli, northern Syria. *Photo by Frederick Lorenz*

Syria is currently "mining" underground water at an unsustainable rate, extracting about 34 million CM per year more than can be replenished. Several studies have indicated this overutilization of underground water is creating a water deficit that will ultimately create a serious problem.[24] During the summer of 2003, one of the coauthors observed groundwater overpumping in the Khabur Basin, with groundwater being used to fill dry streambeds that once provided surface flow for irrigation.

---

[22] Central Intelligence Agency (CIA), "Syria," in *The World Factbook* (Washington, DC: Central Intelligence Agency, 2009), https://www.cia.gov/library/publications/the-world -factbook/geos/sy.html.

[23] Nabil Samman, "Syrian Water Resources: Strategic Issues" (on file with authors), 2.

[24] Ibid., 3.

The Syrian Ministry of Irrigation is in charge of the operation and maintenance of irrigation networks and dams, water resource planning and research, and pollution control. Syria has been burdened by years of inefficient, centrally controlled agricultural policies that have adversely affected agricultural productivity and contributed to land degradation. The ministry is responsible for groundwater monitoring and the issuance of licenses for well drilling, but enforcement and coordination is lax. In some areas with a high concentration of wells, such as parts of the Ar Raqqah and Salamieh areas, the water table has long been declining at a significant rate.[25] Obtaining data on these subjects from the Ministry of Irrigation has not been possible due to governmental security concerns.[26]

Syria's major irrigation potential lies in the Euphrates River valley and its two major tributaries, the Balikh and Khabur Rivers, in the northeast portion of the country. One of the coauthors visited the Khabur basin in the summer of 2003, including the point where it enters Syria from Turkey. The Khabur joins the Euphrates, which then flows southeastward across the arid Syrian plateau into Iraq, where it briefly joins the Tigris River before emptying into the Persian Gulf. The following section describes the major dams and irrigation infrastructure in Syria.

Syrian Dams and Irrigation Works

Syrians have long used the Euphrates for irrigation, but because the major systems were destroyed centuries ago, they have struggled to renew the potential of the river for the people. Several project studies were conducted after World War II. In the 1960s, the Soviet Union agreed to provide financial and technical assistance for the al-Thawrah Dam (also called the Euphrates or Tabaqah Dam), a large hydroelectric power station, as well as for portions of the major Euphrates irrigation project. The al-Thawrah

---

[25] Coauthor Lorenz spent a week in the Khabur basin in August 2003, conducting interviews with a number of local water officials who remain anonymous by mutual agreement.

[26] Multiple efforts by one of the coauthors in Damascus in July and August 2003 failed to yield any data from the Syrian Ministry of Irrigation. In the authors' opinion, this is due to the lack of transparency in the Syrian government and the particular sensitivity of water statistics. The same pattern persisted in 2011; see *The Blue Peace* report discussed and cited in this chapter and in chapter 7.

Khabur River, with debris, near Quamshli, northern Syria.
Photo by Frederick Lorenz

power plant has eight 100-megawatt (MW) turbines for power generation as well as transmission lines to Aleppo. The output of electrical power is 2,500 kWh annually, which is 45 percent of the total electrical power needs of Syria.[27] The al-Thawrah Dam became operational in 1973, when Lake Assad, the artificial lake behind the dam, began filling. Approximately 80 kilometers (km) long, Lake Assad averages about 8 km in width and holds nearly 12 BCM of water. The disappointing performance of the dam led the Syrian government to construct additional dams upstream from al-Thawrah, but new dams will not solve the problem as water quantity and quality diminish.

The Tishreen Dam is situated on the Euphrates north of al-Thawrah Dam, 125 km from Aleppo.[28] It is a sandy dam 1,500 meters long, 290 meters at the base, and 40 meters high. The total area of the lake dammed by the Tishreen is 166 square kilometers (km^2), with a damming capacity of 1.883 BCM. While its main purpose is to generate 630 MW of electrical power, some 237 hectares have also been irrigated with water from the dam. Its maximum drainage capacity is 11,290 CMS, and it has six turbines rated at 105 MW each. In Syria, the dams are considered national security locations where photography is generally prohibited. Indeed, military checkpoints were found in the summer of 2003 on both sides of the dam, but the authors were permitted to take some photographs from designated locations.

The Khabur Dam (also called Bassel al-Assad Dam) was constructed in 1993 on the Khabur River, a tributary of the Euphrates. The dam is 20 meters high, and long and flat with a crest length of 5 km. It is designed to store 605 million CM of water for irrigation in a 92.5-km^2 reservoir, but it has consistently underperformed expectations. It has two pumping stations, each with a capacity of 4.5 CMS, which are meant to feed water from the main canals to two higher level canals. On a visit to the dam in summer 2003, the authors noted that it was filled to only about 10 percent capacity, and the canals exiting the dam and lake were dry. This was a

---

[27] Samman, "Syrian Water Resources," 4.

[28] See Lorenz and Erickson, *Thread of Life*, Tishreen Dam, photo series # 4 E.

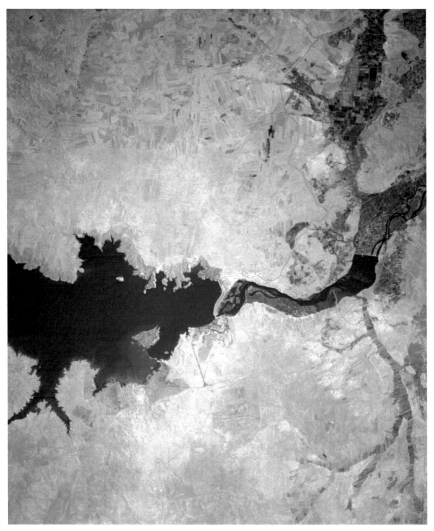

Satellite photo of al-Thawrah Dam (center of image) and Lake Assad, Syria.
Photo by NASA

season when the dam should have been fulfilling its intended purpose, especially since it followed a winter season of higher than normal rainfall.

Challenges for Syria

On 4 June 2002, a major Syrian dam collapsed; even though it was not widely reported, this event raised questions about Syria and the management of its water resources.[29] Although not within the Euphrates-Tigris basin, the Zeyzoun Dam's rupture and collapse brought to light immediate concerns of dam safety and maintenance in Syria. A series of articles appeared in the Syrian press in 2002 about the cause of the dam's failure. There were numerous charges of corruption and neglect. For example, Mikhail al-Ais, an expert in dam construction at Damascus University, presented a memorandum to the Ministry of Irrigation in 2001 showing the existence of serious problems in dam maintenance.[30] He reported that 31 dams in Syria required immediate repair or faced the danger of major failure.[31] In his memo, al-Ais also pointed out a number of structural defects at Zeyzoun, as well as a lack of monitoring equipment for the dam. Reports in the Syrian press in 2003 indicated that there had been a series of indictments of corrupt public officials and that there may have been a scheme to improperly manipulate water levels.[32]

Syria has been plagued by complex and interrelated problems that have frustrated the realization of targeted irrigation and hydropower goals. Without these impediments, extending and improving the nation's irrigation systems could substantially raise its agricultural output. But technical problems with unstable subsoil, which caused irrigation canals to collapse, proved more difficult than at first anticipated. Large cost overruns on some of the irrigation projects made them much more expensive than planned and created difficulties in financing additional projects. These large irrigation projects required several years before returns on the investments began, and the struggling Syrian economy was simply too weak after a major withdrawal of Soviet support in 1989. Moreover, the collapse of Zeyzoun Dam in the summer of 2003 uncovered serious problems in governmental management and corruption. At present, it remains

---

[29] The collapse of the Zeyzoun Dam was recorded in satellite images before and after the event. Some of these images can be found at the following NASA Web site: http://visibleearth.nasa.gov/view.php?id=59623.

[30] Samman, "Syrian Water Resources," 14. Samman was able to visit the site of the dam during the collapse (which took about four hours) and reported the slow speed of the rupture. This allowed for an evacuation of the downstream villages, saving many lives.

[31] Ibid., 15.

[32] Ibid., 16.

to be seen if the Syrian dictatorship has been able to absorb any lessons from these events. Until significant changes are made, long-standing inefficiency will likely continue to plague Syria in making optimal use of its own water resources.

Iran: A New Factor

Iran's contribution to the water balance in the Euphrates-Tigris basin is not insignificant—comprising about 20–30 percent of the flow of the Tigris to Iraq.[33] Thus, increased dam building in Iran in the next 10 years, much of it financed by China, will have an impact on the basin that needs to be assessed. Reports from refugee monitoring agencies in Diyala in eastern Iraq have already noted human displacement and population movement as a result of declining river flows from Iran.[34] A United Nations Educational, Scientific and Cultural Organization (UNESCO) water projects coordinator observed that "Iran has diverted 15 tributaries to the Tigris since 2006 alone." A recent article reported that two new Iranian dams could potentially cut off water to two of Iraq's main dams at Haditha in the northwest and Mosul in the north.[35]

Residents and officials in the Kurdish region of northern Iraq have reported that drought conditions have been aggravated by dam building in Iran. Dams on the Alwan and Sirwan Rivers in Iran are reported to have caused a crisis in the Kurdish Garmian District, with the preparation for evacuation of citizens from affected areas. The Garmian District has a population of 450,000, and recent photos show ancient bridges over completely dry riverbeds. A representative of the Kurdish Ministry of Water Resources stated that the Kurdish Regional Government has repeatedly

---

[33] The number is difficult to calculate, but estimates range from 20 to 40 percent.

[34] See UN International Office of Migration, *Baghdad: Governate Profile, November 2010, IOM IDP and Returnee Assessment* describing drought and low water levels. Available online at http://www.iomiraq.net/Documents/IOM%20Iraq%20-%20Governorate%20Profile%20-%20Baghdad.pdf.

[35] "I visited them [the dams] last summer and [they] were already down to about 50 percent of capacity," said observer Casey Walther in a United Press International (UPI) article from 12 January 2012. The article also mentioned possible "ethnic clashes" if the water situation did not improve. Article is available online at http://www.upi.com/Business_News/Energy-Resources/2012/01/27/Iraq-water-crisis-could-stir-ethnic-clash/UPI-56601327698003/.

warned Baghdad about the negative impact Iran's project was having on the region's water capacity, but nothing was being done.[36]

In March 2011 Iranian and Chinese officials were reported to have signed a $2 billion agreement for the construction of a dam and a power plant in Iran's western province of Lorestan.[37] The agreement will be signed between Sinohydro Corporation, China's largest water project developer, and Iran's Water and Power Resources Development Company. The dam, to be built on the Bakhtiari River in the Zagros Mountains, will reportedly hold Iran's largest reservoir, with a capacity of 4.8 BCM, and will support a 1,500-MW hydroelectric power station. The Bakhtiari is a tributary of the Tigris that flows directly into eastern Iraq.

Iran's water development is certain to collide with water demands in Iraq. For instance, in the summer of 2009 the Iraqi Committee on Agriculture, Water, and Marshes claimed that Iranian actions led to a complete cut off of the al-Karkhah River, causing a decline in the amount of water flowing to the Iraq marshes by 90 percent, thereby increasing salinity and changing the natural and social environment in the marsh areas.[38] The matter was referred to the Iraqi Ministry of Water Resources (MOWR) to "save the inhabitants of the marshes of the danger which threatens to force them out of these areas."[39] However, Iran seems to be deaf to Iraq's concerns, at least on water issues, and there is no international water management mechanism to address the problem. Iraq has reportedly complained to the international organization supervising the Ramsar Convention for Wetlands,[40]

---

[36] *Kurdish Globe*, "Iran Adds to Drought Misery," 14 May 2008, http://www.kurdishglobe .net/display-article.html?id=6F241EA0928DCF7898746DC9703AF8DB. See the photo accompanying this article for an example of a completely dry riverbed.

[37] Report from Press TV Iran, translated by Ladane Nasseri and reported in Bloomberg News, 14 March 2011.

[38] *Iraq Directory*, "Iraq Demanding the Guarantee of Water Rights," 19 September 2009, http://www.iraqdirectory.com/DisplayNews.aspx?id=10404. The joint meeting reportedly made several recommendations, "urging the Iranian side, through the two Committees of Parliamentary Friendship and External Relations in the parliament, to resolve the crisis quickly and demanding the [Iraqi] Ministry of Water Resources to play a bigger role with the Iranian side through the Joint Technical Committee."

[39] Ibid.

[40] See the Ramsar Convention of Wetlands, http://www.ramsar.org/cda/en/ramsar-home /main/ramsar/1_4000_0__.

demanding its "water rights" under a 1971 convention designed to protect and preserve wetlands. Unfortunately, there are no minimum water quantity and quality requirements in the treaty, and no real enforcement mechanisms that can be relied upon by an aggrieved party.

Because of increased development activity and water withdrawals inside Iran, further study is required to evaluate the impact on the flow of the Tigris entering Iraq. What is clear at present is that Iran's role as a riparian country in the Euphrates-Tigris basin and as a significant part of water management in the basin can no longer be ignored.

Iraq: Water and Security

Background

Over the centuries, the plentiful water resources of the Euphrates and Tigris Rivers promoted widespread and organized cultivation along their riverbanks, leading to the development of Mesopotamian civilization. Historically, agriculture was the primary economic activity in the region, but the past century has brought monumental political and economic change. In 1918, after the collapse of the Ottoman Empire, the modern boundaries of Iraq were drawn by the victorious Western powers (see chapter 1). This carving-up of the region was based purely on the self-interest of the great powers, with little regard for the three major ethnic/religious groups living in the region: the Shiites, Sunnis, and Kurds. There was no concern by the Western powers that water resources of the Euphrates-Tigris, once the dominion of the Ottomans, would now be divided among three states. And the failure to provide an independent homeland for the Kurds would lay the groundwork for additional instability.

The population of modern Iraq is currently about 28 million, of which 41 percent is less than 14 years old. The population is growing at an annual rate of about 3 percent. The climate in Iraq is mainly of the continental, subtropical semiarid type, with the north and northeastern mountain regions having a Mediterranean climate. Rainfall is seasonal and occurs mainly between December and February, except in the northern mountains, where it occurs from November to April.

Approximately 25 percent of Iraq's population depends on irrigated agriculture for their livelihood and subsistence. Agricultural products account for a significant proportion of Iraq's exports, and this has been particularly true in the last 10 years when wars and United Nations (UN) restrictions limited oil exports. Agriculture uses about 90 percent of Iraq's average annual water supply and is therefore critical to water development and management. Salination of a large part of the irrigated land results in reduced crop yields and high salinity of the rivers, creating problems in the municipal water supply as well as ecological problems that threaten the restoration potential of marshlands in the south.

Iraqi banknote depicting Dokan Dam (on the right), Kurdistan, northern Iraq.

Iraq was the first state in the Euphrates-Tigris basin to construct a major water project in the twentieth century. Known as the Hindiyah Barrage and completed in 1913, it was intended to resurrect the system of canals that had been inoperable since the Middle Ages. Three dams—the Dokan, Derbendi Khan, and Hamrin—were finished in 1958, 1962, and 1981, respectively. Additional dams were planned for Dohuk and Bikhma in the 1990s, but the Iran-Iraq War, the first Gulf War, and the deteriorating economy delayed the projects. The Mosul Dam is currently in operation, but serious structural deficiencies threaten its integrity. While one of the coauthors was in Baghdad in July 2004, the local U.S. Army engineer for the Mosul District was attempting to secure emergency repairs that would protect several thousand people who live in the floodplain directly below the dam. Those repairs were completed, but in 2010 the Mosul Dam continued to require a half million dollars per year to repair cracks that threaten its integrity and reduce its effective hydropower potential.[41]

---

[41] *Iraq Business News*, "Tenders Soon for Repairs of Mosul Dam," 4 September 2010, http://www.iraq-businessnews.com/2010/09/04/tenders-soon-for-repair-of-mosul-dam/.

Like Syria, Iraq has been burdened by many years of inefficient, centrally controlled agricultural policies that have adversely affected agricultural productivity and contributed to land degradation. Mounting pressures to produce more food for the region's growing population led to the adoption of aggressive but poorly managed water development programs, bringing drastic modification to the Iraqi landscape and habitat in the Euphrates-Tigris basin.

Water management infrastructure in Iraq now consists of 9 large storage dams and 12 major barrages (low water-control structures on main rivers that help to raise the water level to better distribute water via irrigation canals), along with thousands of kilometers of drainage canals, irrigation canals, levees, and dikes. Iraq has over 500 major pumping stations meant to distribute water to farms and cities that cannot be reached by gravity canals. These pumping stations are currently in disrepair due to years of neglect by the Saddam regime and the looting that occurred immediately following the U.S.-led invasion. At the time of the U.S. invasion in 2003, the pumping stations were operating at about 40 percent efficiency, according to a senior advisor to the Iraqi Ministry of Irrigation.[42] By the summer of 2004, there was no improvement; the money allocated for repair had not been spent due to contract inefficiencies and security concerns.[43] Moreover, in September 2004, the United States announced that the original amount allocated for water and sewage in Iraq, $4.15 billion, would be cut to $2.21 billion. This was part of the shift in American priorities in Iraq, and recognition of the seriousness of the security situation.[44] Since then, conditions in the water management sector have not substantially improved; other priorities and internal divisions have prevented the necessary attention to water management.

Iraq's Surface Water Resources and Infrastructure

Since Iraq is the most vulnerable of the four riparian nations on the Euphrates-Tigris, the availability of surface water from the upstream

[42] Eugene Z. Stakhiv, "Fact Sheet" (Iraqi Ministry of Irrigation, 4 July 2003), 1.

[43] Interview with Walleed Abdel-Hammad, planning coordinator, Ministry of Water Resources, Baghdad, 1 August 2004.

[44] James Glanz, "Iraqis Warn U.S. Plan to Divert Billions to Security Could Cut Off Crucial Services," New York Times, 21 September 2004.

countries is of critical concern. The following data on surface water is from the FAO.[45] The average annual flow of the Euphrates as it enters Iraq is estimated at 30 BCM, with a historic fluctuating annual value ranging from 10 to 40 BCM. Unlike the Tigris, the Euphrates receives no flow from tributaries during its passage in Iraq. About 10 BCM per year are drained into the Hawr al-Harnmar marsh in the south of the country. For the Tigris, average annual runoff as it enters Iraq is estimated at 21.2 BCM. All the Tigris tributaries are on its left bank. More details on the Tigris and statistics for northern Iraq are provided in chapter 4.

The Euphrates and the Tigris were at one time subject to large and occasionally disastrous floods. The level of water in the Tigris could rise at the rate of over 30 CM/hour. In the southern part of the country, immense areas were regularly inundated, levees often collapsed, and villages and roads were built on high embankments. Lake Tharthar, a man-made reservoir, was planned in the 1950s to protect Baghdad from the ravages of the periodic flooding of the Tigris by storing extra water discharge upstream of the Samarra Barrage. The completion of the principal Turkish dams in the 1990s has reduced seasonal fluctuations in the basin. In May and June 2003, the U.S. Army Corps of Engineers joined with the Iraq Ministry of Irrigation to perform technical assessments of dams and barrages on the Tigris and Euphrates Rivers. The Dam Assessment Team (DAT) consisted of civil, mechanical, and electrical engineers, and threat assessment and security staff specializing in design, planning, operation, and safety analyses of water containment structures. The purpose of the assessment was to perform physical inspection of the structures, assess dam functionality and operability, determine and prioritize needed actions (immediate, short term and long term), and estimate costs of immediate actions.

The DAT's conclusions and recommendations in July 2003 identified four structures as "high risk" and made specific recommendations for immediate action. There were a number of other recommendations that should have been implemented in the following year. Eight years later, however,

---

[45] See http://www.fao.org/ag/agl/aglw/aquastat/countries/iraq/index.stm.

little of the infrastructure repair work had been accomplished. In the Iraq water treatment sector, waste and inefficiency were the norm during the period of reconstruction following the Coalition invasion. In a misguided reconstruction project for the city of Fallujah, for example, the United States spent nearly $100 million to build a sewage treatment system, according to a government audit report released in October 2008.[46] Sewage continues to flow into the streets, and the Special Inspector General for Iraq Reconstruction found that the system may never be properly connected to individual homes, lacks the necessary fuel to operate, and is unlikely to ever cover the full city.

The U.S.-led invasion and occupation of Iraq had the potential to create major opportunities for the people of Iraq through the reestablishment of their water resources. In the summer of 2003, the senior advisor to the new Iraqi MOWR was optimistic:

> Iraq can become the contemporary "California of the Middle East." A functioning "plumbing system" already exists in Iraq. It has a lot of "wear and tear," as much-needed routine maintenance, primarily on the numerous pumps and pumping stations, has been deferred. There is probably sufficient water flowing through the system to meet current needs, and even future demands, if water were managed more efficiently.[47]

According to the senior advisor of the MOWR, the focus in Iraq was "better operation, maintenance and management of the current system, based on investment decisions that maximize economic efficiency, environmental quality and social equity."[48] It is hoped that the water infrastructure can be made to function more efficiently through improved on-farm management practices, which alone should provide about a 10-percent reduction in water use over the span of a decade. The same should be true for Syria, and by reducing the demand for water in Syria and Iraq, the impact of upstream diversions will be mitigated. In July 2003, the Iraqi MOWR issued

---

[46] Julian E. Barnes, "$100 Million Down the Drain in Iraq," *Los Angeles Times*, 27 October 2008.

[47] Stakhiv, "Fact Sheet."

[48] Ibid., 6.

Iraqi Ministry of Water Resources building, Baghdad.
Photo by Frederick Lorenz

a one-year strategic plan.[49] It included an ambitious schedule for privatization of water facilities, the reestablishment of water use fees, conducting an inventory of all waterworks and pumping stations, and a plan for emergency repairs.

In 2003 and 2004, the water infrastructure of Iraq suffered from looting and damage, further reducing the capacity of the beleaguered system. Reconstruction efforts began under the Coalition Provisional Authority and continued after the transfer of sovereignty at the end of June 2004. On 29 July 2004, the *New York Times* reported that rising security and other overhead costs of Western contractors were cutting into the billions of dollars set aside for some 90 planned water projects, allowing the contractors to

---

[49] Republic of Iraq Ministry of Water Resources, *2003 Strategic Plan.*

supply only half of the potable water originally expected.[50] This reprioriti-zation of resources vastly reduced the benefits for the citizens of a country that generally met no more than 60 to 80 percent of the demand for water before the U.S.-led invasion.

In the fall of 2003, the U.S. Congress approved an $18.4 billion Iraq re-construction program, with about $4.3 billion set aside for water and public works, but by the summer of 2004 the continuing violence from the insurgency prevented real progress in reconstructing the water infra-structure. Administrative costs for large Western firms, when added to the security costs, further reduced the amount available for reconstruc-tion. By the summer of 2004, the new U.S. ambassador was attempting to reallocate funds and streamline procedures to get the money in the hands of Iraqi firms. This was designed to revitalize the process and make prog-ress in spite of the increasing security problems. The process was largely unsuccessful, however, and by the spring of 2011 major deficiencies in the system remained. By the time most U.S. forces departed Iraq in the summer of 2011, the grand vision for a "California of the Middle East" had not been achieved.

Chapter 4 provides more detail on water resources in northern Iraq—in the Kurdish region—and why this will become more important in the years ahead.

Iraq's Groundwater

Although surface water is the main source of water supply in Iraq, groundwater is an essential source of supply in the desert areas (which cover about 58 percent of the country) and in some parts of the south. Groundwater probably represents the most important factor for the future

---

[50] The substance of the *New York Times* article was confirmed by coauthor Lorenz during his trip to Baghdad in July and August 2004. Interviews with the staff of the senior advisor's office, as well as Waleed Abdel Hamaad of the MOWR, indicated that contract inefficiencies and security concerns seriously detracted from Coalition mission effectiveness.

development of areas in the western desert.[51] As of 1950, only a modest number of wells had been drilled in the northern, western, and central parts of Iraq. Between 1960 and 1980, more than 2,500 wells were drilled by different government organizations and foreign firms. The number of hand-dug wells may be several times greater than that of drilled wells, but reliable statistics are not available.

Groundwater quality in the north and the east has been adequate for use as potable and irrigation water. In contrast, water quality is less than favorable in the south and west, and in many places groundwater development is already impossible. Even in areas where groundwater quality is acceptable, excessive pumping is likely to cause intrusion from saline sources nearby. Moreover, water quality can vary tremendously within the subsurface region, with higher salinity levels the deeper one goes.[52]

Today, Iraq is estimated to have approximately 200 BCM of groundwater, but the exploitable amount is estimated to be only about 1.2 BCM, based upon 2009 figures.[53] The "exploitable amount" figure for groundwater is subject to some speculation. It considers such factors as the economic and environmental feasibility of extracting groundwater, the physical possibility of pumping, and the minimum requirements for sustainability and recharge. Groundwater interchanges regularly with surface water as part of the hydrologic cycle, and it is vulnerable to the same threats from decreasing water quantity and quality. Regulation and measurement of groundwater extraction in Iraq faces the same problems evident in all sectors, such as a shortage of funding, high rates of inefficiency, and a questionable security environment. Ultimately, groundwater resources in Iraq are important, but a lack of data and monitoring makes their contribution difficult to consider.

---

[51] Sameh Wisam al-Muqdadi, "Groundwater Investigation and Modeling in the Western Desert of Iraq" (PhD thesis, Freiberg [Germany] Technical University, 2012), section 1.1, http://www.qucosa.de/fileadmin/data/qucosa/documents/8747/Sameh%20Al-Muqdadi%20 May%202012.pdf.

[52] FAO Aquastat Database, "Iraq," http://www.fao.org/nr/water/aquastat/countries/iraq /index.stm.

[53] Strategic Foresight Group, *The Blue Peace: Rethinking Middle East Water* (Mumbai: Strategic Foresight Group, 2011), 112.

Proposal for a Water Master Plan for Iraq

In 2003 the United States identified an important project for the Iraqi MOWR—the preparation of an updated water resources master plan. The issues noted above clearly need to be addressed in a comprehensive manner in a national-level water plan update. The plan update was designed to be a phased undertaking comprising a first year (Phase I) that puts the issues in context and priority, followed by four years of detailed sector studies, coordinated planning, and investment studies. The proposal below is taken from a recommendation made by the office of the U.S. senior advisor to MOWR in April 2003.[54] When looking at the cost of the proposed master plan, the scope and complexity of the undertaking become clear. The proposed master plan would consist of the following phases:

a. <u>Phase I.</u> The study would assess the status of water and land resources data available for plan update, compile such data as possible into usable form, assemble and activate appropriate models (water system, economic sector, agriculture, environmental, etc.), and prepare detailed work plans and schedules for subsequent detailed sector and overall plan studies and documentation. Preparatory to development and prioritization of the sector work plans and schedules, intense, short-duration studies would be performed for each significant issue discussed above as well as others that might arise during such studies.

b. <u>Phase II.</u> A series of studies that provide definitive assessment of the needs and opportunities for investment in water and related land resource projects that achieve the objectives of water management in Iraq. The planning horizon would be 50 years from the date of initiation. An overall phased plan of investments and general financing and repayment would be developed; documented; vetted in the local, regional, and in-

---

[54] At that time, the Coalition Provisional Authority had ceased operation, and the senior civilian advisor from the U.S. Army Corps of Engineers, Edwin Theriot, was making the transition to the U.S. embassy staff.

ternational communities; and adopted as the general basis for water management in Iraq. Phase II duration—four years. Cost of Phase II was estimated in 2004 to be $4 million per year for a four-year total of $16 million.[55]

The master plan proposal made in 2003 was never completed, but in the spring of 2011 a similar project seemed to be finally underway. The government of Italy provided most of the funding, and of course the money came back to the Department of Agricultural and Forest Engineering of Florence University.[56] The project is designed to assist with redevelopment of the marshlands in the south of Iraq, although monitoring stations will be located throughout the country and on both the Euphrates and Tigris. This illustrates an important limitation of foreign aid: each nation acts essentially in its own interest, awarding foreign aid dollars to its own citizens. International planning and cooperation in Iraq's reconstruction has been lacking and is one of many reasons for the lack of progress in the water sector. A strategic plan and national monitoring is essential, but it would be a mistake to wait for the results of the plan before making the next important decisions to protect Iraq's water supply.

Iraqi Challenges

Agricultural products traditionally accounted for a significant proportion of Iraq's exports, but this has been reduced by the recent turmoil related to the U.S.-led war. Agriculture still uses about 90 percent of Iraq's average annual water supply and is therefore critical to freshwater development and management.[57] As noted previously, salination of much of the irrigated land results in reduced crop yields and high salinity in the rivers, which creates problems for the municipal water supply as well as ecological

---

[55] Phases I and II paraphrased from document provided to coauthor Lorenz by the office of the U.S. senior advisor to Iraq MOWR in Baghdad, 2004. On file with author.

[56] Italian Ministry of Foreign Affairs, "Agriculture," Task Force Iraq, http://www.italyforiraq .esteri.it/ItalyForIraq/EN/iniziative/Agricoltura.asp (accessed 14 July 2012).

[57] FAO, "Iraq," note 5 (reporting that in 1990, Iraq used 92 percent of water withdrawal for agricultural purposes, while more recent estimates list this figure at 85 percent).

issues that threaten the restoration potential of the marshlands drained by Saddam Hussein.[58]

With U.S. assistance after the 2003 invasion, Iraq was able to make some advances in the long-term planning stages of water resource management. The Iraqi leadership recognized the threat of reduced water supply in the Iraqi national security strategy for 2007–10.

> The problem of decreasing water levels in the Tigris and Euphrates Rivers is a dangerous phenomenon that directly threatens environmental and nutritional security. . . . This problem stems essentially from the fact that there are large dams in Turkey and Syria for storing the water of the two rivers that do not take into consideration the rights of Iraq to water resources and the longer stretch of these rivers on its territory. Therefore, . . . this problem . . . leaves Iraq subject to a catastrophe that threatens its current and future national security.[59]

Nevertheless, having a strategic plan provides little without the resources and political will to carry it out. For all the ministries of the Iraqi government, progress in reconstruction and development is far behind schedule. The MOWR is no different, with little to show in the way of infrastructure improvement and international support to safeguard its strategic water. Internal issues and lingering security problems continue to delay progress.

On the eve of World Water Day, 22 March 2011, the UN reported that 50 percent of water resources are wasted in Iraq, where six million people have no access to clean water.[60] "Iraq faces difficulties in meeting the target of 91 percent of households using a safe drinking water supply by 2015,"

---

[58] Nurit Kliot, *Water Resources and Conflict in the Middle East* (New York: Routledge, 1994). In this work, Kliot names soil salinity as the greatest obstacle to Iraqi agriculture and notes that, as early as 1949, an estimated 60 percent of the irrigated land was seriously affected by salt.

[59] Republic of Iraq Cabinet and National Security Council, *Iraqi National Security Strategy*, 16.

[60] *Iraq Business News*, "Half of Iraq's Water Is Wasted," 22 March 2011, http://www.iraq-businessnews.com/2011/03/22/half-of-iraqs-water-is-wasted/.

reported the UN Inter-Agency Information and Analysis Unit in 2010.[61] Decades of conflict, sanctions, and neglect had taken their toll. In the first six months of 2010, over 360,000 diarrhea cases were reported as a result of polluted drinking water and a lack of hygiene awareness among local communities in Iraq. "Every day at least 250,000 tonnes of raw sewage is pumped into the Tigris river threatening unprotected water sources and the entire water distribution system," according to a UNICEF report.[62]

There are additional problems in Iraq with interaction between ministries and coordination of overlapping responsibilities for water issues.[63] The next few years will be critical, and only a stable government can support major progress in the water sector. As mentioned by the first U.S. senior water advisor, Iraq could be viewed as another California, with the potential for large-scale development of hydropower and irrigation. But without security and stabilization, conditions in all sectors will deteriorate. This makes it all the more difficult to plan for the future and to estimate requirements for water in the region.

The government of Iraq outlined strategic goals in the water resource management sector in a 2007 report.[64] At the top of the list is the plan for the construction of nine large dams, the largest of which would be the Bakhma Dam with a capacity of 14.4 BCM and a seven-year construction phase. Fourteen small dams are planned as well, in addition to dams in the Kurdish areas. The plan also calls for land reclamation and the improved maintenance of more than 126,000 km of drainage networks that need constant attention. Despite some gains in strategic planning, there is no overarching policy or strategic framework that links the Iraq water sector together, and no integrated planning framework for water resources.[65] The reliance on supply-side dam building rather than demand-side efficiency and conservation measures is a problem typical in develop-

---

[61] Inter-Agency Information and Analysis Unit, *Iraq Factsheet.*

[62] Reported in UNICEF, "World Water Day 2011 (22 March)," 3, http://iq.one.un.org /documents/155/UNICEF%20media%20advisory%20and%20facts.pdf.

[63] Geopolicity, *Managing the Tigris Euphrates Watershed,* http://www.geopolicity.com/upload /content/pub_1293090043_regular.pdf.

[64] Ibid., 40.

[65] Ibid., 45.

ing countries.[66] In the case of Iraq, the strategic water and land resources project, which was recently initiated, should be of assistance. Also, the use of better technology, including basinwide modeling, should help the government of Iraq make the right choices when it comes to developing its water resources. But the right choices for an outside analyst are not always the same when viewed from the perspective of an Iraqi politician. This is a sensitive topic that will be discussed later in chapter 6.

The Real Threat: Salinity and Other Chemicals

Salinity has long been a significant but rarely measured threat in the basin. High water-salinity levels were largely responsible for the decline of the Sumerian civilization (see chapter 1), and the same mistakes are being repeated today. Local leaders focus on obvious water infrastructure, such as dams and canals, without looking carefully at the long-term consequences of construction. Unfortunately, the hidden threat from salinity and other chemicals is not fully understood by local leaders or used in the planning process.

Salt-affected soils in Colorado. *Photo by USDA Natural Resources Conservation Service*

High salt levels pollute drinking water and can make agriculture impossible. Salt levels are related to water quantity; during low water levels, salt levels tend to increase, aggravating the situation. Other parameters such as heavy metals, nutrients (phosphorus and nitrogen), bacteria, and biota characteristics in the Euphrates and Tigris are not well known, but will eventually be essential in order to perform a complete assessment. But even with limited monitoring capability, it is unnecessary to wait for a full assessment because the salinity figures alone are enough to justify alarm.

Salinity is the saltiness or dissolved salt content of a body of water and is a general term used to describe the levels of different salts, such as sodium chloride, magnesium, calcium sulfates, and bicarbonates. *Total*

---

[66] Allan, *Middle East Water Question*, 185.

dissolved solids (TDS) are a measure of the combined content of inorganic and organic substances contained in a liquid in suspended form. TDS is a common water quality measurement in freshwater systems, and salinity is usually the major factor in the definition of TDS. Although TDS itself is not generally considered a primary pollutant, it is commonly used as an indicator of the presence of a range of chemical contaminants. Freshwater is generally considered to have less than 1,500 milligrams per liter (mg/L) of TDS; brackish water 1,500 to 5,000 mg/L; and saline water more than 5,000 mg/L.[67] The United States established a secondary water quality standard of 500 mg/L to provide for the potability of drinking water. Basin models are used to more comprehensively evaluate TDS within a river basin and dynamically along its various tributaries. Models can be programmed to show current conditions and project future conditions based on historic data and estimates of future withdrawals and return flow to the rivers.

Data indicating salinity levels in the Euphrates-Tigris basin is difficult to obtain from the riparian parties, and Turkey is naturally reluctant to release data that might show the extent of pollution released to downstream countries. Even historic data is a national security matter for Turkey, for that will show a "baseline" upon which all future discharges must be measured. Agricultural return flow is only one part of the problem; increasing population along the river and the flow of untreated sewage in Syria also contribute to the predicament for Iraq. But the primary cause of man-made salination is the salt conveyed through irrigation return flows. All irrigation water derived from rivers or groundwater, however "sweet" or fresh, contains salts that remain in the soil after the water has evaporated. Ultimately farmland becomes unworkable, and this is already occurring in many parts of Syria and Iraq.

A number of recent studies, including the development of sophisticated models, indicate the critical nature of the problem. The most significant study was conducted by Jon Martin Trondalen and published as part of the UNESCO Water and Conflict Resolution Series.[68] This independent study focuses primarily on the Euphrates, principally due to the avail-

---

[67] Gilbert M. Masters and Wendell P. Ela, *Introduction to Environmental Engineering and Science*, 3d ed. (Upper Saddle River, NJ: Prentice Hall, 2007).

[68] Trondalen, *Water and Peace*.

ability of historic data and opportunities for sampling. One important observation of this book was the fact that the large reservoir volumes in the Euphrates-Tigris basin (mostly in Turkey and Syria) have contributed to lower water quality. The longer detention periods, as compared to natural runoff, allow for increased stagnation and an increase in TDS levels.

FIGURE 3.1. **Model structure and annual average input data for natural run-off and salinity**

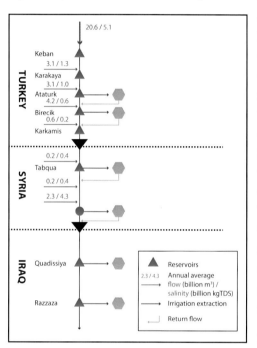

The Trondalen report looks at a number of scenarios, with different flow levels as the Euphrates enters Syria and then Iraq and varying concentrations of TDS as the agricultural return flow reaches the river. In figure 3.1, runoff data and salinity data are representative of the situation before construction and operation of reservoirs and before extensive irrigation withdrawals. The model irrigation extraction sites and corresponding return flow sites are also shown in this figure.

In table 3.2, the model shows that with Turkey and Syria's "full irrigation target" of 10 BCM each, the salinity levels at the Turkey-Syria border could average 317 mg/L and

Reproduced by permission from CESAR, *The Euphrates River and the Tigris River Water Resources Management: Water Resources Analysis Methodology*, 2006, figure 8-1. Second reference document in Jon Martin Trondalen, *Water and Peace for the People: Possible Solutions to Water Disputes in the Middle East.*

1,395 mg/L at the Syria-Iraq border. Trondalen concludes that "unless a river basin agreement is reached in a relatively short time, the water quality will reach a level in which water from the Euphrates is no longer suitable for *drinking or agricultural purposes*" (emphasis added).[69] Figure

---

[69] Ibid., 165.

TABLE 3.2. **Simulation statistics on selected scenarios**

Parameter	Natural runoff	Full irrigation target		60% irrigation target	
		A1	A2	B1	B2
Assumptions/input data					
Minimum flow at Turkish-Syrian border (m³/s)	-	450	450	450	450
Return flow concentration (mg TDS/l)	-	700	3,500	700	3,500
Return flow ratio (%)	-	20	20	20	20
Initial salinity concentration in reservoirs (mg/l) (Turkey/Syria/Iraq)	-	300/400/500			
Net irrigation target (billion m³/year)					
Turkey	-	10	10	6	6
Syria	-	10	10	6	6
Iraq	-	36	36	21.6	21.6
Net irrigation obtained (billion m³/year)					
Turkey	-	9.2	9.2	6	6
Syria	-	9.4	9.4	6	6
Iraq	-	9.7	9.7	15.1	15.1
Flow at borders (m³/s)					
Turkish-Syrian border:					
Average	1,006	681	681	781	781
Min.	493	450	450	463	463
Syrian-Iraqi border:					
Average	1,091	467	467	671	671
Min.	535	264	264	331	331
Calculated salinity concentrations at borders (mg TDS/l)					
Turkish-Syrian border:					
Average	268	317	517	303	434
Max.	330	369	623	352	533
Syrian-Iraqi border:					
Average	400	746	1,395	573	906
Max.	493	967	1,841	753	1,295

Notes:

1. The results presented in the table are annual average values based on dynamic simulations with a time step of 1 week over a 40-year period. The results will diverge from simple steady state calculations.

2. In addition to the results presented in table A, calculations have been performed on the Euphrates River in Iraq to the point of confluence with the Tigris River. The model calculations show no significant changes from the border to the point of confluence, but this is mainly due to the assumptions made (no return flow, no increased evaporation). In practice, return flow will occur and the river will become more saline downstream.

Adapted from CESAR, *The Euphrates River and the Tigris River Water Resources Management: Water Resources Analysis Methodology*, 2006, table A. Second reference document in Jon Martin Trondalen, *Water and Peace for the People: Possible Solutions to Water Disputes in the Middle East.*

3.2 shows the dangerous salinity levels for the Euphrates at the Turkish-Syrian and Syrian-Iraqi borders. Further research is needed to determine the full impact of the predicted level of salt on the agrarian economy and human health in the region. But one thing is clear: if all the parties continue to develop their own agriculture as planned, salinity levels are certain to reach levels that will significantly affect agriculture and human health, particularly in Iraq.

The Impact of Climate Change

Climate change is likely to have numerous and diverse impacts, including impacts on human health, natural systems, and the built environment.[70] Since global climate change will likely affect fundamental drivers of the hydrological cycle, it may have a large impact on water resources

FIGURE 3.2. **Average salinity concentration bands at the Turkish-Syrian (T-S) border and at the Syrian-Iraqi (S-I) border with variable return flow concentration**

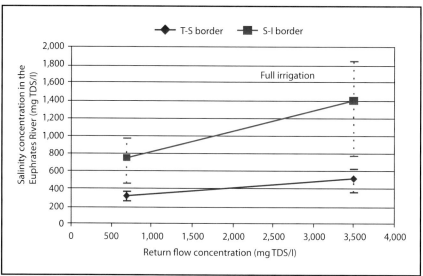

Reproduced by permission from CESAR, *The Euphrates River and the Tigris River Water Resources Management: Water Resources Analysis Methodology,* 2006, figure 8.5a. Second reference document in Jon Martin Trondalen, *Water and Peace for the People: Possible Solutions to Water Disputes in the Middle East.*

---

[70] See the reports of the Intergovernmental Panel on Climate Change for more information. For example, the *Climate Change 2007: Synthesis Report* is available online at http://ipcc.ch /publications_and_data/ar4/syr/en/spms1.html.

and water resource management. This section will explore the possible impacts and describe some alternative strategies to improve water management by tracking, anticipating, and responding to climate change.

An understanding of the problem begins with a basic understanding of the science and the potential implications of climate change on the realm of water resources. The following is a summary of the worldwide consequences as described in one report:

- increased runoff and earlier spring peak discharge in many glacier-and snow-fed rivers;

- warming of lakes, reservoirs, and rivers in many regions, with effects on thermal structure and water quality;

- decreased river flow in dry regions by 10–30 percent at midlatitudes, much of this in already water-stressed latitudes;

- increased extent of drought-affected areas;

- short-term heavy precipitation to increase flood risk; and

- increased number, duration, and intensity of heat waves.[71]

As indicated, millions of people are now impacted by droughts and floods, and climate change is likely to increase both the magnitude and number of hydrological extremes. Information about climate change is not only essential for water managers and planners, it is increasingly important as a security factor in national planning (see the introduction of this book). Scientists are now developing means and methods of adaption in dealing with consequences that are not easy to predict.[72] Nevertheless, international organizations have begun to gather data and make generalized observations.

---

[71] Carol Howe, Joel B. Smith, and Jim Henderson, eds., *Climate Change and Water: International Perspectives on Mitigation and Adaptation* (London: IWA Publishing and American Water Works Association, 2009), 6.

[72] Fulco Ludwig and others, eds., *Climate Change Adaptation in the Water Sector* (London: Earthscan Publishing, 2009), 3.

FIGURE 3.3. **Water resources development estimates for 2050**

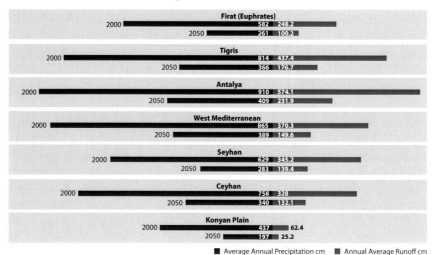

Adapted from Strategic Foresight Group, *The Blue Peace: Rethinking Middle East Water* (Mumbai: Strategic Foresight Group, 2011), figure 8-h.

For Turkey, a number of UN reports predict major climate change–related impacts, with temperatures expected to rise by 2–3 degrees Celsius by the end of the century.[73] Temperatures in the eastern regions of Turkey, which contain the headwaters of the Euphrates and Tigris, are expected to increase during summer seasons by 4 degrees Celsius by 2061. As a result, the amount of water in the Euphrates could eventually decline by 30 percent by the end of the century. In a more pessimistic report on annual precipitation and annual runoff in the Euphrates watershed, comparing the year 2000 with the year 2050, a 60 percent decline was predicted (see figure 3.3).[74] In an even worse scenario, the decline in the Tigris watershed is predicted to be more than 60 percent. If these figures are accurate, the amount of water reaching Syria and Iraq will show massive declines even without the impact of increasing population and the development of the GAP described in this book.

It is wise to be skeptical of water figures released by a government, particularly when the government has an interest in demonstrating that it has

---

[73] Strategic Foresight Group, *Blue Peace*, 121.

[74] Ibid., 122, figure 8-h.

no "excess water" to share, and to bear in mind that climate change predictions require a certain degree of conjecture. The Turkish DSI released a report that showed an overall 13 percent decrease in water availability by 2030 and a 22 percent decline by 2050 due to climate change.[75] Turkey has a longstanding position that it is not "water rich," and this report certainly supports that position. Turkey treats detailed water data as a state secret and knows that a release of (even accurate) data will rarely serve its own self-interest. As an example, the work of Trondalen mentioned earlier in this chapter is unlikely to be embraced by Turkey because it shows in stark detail the negative impact of Turkish agricultural policies on Syria and Iraq. But Turkey can use the climate change data (even though speculative) to support its own longstanding positions.

Climate change impacts on Iraq are difficult to quantify, but some observations can be made. The Iraqi government ratified the Kyoto Protocol in January 2008, and there was some hope that this could be a step toward creating policy to counter the effects of climate change.[76] One of the biggest problems for Iraq is desertification, and large sections of once-productive farmland have already been abandoned.[77] This has been aggravated by drought over the past several years, as well as by government inability to provide mitigation. Dust storms in Iraq, a normal phenomenon, have increased in frequency from 19 to 40 days per year over the past few years; this could be part of a global trend that is difficult to predict or measure.

Salination of agricultural lands has been mentioned earlier in this chapter, and Iraq seems condemned to relive the same problems faced by the Sumerians (see chapter 1). Poor drainage networks and primitive irrigation methods lead to salt accumulation in the soil. Leaders make poor decisions based on self-interest and a lack of careful planning. All this is likely to be aggravated by climate change, which will result in decreased soil moisture, increasing soil erosion and wetland modification. This will necessarily have an impact on food production and the overall economy.

---

[75] Ibid., 123, figure 8-i.

[76] Ibid., 113.

[77] Campbell Robertson, "Iraq Suffers as the Euphrates River Dwindles," *New York Times*, 13 July 2009, http://www.nytimes.com/2009/07/14/world/middleeast/14euphrates.html.

Iraq seems beset by a "perfect storm" of conditions, both man-made and natural, that will challenge every effort to improve the lives of the Iraqi people.

Projections for Freshwater Availability: 2025 and Beyond

Computing future water availability and demand is an inexact science, and it is in the interest of each state to overstate demand. Upstream parties are likely to understate water availability within their own borders and criticize downstream parties for waste and inefficiency. Computations should start with a determination of current and recent flow levels, but this data is very difficult to find.[78] International agencies have nonetheless developed a number of studies looking at global water demand, and the results are specific enough to reach some conclusions.

One of the major factors in computing water demand is population, and the future populations of the three countries dependent on the Euphrates-Tigris are comparatively easy to predict. The total population of these countries was less than 30 million in 1950 but had climbed to 106 million by 2000. This number was approximately 134 million in 2011[79] and is likely to be 150 million in 2020. These potential changes will pose problems for food security, especially for a basin that has no significant water-sharing agreements.

Annual internal renewable water resources refer to the average annual flow of rivers and the recharge of groundwater generated from precipitation within a country. In other words, this concept excludes the water that flows from other countries or is imported. Caution must be used when comparing the internal renewable water resources of different countries because the estimates are based on differing sources and dates, and are often influenced by competing national interests. Annual averages also disguise large seasonal and long-term variations. Concerning the per capita annual share in the three states in the Euphrates-Tigris basin, the optimistic 1995 estimates divide the renewable water as follows: 2,967 CM

---

[78] In multiple trips, coauthor Lorenz was consistently rebuffed in his attempts to gather data in Ankara and Damascus. Turkey has been more forthcoming in the past three years, but the information is still inadequate.

[79] CIA, "Syria."

in Turkey; 1,791 CM in Syria; and 3,688 CM in Iraq. Estimates for population increases by 2025 reduce the shares to 2,090 CM in Turkey; 990 CM in Syria; and 1,845 CM in Iraq. The "dependency percentage" of water resources with neighboring states also varies. This indicates the degree to which the population is dependent on external resources of water. For the Euphrates-Tigris basin, the lowest is that of Turkey, which is less than 2 percent; for Iraq, it is more than 53 percent; and the highest is in Syria, where it reaches 80 percent. It is important to note that self-sufficiency in food per person is generally considered to require 10,000 CM of water.[80]

TABLE 3.3. **Renewable per capita freshwater availability for Iraq**

Year	Population (in millions)	Availability (BCM/Yr)	Per Capita (cubic meters/yr)
2010	28	57	2,035
2020	34	50	1,470
2030	42	43	1,023

Adapted from Strategic Foresight Group, *The Blue Peace: Rethinking Middle East Water* (Mumbai: Strategic Foresight Group, 2011), figure 7-b.

In a report released in 2011, a water expert at the University of Baghdad estimated the renewable per capita freshwater availability (in cubic meters per year) for Iraq.[81] This report predicts that the amount available in Iraq will decline from 2,035 CM in 2010 to 1,470 CM in 2020 and 1,023 CM in 2030 (shown in table 3.3). This estimate is based on current population increase projections from 28 million to 42 million in 2030, as well as a steady decrease in water flow as a result in upstream development. All such estimates involve a certain amount of conjecture, but the dangerous potential for Iraq is clear.

In 1990, John F. Kolars and William A. Mitchell conducted a study of the GAP in Turkey and developed an estimate of water availability until the year 2040.[82] Kolars and Mitchell cautioned that the projected data is highly conjectural and depicts a "worst case scenario." It should also be noted that figure 3.4 (adapted from their book) deals only with the Euphrates, but it has significance because of Syria's heavy reliance on the waters

---

[80] Ali Aziz Hnoush, *Water Security and Environmental Security of States of the Euphrates and Tigris Basins: Towards a Strategy of Sustainable Development* (on file with authors), 14.

[81] Strategic Foresight Group, *Blue Peace*, 111.

[82] John F. Kolars and William A. Mitchell, *The Euphrates River and the Southeast Anatolia Development Project* (Carbondale, IL: Southern Illinois University Press, 1991), 131.

FIGURE 3.4. **Projected sequential depletion of the Euphrates River, 1990–2040**

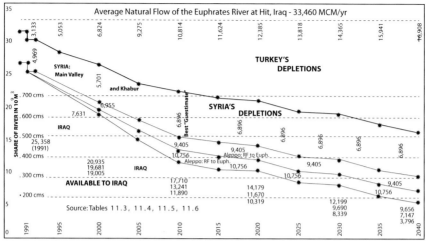

Reproduced by permission from John Kolars and William Mitchell, *The Euphrates River and the Southeast Anatolia Development Project* (Carbondale: Southern Illinois University Press, 1991), figure 2.

of the Euphrates and the relative capacity of the Euphrates in the basin. Despite these qualifiers and over 20 years after the chart was produced, it still seems reasonably accurate and, given the lack of publicly available data produced by the three riparian countries, retains its value.

The GAP has developed more slowly than predicted in 1990, but declining flows in the Euphrates and Tigris have nevertheless been noted. In Kolars and Mitchell's chart, the average natural flow of the Euphrates is designated by the constant line at the top of the chart, given as 33,460 MCM/yr (million cubic meters per year). The increasing depletion of the Euphrates is evident by reading the chart from left to right. The intersections of the cubic meter per second measures—shown by "cms" dash lines—denote the years in which certain levels of flow may be reached. The solid lines (with stars for years) indicate the amount of water predicted to reach Syria and Iraq in the Euphrates main channel that flows from Turkey. The three alternate lines in the center of the chart represent differences for possible diversions by Syria for irrigation near Aleppo, but since that project failed to materialize, the upper line should be more accurate. Although river gauge data is not available to compare to actual flow and use in 2011, the figures in this chart are supported by more recent scientific modeling data in the CESAR report mentioned earlier in this chapter.

A number of publications have compiled charts indicating the water potential for the Euphrates-Tigris basin compared to the consumption projections for the riparian states. In an ambitious 2011 report, the Strategic Foresight Group made an attempt to analyze the "Present and Future Water Balance" for several Middle Eastern countries.[83] Data was provided by voluntary participants in the study, and government officials were notably absent on the Syrian side. In terms of freshwater supply, Syria and Iraq are fully dependent on the waters of the Euphrates and Tigris, while Turkey has a number of other basins within its borders.

Below is the Strategic Foresight Group's summary of Syria's water resources:

> Syria is facing a serious problem of reduction in its available water resources due to climate change, variations in precipitation levels, pollution and related factors. Syria plans to develop additional water capabilities, utilize available storage facilities as well as introduce demand management policies and curb excessive utilization. The implementation of this strategy is difficult to assess due to secrecy regarding data on water resources.[84]

The 2011 water demand in Iraq is estimated to be 55 BCM per year, with a total supply of 57 BCM, leaving a presumed surplus of 2 BCM.[85] But this figure is meaningless in the sense that Iraq is unable to harness the additional 2 BCM of freshwater. The water that flows past Baghdad to the sea is already of such low quality that it provides no real advantage to the Iraqi people. Today the demand for domestic consumption and agriculture is rising but fluctuating each year due to poor supply systems; recent severe drought; and less water flowing from Turkey, Syria, and Iran.[86]

---

[83] Strategic Foresight Group, *Blue Peace*, 101–25.

[84] Ibid., 108.

[85] Ibid., 112.

[86] Ibid., 114.

The marshlands in southern Iraq once comprised the largest marsh system in the Middle East and western Eurasia.[87] Satellite imagery collected in 1970 showed the marshes covering an estimated area of 15,000–20,000 km². A United Nations Environmental Programme report estimated in the spring of 2000 that an area of 1,000 km² in the al-Hawizeh Marsh system was all that remained. In March 2003, it was estimated that the Mesopotamian Marsh system had been reduced to a mere 7 percent of its 1970 area. This was due to the efforts of Saddam Hussein that could be described as "punitive hydro-engineering"(map 3.4).[88] There have been a number

MAP 3.4. **Former marshes and water diversion projects in southeastern Iraq, 1994.**
Reprinted from Central Intelligence Agency, The Destruction of Iraq's Southern Marshes *(1994)*

[87] Hassan Partow, *The Mesopotamian Marshlands: Demise of an Ecosystem* (Nairobi: United Nations Environmental Programme, 2001), 11.

[88] *Economist,* "The Marsh Arabs of Iraq: Do They Want to Go Back in Time?" 5 June 2003, http://www.economist.com/node/1827561.

of efforts to refill and reclaim the marshes over the past eight years, with limited success. By some estimates, it would take an additional 20 BCM per year to restore the marshes, and this is unlikely to be available in view of declining water levels.

FIGURE 3.5. **Water balance with increasing demand**

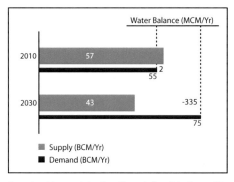

Reproduced by permission from Strategic Foresight Group, *The Blue Peace: Rethinking Middle East Water* (Mumbai: Strategic Foresight Group, 2011), figure 7-c.

In figure 3.5, a projected water deficit in Iraq in 2030 is expected to reach 12 BCM, and that does not include an additional 20 BCM needed for marsh restoration.[89]

In a factsheet produced by the UN Inter-Agency Information and Analysis Unit in October 2010,[90] the following per capita levels of freshwater availability in CM per year were indicated: Turkey 2,890; Iraq 2,400; Iran 1,876; and Syria 791 (figure 3.6). These figures can be misleading, however, because they do not take into account declining flows, growing populations (Iraq's tripled between 1970 and 2007), water quality, and the relative economic strength of each country. For example, although Saudi Arabia has only 95 CM per capita, it is able to maintain a high standard of living by the importation of "virtual water" and using desalination to create "new" water. But desalination is rarely an answer for developing countries due to the tremendous cost and potential environmental concerns in releasing salt back into the environment. Even with more efficient technology, there is no breakthrough on the horizon that would make inexpensive desalinated water available in Iraq.[91] One analyst has recommended the construction of a desalination plant in the Euphrates River as a partial

---

[89] Strategic Foresight Group, *Blue Peace*, 112, figure 7-c.

[90] Inter-Agency Information and Analysis Unit, *Iraq Factsheet*.

[91] See Allan, *Middle East Water Question*, 92, for a description of the cost benefit analysis of desalination.

FIGURE 3.6. **Water availability (m³ per capita)**

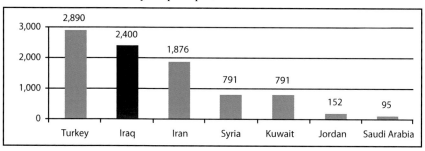

solution to the problems facing Iraq. That proposal is described in more detail in chapter 7.

Turkey has extremely ambitious plans to ensure that adequate water is supplied to all sectors by 2023. Turkey also takes the position that there is no real problem if the waters are used efficiently:

> The combined water potential of the Euphrates and the Tigris Rivers is, in the view of the Turkish authorities, sufficient to meet the needs of the three riparian states provided that water is used in an efficient way and the benefit is maximized through new irrigation technologies and the principle of "more crop per drop" at the basin level.[92]

The Dilemma: Managing Supply versus Managing Demand

In dealing with a potential water deficit, a government has several options. In the Middle East, there is a tendency to look to "new water" or building infrastructure such as dams and canals to remedy the problem. The United States went through this phase from the 1930s until the 1970s, before the U.S. environmental movement took hold and slowed it down. The shortcomings of the United States' approach only became apparent years later, and it might be said that lessons learned in those years could be useful to developing countries facing some of the same issues.[93] The United States

---

[92] Republic of Turkey, *Turkey Water Report 2009*, 16.

[93] One of the classic books describing the water situation in the American West is Marc Reisner's *Cadillac Desert: The American West and Its Disappearing Water* (New York: Penguin Books, 1986; rev. ed. 1993).

is now in the somewhat unique position of removing dams that were built during the boom years of dam construction.[94]

It is often more politically palatable to build a dam—it gives obvious results and is often a sense of national pride. It is much more difficult to deal with water conservation and control demand, particularly when there may be vested interests such as farmers, politicians, and landowners who benefit from the status quo. In an authoritarian country like Syria, the most obvious solution is to build more dams, even when there is insufficient water to make the dams effective and productive. Ruling parties will typically promote public works projects as a means of garnering and maintaining support. In Iraq there are ambitious plans to build more dams despite studies (such as the CESAR report cited previously) indicating that additional dams will not reduce the anticipated water deficit. Scientific methods and models suggest that more can be achieved by improving the efficiency of existing systems than by building new ones.

In Syria only 16 percent of the farmers use modern irrigation systems, and water losses from seepage and evaporation are more than 40 percent of the water used. Yet Syria engages in the same type of decision making, favoring dams and major new projects rather than improving the efficiency of existing ones. Without a change in direction and an adoption of new approaches, both Syria and Iraq will continue down the same nonproductive path when it comes to their water resources.

A Summary of the Water Deficit

Predictions always entail some degree of guesswork, but the evidence is clear that in the next 10 to 20 years water demand in the region, and particularly in Iraq, is certain to exceed supply. The chart produced by Kolars and Mitchell for the Euphrates in 1991 is consistent with new data currently available and graphically illustrates this concern. As the development of the GAP in Turkey nears completion, there will be an inevitable reduction in both quantity and quality of water to the downstream countries. Syria is vulnerable and contributing in its own way to the difficulties

---

[94] For a current description of the Elwha Dam removal, see the Olympic National Park Web site at http://www.nps.gov/olym/naturescience/elwha-ecosystem-restoration.htm.

downstream in Iraq. Iraq's increasing reliance on the Tigris has advantages, but the new dams under construction by Iran will further reduce the flow. Based on these considerations, the situation for Iraq in the next 10 to 20 years appears to be grave.

In the past 10 years, a number of sophisticated computer models have been developed to provide planning tools for water managers. Chapter 6 provides a more detailed description of these models with recommendations for their use in the region. The CESAR report, mentioned earlier, has made a significant contribution, but more work needs to be done. Water quality will certainly decline as agricultural production increases and Turkey and Syria fully develop their water resources by 2023. The immediate threat will be increasing salinity in the next 10 to 15 years as much of the water in Iraq could become unusable.

A review of the available data seems to favor the "water pessimist" approach described at the beginning of this chapter. For Iraq, the authors of this book predict special challenges because the country is faced with dysfunctional politics and a crisis of governance. If Iraq can solve these problems, and the economy improves, it should be able to satisfy the needs of a growing population. In a best-case scenario, Iraq could have a positive water balance and the ability to harness and store water. But Iraq will have to overcome many obstacles, both internal and external, to make progress.

Although the level of water scarcity (or water deficit) in the next 20 years is difficult to measure precisely, Syria and Iraq can be expected to experience crisis conditions as available freshwater declines. Yet, while a crisis is certainly looming on the horizon, it may not look like the "rivers of flame" predicted by Jon Martin Trondalen,[95] though it will probably be a grave danger nonetheless. Another point can be made here: a failure to deal with the problems at a relatively early stage will "eventually multiply problems beyond the reach of realistic remedial action."[96] It remains to be seen what the crisis will look like, or what the implications will be for regional security.

---

[95] Trondalen, *Water and Peace*, 160.
[96] Ibid., 206.

CHAPTER 4
IRAQ AND THE HIDDEN ISSUE: KURDISH CONTROL OF THE TIGRIS

The question of Kurdish autonomy and possible independence in Iraq has been the subject of much debate, and the sharing of oil resources has been a central factor in that discussion. Yet the sharing of water resources within Iraq is rarely reported, despite the fact that the Kurdistan Regional Government (KRG) in the north controls a major part of the Tigris River, as well as major dams. Expanding irrigation and agriculture in northern Iraq, or building new dams, will further complicate the already tenuous water situation in the southern non-Kurdish provinces of Iraq. This chapter will analyze this situation and attempt to answer the following questions:

1. Do the KRG's water and agricultural policies compete with or complement those of the Iraqi federal state?

2. When completed, will the KRG's projected water projects harm the downstream Arabs of Iraq?

3. In terms of water management, should the KRG be treated as a full partner or is it viable to work with the KRG through the Baghdad government?

4. In reality, is there a fourth riparian (and perhaps a fifth, counting Iran) in the Euphrates-Tigris basin?

Geography and Water Resources

The three Kurdish governorates in northern Iraq border Turkey to the north, Iran to the east, and Iraq proper to the south (map 4.1). Elevations in the Kurdish mountains average about 2,400 meters and rise to over 3,600 meters in the Zagros Mountains.[1] The region can be divided into three geologic zones: the northern range of the Zagros Mountains, the central transitional mountain range, and the southern plains along the Tigris River.[2] In millimeters, annual precipitation totals corresponding to the zones are above 500, 300–500, and below 300, respectively.[3] The region has a Mediterranean climate with hot, dry summers and cool, wet winters. Approximately 80 percent of the region's precipitation falls between the months of December and March.[4]

The four major rivers in the Kurdish region are the Tigris, Great Zab, Little Zab, and Diyala. The Tigris, which forms the border of Dohuk governorate for 138 kilometers before leaving the region, and the Great Zab have their headwaters in Turkey; the sources of the Little Zab and the Diyala are in Iran.[5] The flow of the Tigris as it enters Iraq is 21 billion cubic meters (BCM),[6] and an additional 23 BCM is added from runoff within Iraq, nearly all of which comes from rivers in the Kurdish region.[7] All tributaries to the Tigris enter from its left bank. The Great Zab contributes a flow of 13 BCM at its confluence with the Tigris; the Little Zab, 7 BCM; and the Diyala, 5.5 BCM. The al-Adhaim, a minor river, contributes less than 1 BCM.[8] These numbers are all approximations of annual averages, and totals from one source may not accurately compare with numbers from another due to temporal variance and instrumental imprecision.

---

[1] Kurdistan Regional Government (KRG), "About Kurdistan Region," KRG, http://www.krg.org/articles/?lngnr=12&rnr=140&smap=03010300.

[2] Carlo Travaglia and Niccolo Dainelli, *Groundwater Search by Remote Sensing: A Methodological Approach* (Rome: Food and Agriculture Organization of the United Nations [FAO], 2003), 3.

[3] Zoran Stevanovic and Miroslav Markovic, *Hydrogeology of Northern Iraq*, vol. 1, *Climate, Hydrology, Geomorphology and Geology* (Rome: FAO, 2004).

[4] Ibid., chapter 2.

[5] Travaglia and Dainelli, *Groundwater Search by Remote Sensing*, 4.

[6] Stevanovic and Markovic, *Hydrogeology of Northern Iraq*, vol. 1, 25.

[7] Ibid., 28.

[8] Ibid., chapter 2.

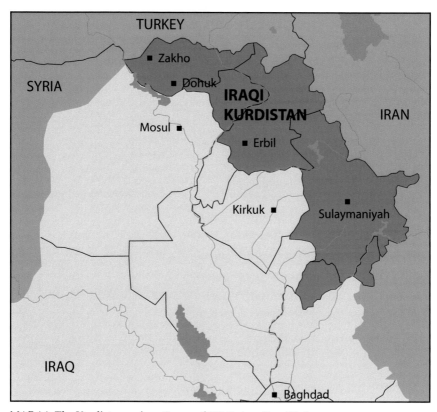

MAP 4.1. **The Kurdistan region.** *Courtesy of U.S. Business Council in Iraq*

For surface water storage, the Kurdish region has two major dams: Dokan Dam on the Little Zab has a potential live storage capacity of 6.8 BCM, and Derbendi Khan Dam on the Diyala can store 3 BCM.[9] Dohuk Dam has a capacity of 52 million cubic meters, and 12 small dams in the region have capacities ranging from 35,000 to 380,000 cubic meters.[10] Total storage capacity in the Kurdish region is an estimated 10 BCM.[11] However, the current drought in the region has reduced the amount of water in the reservoirs. According to figures from the KRG's Ministry of Water Resources, water stored in the Dokan Reservoir in November 2008 was 1.5 BCM and

---

[9] Ibid.

[10] KRG Ministry of Agriculture and Water Resources, http://en.moawr-krg.org.

[11] Stevanovic and Markovic, *Hydrogeology of Northern Iraq*, vol. 1, 32.

1 BCM in the Derbendi Khan Reservoir.[12] The dams associated with these reservoirs have electricity-generating capabilities of 120,000 and 37,000 kilowatt hours, respectively. The partially completed dam on the Great Zab would have a storage capacity of 8.3 BCM and produce 2,500 megawatt hours of power.[13] The KRG also has tenders for feasibility studies for three dams: one on the Great Zab, one on the Shamdinan (a tributary of the Great Zab), and one on the Little Zab.[14]

The Kurdish region is part of the foothills aquifer system, one of five major systems in Iraq.[15] Current renewable groundwater recharge in northern Iraq is 1.1 BCM/year.[16] Karst formations in the border folds zone show the potential to hold significant groundwater reserves.[17] In fact the Kurdish region is the most promising area of Iraq for groundwater development, having water quality sufficient for potable and irrigable uses. However, the transmissivity, or flow, in the region is high, meaning that depletion of the aquifer can easily occur if recharge rates are poorly understood.[18]

Water management and water use throughout Iraq are critically dependent on the north, where the main water resources of the Tigris are located. The Tigris receives a significant amount of water from its left-bank tributaries that drain the Zagros Mountains. The average annual flow of the Tigris entering Iraq is estimated at 21 BCM, and it is assumed that up to 50 percent of the Tigris's yield downstream of Baghdad originates in Iraq.[19] Water resource studies in the north were carried out in the past by outside companies, but limited documentation is available for analysis today because previously operational and well-equipped hydrological

---

[12] Ibid., 18.

[13] Ibid., chapter 2.

[14] KRG, "Invitation to Tender Deadline Extended: Feasibility Study for Three Hydropower Plants," press release, 21 October 2008, http://www.krg.org/articles/detail.asp?smap=020101 00&lngnr=12&asnr=&anr=25710&rnr=223.

[15] Stevanovic and Markovic, *Hydrogeology of Northern Iraq*, vol. 1, chapter 1.

[16] Ibid., chapter 1.

[17] Travaglia and Dainelli, *Groundwater Search by Remote Sensing*, 4.

[18] Stevanovic and Markovic, *Hydrogeology of Northern Iraq*, vol. 1, chapter 1.

[19] Ibid., chapter 3.

stations were destroyed. A water resources and irrigation project, which began under the United Nations' oil-for-food program in 2002, planned for at least 30 hydrologic recordings for northern Iraq's major rivers,[20] but this work was not started and several years of network observations, such as collecting data analysis and correlation with the historical data, are still required.

In 2008 the KRG began the bidding process for a feasibility study for three additional dams—one on the Great Zab, one on the Shamdinan (main tributary of Great Zab), and one on the Little Zab.[21] It is not clear if these projects were coordinated with the central Iraqi Ministry of Water Resources, but the KRG seems to have its own plans and the resources to carry them out. Continued development within the boundary of the KRG is bound to have an impact on the south, although it is difficult to quantify at this time (map 4.2). Increased salinization of the Tigris in southern Iraq has already been attributed to reduced flow due to upstream and northern tributary use.[22]

The Kurdistan Regional Government

The peculiar nature of the Iraqi federal state regarding the Kurdish areas has created "a state with a state." The language of the KRG's official Web site captures some of what might be called the siege mentality of the Kurdish state: "The KRG is the authority that rules over much of the liberated area of Iraqi Kurdistan. Its domain includes the provinces of Erbil and Dohuk, and the city of Erbil serves as its capital. In its present form, the KRG is comprised of the Cabinet, first formed in September 1996, and the Kurdish Parliament, which was elected in May 1992."[23] Phrases such as "much of the liberated area" imply the future acquisition of additional

---

[20] Ibid. River locations and technical specifications were revised in December 2010.

[21] KRG, "Invitation to Tender."

[22] Sadik B. Jawad, "Integrated Water Resources Management of Diyala River Basin in Central Iraq Using System Dynamics Modeling," (research proposal, 2005), 15, https://waterportal.sandia.gov/iraq/documents/W03%20full%20proposal%2C%20Diyala%20modeling.doc/view.

[23] KRG, "About KRG: Structure and Mission," http://old.krg.org/about/background.asp (accessed 19 March 2011).

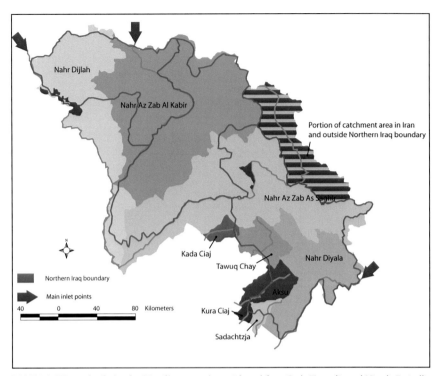

MAP 4.2. **Watersheds in the Kurdistan region.** *Adapted from Carlo Travaglia and Niccolo Dainelli.* Groundwater Search by Remote Sensing: A Methodological Approach (*Rome: Food and Agriculture Organization of the United Nations, 2003*).

areas inhabited by Kurds, and the phrasing of "in its present form" may indicate an expectation of a new governmental structure in the future.

Increasingly the KRG is acting as an independent player in affairs related to natural resources, especially oil and water. This is the result of its status as a nearly autonomous region as established under the articles of the Iraqi constitution. The relationship between the KRG and the central Iraqi government is fragile and can be expected to evolve in the next 10 years.

The Kurdish Areas and the Iraqi Constitution

The 2005 Iraqi constitution was a bitterly contested and controversial document that pushed the debate and resolution of many key issues into the future. The constitution that emerged was a weak compromise solution that became necessary to achieve ratification.[24] The government that was created follows a parliamentary model with a ministerial cabinet system. The prime minister is the country's executive while the country's president possesses largely ceremonial power. There are overlapping checks and balances that exceed those found in the U.S. Constitution, and the Iraqi central government can be characterized as weak and decentralized.

Section 4 of the Iraqi constitution outlines powers of the federal authorities. Of interest to this study is article 110, which contains powers that are exclusive to the federal authorities. Relevant passages are quoted below.

> Article 110: The federal authorities will have the following exclusive powers:
>
> 1st—drawing up foreign policy, diplomatic representation, negotiating international accords and agreements, negotiating and signing debt agreements, drawing up foreign sovereign economic and trade policies.
>
> 8th—planning policies connected to water resources from outside Iraq and guaranteeing levels of water flow into Iraq, according to international law and custom.

Article 111 deals with oil and gas revenues and mandates that such resources and revenues are the property of the Iraqi people.

Section 5 of the Iraqi constitution (titled "Powers of the Regions") was included in the 2005 version in order to rally the Kurds of northern Iraq to the cause of the central government. Under this section, provinces have the right to hold referendums so that they may form a united region.[25] Regions have a legislative council and a president, which are elected by secret popular ballot. Under the constitution, regions may manage internal affairs such as education, social planning, cultural affairs, and local development projects, but they are prohibited from assuming powers reserved exclusively to the federal government.

---

[24] Republic of Iraq, Iraqi Constitution (English version), 2005, http://www.uniraq.org /documents/iraqi_constitution.pdf.

[25] Ibid., section 5, chapter 1, article 119.

The Kurdish Regional Government and the Iraqi State

The foundations of the KRG originate from the time of the Gulf War in 1991 when the Kurds, supported by the United States, established what amounted to an independent national state. Protected, encouraged, and heavily subsidized by America, the Kurds built a secure and stable government between 1991 and 2003. Kurdish expectations in a postinvasion Iraq included a spectrum of possibilities that ranged from independence to autonomy within a federal Iraq dominated by Kurdish politicians. The Kurds maintained and refused to disarm the Peshmerga, security forces that were trained and equipped in the American style as a conventional army. During the transitional period from 2003 through 2005, as the rest of Iraq devolved into anarchy, the Kurdish region remained stable. U.S. policy in this period discouraged autonomy and sought to bring the Kurds into the Iraqi government as a secular moderating force that might combine with an increasingly marginalized Sunni population to balance a hostile Shia population.[26] This was consistent with American policy toward Turkey, a NATO ally that has long opposed an autonomous or independent Kurdish entity.

The two principal Kurdish political parties, the Kurdistan Democratic Party (KDP) and the Patriotic Union of Kurdistan (PUK), orchestrated the formation of the region in 2006, becoming the first Iraqi federated region formed under the new constitution. In an unusually friendly manner, the KDP and PUK alliance produced Massoud Barzani as the region's president while Jalal Talabani became the country's first Kurdish president. These men, formerly bitter tribal enemies and competitors, appear well matched and complementary in these roles (the diplomatic and suave Talabani is a fluent English speaker, whereas the nationalistic Barzani dresses in a military uniform with a traditional Kurdish headscarf). The KRG government rapidly established itself by creating a bureaucracy mirroring the federal government that appears to exceed the limitations imposed on "regions" in the new constitution. For example, the KRG has established quasi-consulates in Tehran and Ankara.

---

[26] Aram Rafaat, "U.S.-Kurdish Relations in Post-Invasion Iraq," *MERIA* (*Middle East Review of International Affairs*) 11, no. 4 (December 2007).

Despite the Talabani presidency and significant Kurdish representation in the Iraqi parliament, relations between the KRG and the central government continued to erode between 2008 and 2012. The status of Kirkuk (to be determined by a referendum conducted under the rules of article 140 of the Iraqi constitution) remains a thorn in the side of Iraqi politics. Having missed the constitutionally mandated deadline of 31 December 2007, the referendum now seems doomed to an endless series of six-month delays. One report concludes that there can be no successful resolution of the Kirkuk issue because of the competing sensitivities of the Arabs, Kurds, and Turks.[27] This line of thinking leads some to speculate that the best solution for Kirkuk is to place the city under some form of federal control, perhaps similar in governance to Baghdad, which enjoys an independent status under the Iraqi constitution.[28]

Kurdish Policies and Agendas

The policies of the KRG appear at odds with the concept of a national unity government and strong central state. The 2005 constitution established Kurdish and Arabic as the two official languages in Iraq. In fact, schools in the Kurdish-controlled regions have taught the curriculum in Kurdish since 1991, and an entire generation of young Kurds is unable to speak Arabic today. Moreover, not all of the well-trained and heavily armed Peshmerga have been fully integrated into the Iraqi armed forces, and they remain largely outside the authority of the Iraqi ministry of defense. The KRG is avowedly expansionistic and has set its sights on annexing the oil-rich city of Kirkuk into the region. To accomplish this, the Kurds have been actively engaged in population engineering aimed at changing the demographics of the city to achieve a Kurdish majority in a referendum originally scheduled for 2007 but currently on hold. There are even hints that the Kurds desire to annex portions of the northern

---

[27] International Crisis Group, *Turkey and the Iraqi Kurds: Conflict or Cooperation?* Middle East Report no. 81-13, November 2008, 19–21.

[28] Ibid., 21.

metropolis of Mosul as well.[29] Mosul—capital city of Ninawa Province in Iraq, near the border with Kurdistan region—lies 405 kilometers north of Baghdad. Some 350,000 Kurdish Yazidis (primarily ethnic Kurds) live in villages around Mosul.

Of concern to their U.S. allies is the fact that the Kurds have developed strong ties to neighboring Iran. Trade links between the KRG and Iran are solid, and there are Iranian consulates in Erbil, the KRG capital and KDP stronghold, and in Sulaymaniyah, hub of the PUK. Even more important, the KRG has offices in Tehran, which is construed by some as de facto recognition of the KRG by the Iranian government.[30]

Of note to this study are the policies of the KRG relative to natural resources, particularly oil and coal. The KRG began in 2007 to supplant the role of the federal government's constitutional mandate as the controlling entity over the region's oil fields and reserves. In 2008, the KRG ministry of oil opened bids for oil and gas exploration and development independently of the federal ministry of oil resources and within a year began to export oil.[31] This has become the cause of much internal discord between the Kurds and the central Iraqi government because, under the constitution, oil is a national resource. Moreover, little of the KRG's oil revenue reaches the coffers of the central government, further exacerbating ill will and tensions between parties.

In 2007, the KRG's ministry of water resources opened tenders for hydro projects, some of which affect the Tigris River basin. As in the case of oil, the Kurds appear to be overstepping the limitations imposed by the 2005 Iraqi constitution and expanding into areas reserved for the central government. In 2010, the KRG began withholding oil revenues in an effort to force the central government to ratify the previous oil deals made inde-

---

[29] *Kurdish Globe*, "Protests in Mosul over Annexing Parts of City to Kurdistan," 4 July 2009, https://www.kurdishglobe.net/display-article.html?id=89AD4FF14A94095FCA0504885F8 AFDA7.

[30] Rafaat, "U.S.-Kurdish Relations," 5.

[31] Economist Intelligence Unit, *Country Report—Iraq*, 4–5.

pendently.[32] If successful, it is likely that the KRG will use this carrot and stick approach to manage their water relations with Baghdad as well.

The Kurdish Ministry of Agriculture and Water Resources

The Kurdish Ministry of Agriculture and Irrigation is sometimes seen in print as the Ministry of Water Resources. The ministry's mission has three main components:

- to introduce programs and projects that will guarantee the food security of the 3.5 million people living in the region;

- to provide assistance for farmers that will encourage and support them to remain on their land or to return to their reconstructed villages; and

- to work toward introducing farming and agricultural practices that will protect the environment for the future.[33]

The ministry has established a protective position for its agricultural industry by passing regulations that "ban the import of vegetables into the region for the purpose of protecting domestic agricultural production and promoting farmers to increase their production, and at the same time help them market their products."[34] The ministry has also been very active in bringing foreign technical advisors and funding into the KRG. In 2010, the French trade minister opened the House of Agriculture and the Environment in Erbil, paving the way for French firms to work on agricultural, water, and environmental projects.[35] It is clear from these kinds of efforts that the KRG intends to revive its agricultural industry with a view

---

[32] *Washington Times*, "Iraqi Kurds Demand OK for Oil Deals Made in Self-Ruled Areas," 29 December 2010.

[33] KRG, "Ministry of Agriculture and Irrigation," http://old.krg.org/about/ministries/moai /index.asp (accessed 19 March 2011).

[34] Ayob Mawloodi, "Vegetable Imports Banned," *Kurdish Globe*, 26 April 2010, http://www .kurdishglobe.net/displayArticle.jsp?id=B9AA82BED53BEA9E3F47F97DC7A3337A (accessed 19 March 2011).

[35] KRG, "France's Trade Minister Opens Agriculture and Environment House in Erbil," press release, 2 November 2010.

toward self-sufficiency, which is certain to bring a corresponding increase in water usage.

The Challenges Facing Iraq

The problem is well summarized in a recent report by an international management and consultancy group looking at Iraq and the management of its water resources.

> If the Federal Constitution of 2005 were to be fully implemented, and new regional entities evolved within Iraq, then the complexity of managing the utilization of water resources would potentially increase immeasurably, with each upstream administrative division enhancing the risk that they divert water in an unsustainable way, to the eventual detriment of downstream users. This does not mean that all functions of water resource management should remain high[ly] centralized, but the report identifies increasing administrative divisions, as potential driver[s] of riparian conflict should water stress levels increase as predicted.[36]

This report emphasizes that the central government in Iraq has been unable to achieve the level of coordination urgently required to place Iraq on the road to sustainable water resource management. That would require an integrated approach that is shaped by a political and institutional process that is lacking in Iraq today.[37] The lack of an integrated approach is all the more dangerous when Iraq's water use is basically unregulated and Iraq "continues to allow free access to water for both irrigation and potable water purposes." The report concludes that this overconsumption of a declining resource "would appear to set Iraq on a course for environmental disaster."[38]

Assessment of Kurdistan-Related Water Issues in Iraq

Based on our research, we can provide some tentative answers to the questions posed at the beginning of the chapter:

---

[36] Geopolicity, *Managing The Tigris Euphrates Watershed*, i.

[37] Ibid., 2.

[38] Ibid., 3.

1. *Does the KRG's water and agricultural policy compete with or complement those of the Iraqi federal state?* In the short term (less than five years), the policy is more competitive than complementary. Because the management of water resources for now (at least on paper) resides with the Iraqi central government, the problem is not yet acute. But as the KRG begins to operate more independently, the challenges in developing and maintaining effective water and agricultural policies for Iraq will increase. In the long term (10 to 15 years), it will be increasingly important for Iraq to maintain a centralized water management system.

2. *When completed, do the KRG's projected water projects harm the downstream Arabs of Iraq?* Although the short-term impact may be minimal, the long-term impact will be significant. Although there are many variables, such as the speed of economic recovery, maintenance of security, and the rate of population growth, increased KRG development will certainly have a negative impact on the south. As water becomes more polluted and scarce, the perception in southern Iraq that the Kurds are overusing the waters of the Tigris is certain to have a destabilizing effect, and is likely to further erode the working relationship between north and south.

3. *In terms of water management, should the KRG be treated as a full partner or is it viable to work with the KRG through the Baghdad government?* In the short term, the KRG's economy will remain stronger than the south's, and stability will draw continued private investment to the north. The independent nature of the KRG relationship with outsiders on oil issues has been mirrored to some extent in the water sector. But it will be important for the United States and the international community to support a strong central government in the water sector, if only to support stability and a more effective management system.

4. *In reality, is there a fourth riparian (and perhaps a fifth, counting Iran) in the Euphrates-Tigris basin?* For now we can consider Iraq a single riparian state, but it will be important to monitor developments in terms of de-facto changes in the federal structure of Iraq. The United States has been providing assistance to Iraq in water management training, and in future sessions it is important to emphasize that a strong central government will be essential to effectively managing the water resources of Iraq.

CHAPTER 5
HYDROPOLITICS

Politics plays an important role in the decision to develop water resources and often hampers parties from reaching reasonable solutions to transboundary disputes. *Hydropolitics*—that is, politics affected by the availability of freshwater resources—is an intricate multilevel interaction between riparian states that involves domestic political and strategic international concerns. Domestic politics plays both an obvious and often more subtle role. Ruling parties will typically promote public works projects as a means of garnering votes. Cultural differences must be considered as well; in the Arab world, in particular, the ruling powers prefer to appear consistently strong, and admitting a weak or inferior position on water issues may not be in the best interests of any regime.

This chapter reviews the political, economic, and military factors that influence the hydropolitics and security in the Euphrates-Tigris basin. The positions of the affected parties on water issues will be described, as well as two incidents that demonstrate the potential for conflict. In the 1975 incident between Syria and Iraq, the nations nearly went to war over water, and during the 1998–99 crisis between Turkey and Syria there was a claim that Turkey was using water as a weapon. Iran will not be discussed at length in this chapter; it is a minor player for now in the water sector, but its future importance should not be underestimated. Iran's role in the region's political, economic, and security spheres will remain important in the short and long term. At the time of this writing, the landscape was changing daily, with continued instability in Iraq, a threatened regime change in Syria, and increasing reports of water problems in the region.

A Multilayered and Complex Game

Power dynamics at the international level were described in chapter 2. Chapter 3 demonstrated that all three riparian states on the Euphrates and Tigris face serious issues of decreasing water quantity and quality, and chapter 4 described the possibility of yet another riparian in the basin. This chapter looks beyond geopolitics to examine the subject of hydropolitics—or water politics—providing a close investigation of the basin to look at the positions of the parties and the potential for conflict.[1] River basins that cross international boundaries present increased challenges to effective water management, where solutions are beyond the power of a single riparian. Water resources and water flows vary in space and time and political boundaries often ignore the critical resource, creating the potential for conflict.

This book looks at water through an international security lens, and the ultimate question is whether the conditions in the Euphrates-Tigris basin will lead to conflict or cooperation. Thus, the ability of the concerned states in the region to resolve these questions in a peaceful manner is the next issue. Can the disparate positions described above be reconciled in the foreseeable future?

For our purposes, hydropolitics can be considered a specialized subject within international relations, and there has been a long-term debate on whether the "low" politics of water can be addressed in advance of "high" politics based on national sovereignty.[2] The functionalist theory of international relations argues that states will willingly transfer sovereignty over matters of public concern to a common authority.[3] The European Union (EU) is perhaps the most successful example of this approach; although

---

[1] Water Encyclopedia, "Hydropolitics," Advameg, http://www.waterencyclopedia.com/Hy-La /Hydropolitics.html.

[2] Delli Priscoli and Wolf, *Managing and Transforming Water Conflicts*, 34.

[3] David Mitrany, *The Functional Theory of Politics* (New York: St. Martin's Press, 1975).

it was originally based upon limited economic cooperation, it eventually grew into a system of "pooled sovereignty" with its own courts and even a common foreign policy.

In contrast to the functionalist approach, the "realists" respond that state adversaries on the high political level will generally not cooperate on lower levels such as the economy, welfare, and water. This debate continues in the Jordan basin today, and some argue that the issues of regional water sharing cannot be broached until the larger political issues of territory and refugees are resolved between Israel and the Palestinians.[4] But every basin is different and, compared to the Jordan, the prospects for the Euphrates-Tigris are relatively good. This book will take the position in the following chapters that progress can be made on the "low" politics of water, and that this could eventually lead to an overall improvement in stability and regional relations.

Water politics plays out at many levels, and the dynamics at the domestic or internal level is important to understand the international issues. At the local level, water will not play a political role unless it is *evident*.[5] Users must be aware that the resource is limited, and there is a need to compete for access. In some Middle East countries, there is a lack of recognition of the problem because the government has been able to import virtual water (see the introductory chapter for further discussion of this term), and this is supported by a robust political economy.[6] In the Euphrates-Tigris basin, water scarcity will not be evident when the problem is not yet severe even though the government fails to properly regulate the resource. If a farmer is overpumping the aquifer—with no charges or fees, and there is enough water (for now)—the problem is not evident and the government knowingly tolerates a blind spot on water deficits. Vested interests control the water sector, and they are not comfortable with bad news. When the government is beholden to these interests, developing a clear plan to deal with water deficits may not be politically feasible. With

---

[4] Miriam R. Lowi, *Water and Power: The Politics of a Scarce Resource in the Jordan River Basin* (Cambridge: Cambridge University Press, 1993).

[5] Allan, *Middle East Water Question*, 163.

[6] Ibid., 41.

Syrian boys on a pipe near Ar Raqqah, northern
Syria, with a Turkish border post in the background. *Photo by Frederick Lorenz*

an autocratic government, there is no interest in raising the issue, either internally or externally.

In the "constructed politics" surrounding national water resources, the first duty of government should be to *assert* water rights, gain *recognition* of them, and then attempt their *attainment*. But on the decentralized and chaotic international stage, the first phase is still underway, and the last stage is "*impossible*," according to J. A. "Tony" Allan (emphasis added).[7] This is particularly true in the Euphrates-Tigris basin, and Allan observes that Turkey is still making "facts on the ground" as a means of asserting its own water rights.

> As Turkey is the upstream riparian the impact of such facts are particularly emphatic. The engineering works have had negative impacts in reducing the average, albeit unreliable flow at the Syrian border by almost 45 percent, from approaching 30 cubic kilometers [same as billion cubic meters (BCM)] per year to under 16 cubic kilometers per year. The positive impact is that the flow has become a reliable average flow.[8]

Even when a position is argued at the international level, the public version may not reflect the actual position or the position that is asserted between diplomats of the concerned countries. When the Iraqi legislature makes a demand of Turkey, or the Arab League calls for recognition of Syria's historic water rights, the real audience may be an entity other than Turkey. Asserting water rights, if it is done at all, may be aimed at a domestic audience, or even international agencies that have the potential to provide resources.

The positions of the three riparians on water resources are provided below, but it should not be assumed that all the parties have clear and consistent positions. Even with Turkey, the easiest of the three to determine, the positions have shifted over time. In the case of Syria, the positions have been very difficult to determine due to the autocratic and opaque nature of the regime. Recent events in Syria could lead to regime change that would in

---

[7] Ibid., 216.

[8] Ibid., 217.

turn herald an entirely new set of priorities, and a new approach to water issues. In the case of Iraq, the position is rapidly developing and shifting as the government of Iraq becomes organized and begins to develop a more assertive foreign policy.

Turkey's Position on Water Resources

The Turkish position on transboundary waters has been consistent and open, and it can be found on the Turkish Ministry of Foreign Affairs Web site.[9] Its position begins with the argument that Turkey is not a country with excess water capacity:

> Contrary to the general perception, Turkey is neither a country rich in freshwater resources nor the richest country in the region in this respect.

> Turkey is situated in in a semi-arid region, and has only about one fifth of the water available per capita in water rich regions such as North America and Western Europe. Water rich countries are those which have 10,000 cubic meters of water per capita yearly. This is well above the 1,500 cubic meters per capita in Turkey.[10]

Today Turkey maintains that it utilizes only 40 BCM of water, leaving 70 BCM unused. But due to "infrastructural constraints" the unused water represents "a resource which Turkey's economy needs and plans to draw upon with increasing efficiency in the future."[11] For more details on Turkey's plan to exploit its water resources, see chapter 3. In that chapter, it was explained that the irrigation infrastructure of the GAP (Southeastern Anatolia Project) is behind schedule and completion of the project will result in a much higher diversion of water flow from the Euphrates and Tigris.

---

[9] See Republic of Turkey Ministry of Foreign Affairs, "Turkey's Policy on Water Issues," Republic of Turkey Ministry of Foreign Affairs, http://www.mfa.gov.tr/turkey_s-policy-on -water-issues.en.mfa.

[10] Ibid.

[11] Republic of Turkey Ministry of Foreign Affairs, "Water: A Source of Conflict of Coopeariton [or Cooperation] in the Middle East," section titled "The Facts," http://www .mfa.gov.tr/data/DISPOLITIKA/WaterASourceofConflictofCoopintheMiddleEast.pdf.

Regarding the GAP, the Turkish position is clear:

> For many decades, southeastern Anatolia was the least economically developed region in Turkey, lagging far behind the rest of the country. Thanks to the Southeastern Anatolia Project (GAP) this situation is now starting to change. . . . The impact on the economy of the region is dramatic. Many Turkish crops will double or even triple. GAP will provide food self-sufficiency in Turkey and will create 3.3 million jobs.[12]

Turkey is aware of the water pollution question and the concerns being raised about high salinity levels in Turkey's agricultural return flow to the rivers mentioned earlier in chapter 3. Turkey claims that it is working to alleviate the problem and that the downstream parties themselves are largely responsible for the pollution levels:

> In point of fact, both Syria and Iraq have a poor environmental record where water is concerned. Both countries use the Euphrates to drain off industrial pollution and sewage, thereby creating an alarming level of pollution in the lower courses of the river and the [Persian] Gulf.[13]

Turkey has often looked to U.S. history for policy justification, comparing Turkey's level of development to the great era of U.S. water infrastructure development. This is also a way to respond to perceived U.S. (and EU) criticism of Turkey's development policies:

> The universal nature and relevance of the GAP has been highlighted by various authorities and experts, one of whom is Dennis Avery, the former Head of the Global Food Policy Institute and who is also an agricultural economist. He pointed out the importance of the GAP by stating, "We are on the eve of the greatest farming opportunity in history and it is precisely at that moment that Turkey is creating a new California."[14]

---

[12] Ibid., section titled "The Southeastern Anatolia Project."

[13] Ibid., under the heading "Water Pollution."

[14] Mithat Rende, *The Global Water Shortage and Turkey's Water Management* (Ankara: Ministry of Foreign Affairs of Turkey, 2004), 5, http://www.rcuwm.org.ir/En/Events /Documents/Workshops/Articles/3/11.pdf.

Turkey also makes it clear that the GAP is more than just an agricultural development; it represents a key part of Turkey's plan for hydropower and energy production. It is further emphasized that "per capita energy consumption in Turkey is only one sixth of that of the EU average and [an] increase in the energy consumption means improving the quality of life of the Turkish citizens. Turkey, which is neither [an] oil nor natural gas producer, plans to meet the rising energy need in several ways. Hydro-power is especially appealing in that it is cheap and clean."[15]

An essential component of Turkey's position on water resources is that the Tigris-Euphrates must be viewed as a single basin. In this view, shortages of water from one river must be compensated by taking water from the other. This has an important strategic benefit for Turkey, particularly with respect to Iraq, because the Tigris provides Iraq with a significant volume of water. Moreover, Iraq has already constructed a canal to bring water from the Tigris to the Euphrates basin, a strategy that seems to support Turkey's position on this point. Although Syria draws little from the Tigris, an argument could be made that the Tigris would have to be used to make up for any shortages in the Euphrates in that country as well.

Turkey approaches its water resources from a position of strength. It relies on a principle similar to the Harmon Doctrine that originated in the United States and that views water as a natural resource. (The legal basis of this theory is discussed in more detail in chapter 6.) Turkey asserts that the purpose of the existing and planned dams on the Euphrates and Tigris Rivers is to contribute to its own energy and irrigation needs. Dams in Turkey, according to this theory, will also control the variance in water flows, avoid floods, and prevent surge conditions downstream. Turkish dams on the Euphrates River are excellent water management installations due to their effective reservoirs, low evaporation losses, and geographical and topographic characteristics. Turkey argues that this has and will continue to benefit the downstream nations who will receive more consistent flow due to its dams.

---

[15] See Turkey Ministry of Foreign Affairs, "Water: A Source of Conflict," under the heading "Water for Energy."

Karkamis Dam on the Euphrates River, southern Turkey. *Photo by Frederick Lorenz*

In 1987, during the filling of the lake behind Ataturk Dam, Turkey agreed with Syria to provide a minimum of 500 cubic meters per second (CMS) at the point where the Euphrates enters Syria. This was designed to be only a temporary measure, but it has assumed greater importance in the absence of a comprehensive agreement concerning water allocation. Turkey has at various times restated its nonbinding commitment to providing the 500 CMS flow in the Euphrates, although accurate data on the amount of flow has not been made available.[16] Turkey now maintains that it is in fact providing more than double the amount of Euphrates water promised, but it relies on 1996 data to support the claim.[17] Moreover, it is impossible for an outsider to obtain data to verify Turkey's position. There is no Turkish commitment regarding flows of the Tigris, and Turkey's contribution to the flow of the Tigris is comparatively less important to Syria and Iraq than its contribution to the Euphrates. See chapter 1 for more details on Turkey and the Tigris.

In terms of water quality, no comprehensive study has ever been completed, and Turkey maintains that the GAP will have no significant environmental impact on its downstream neighbors (for more details on water quality, see chapter 3). Nevertheless, there is great concern about water quality in Syria and Iraq, where the waters of the Tigris and Euphrates are considered the lifeblood of these countries, and recent independent studies shed light on what may be the real threat: high salinity levels that will make the water unusable for drinking and agriculture. If Syria and Iraq have their own data to support their claims of deteriorating water quality, they have not made it available to interested parties outside the

---

[16] In August 2003, one of the coauthors visited the Karkamis Dam, the last dam on the Euphrates in Turkey before the river enters Syria. Records of hourly flows were observed in the administrative office there, but a request for data was referred to the State Hydraulic Works headquarters in Ankara, which would not release the data. On the day of the visit to the dam, water release from the dam fluctuated between 200 and 1,300 CMS and was carefully controlled to achieve maximum hydropower capacity. This illustrates some of the difficulties in obtaining useful data. Daily fluctuations at the different stations are great, and the Turkish government treats the comprehensive flow data as a state secret.

[17] See Turkey Ministry of Foreign Affairs, "Water: A Source of Conflict," under the heading "Turkey Fulfills Her Pledge."

Arab world. This contributes to an atmosphere of charge and denial, with little hard evidence available to support the respective positions.

From Turkey's perspective, the success of the GAP can be easily used as a way to boost national pride through the effective use of the media, and it can thus be translated into electoral gains. In short, from economic regional discrepancy to the Kurdish question, the GAP embodies a series of salient issues from an electoral perspective for the ruling parties, and thus it constitutes an integral part of domestic political strategies.[18]

Turkey's Three-Stage Plan has long been a foundation of its position on the water question. The plan was originally proposed during the joint technical committee meetings between Turkey, Syria, and Iraq.[19] The full name of the plan is the Three-Stage Plan for Optimum, Equitable and Reasonable Utilization of the Transboundary Watercourses of the Tigris-Euphrates Basin, and it was first introduced during the fifth meeting of the joint technical committee between 5 and 8 November 1984. The stages of the plan are as follows:

- Stage 1: inventory studies for water resources to involve the exchange of available data, including water use and loss at various agreed sites.

- Stage 2: inventory studies for land resources, including soil classification, crop patterns, irrigation, and requirements for existing and planned projects.

- Stage 3: evaluate land and water resources, including total water consumption and the "economic viability" of planned projects.

Of course Turkey is confident that when the final evaluation is completed, its superior efficiency, economic capacity, and geographical features will place it in the strongest position to ensure "equitable utilization" of

---

[18] Ali Carkoglu and Mine Eder, "Domestic Concerns and the Water Conflict over the Euphrates-Tigris River Basin," *Middle Eastern Studies* 37 (January 2001), 41.

[19] For a detailed examination of the plan, see Ayşegül Kibaroğlu, *Building a Regime for the Waters of the Euphrates-Tigris River Basin* (The Hague: Kluwer Law International, 2002), 252.

An ancient ruin on Birecik Lake above Birecik
Dam, Euphrates River, southern Turkey. *Photo by
Frederick Lorenz*

the waters. For their part, the downstream states have been reluctant to engage in a basinwide planning process. Factors driving this reluctance, which are discussed in chapter 3, have provided additional obstacles to cooperation on the water issue. Without some agreement on reliable data and fundamental needs for each party, integrated management of the Euphrates-Tigris basin will not be attainable.

Syria's Position on Water Resources

Syria's position can be pieced together over time, and of the three riparians, Syria is the least likely to have a clear and unified approach to water issues. Syria maintains that through thousands of years of water usage it has "acquired rights" that were upheld even during the Ottoman era.[20] Syria also claims that the Euphrates and Tigris Rivers are international watercourses that can be classified as shared resources between the riparian countries; see chapter 6 for more detail on the legal claims.

Syria claims that Turkey acted against the spirit of good neighborliness and caused significant damage to Syrian agriculture, hydropower generation, and water supply facilities during the initial impounding of the Ataturk Dam. At that time, water flow to Syria and Iraq was significantly reduced while the dam was being filled. Syria believes that Turkey aims at exerting political pressure on its neighbors through such actions.

In response to Syrian and Iraqi criticism, Turkey launched the so-called Peace Pipeline proposal in 1989, which would have diverted a large percentage of the Ceyhan and Seyhan Rivers in Turkey to Syria, Lebanon, Jordan, Iraq, and Saudi Arabia, as well as Israel, for a fee. However, this proposal still left Syria and Iraq dissatisfied since they would have been required to pay for pipeline water in place of Euphrates River water, to which they used to have unlimited free access. Although this project is no longer considered viable, there are a number of proposed projects for Turkey to supply Israel with "excess" water from outside the Euphrates-Tigris basin. Syrian officials maintain that the Peace Pipeline and other water-selling schemes can be interpreted as a product of Turkey's dreams

---

[20] Trondalen, *Water and Peace*, 171.

of gaining a leadership position in the Middle East. Syria has further argued that Turkey's secret goal is to dominate the countries of the region economically and politically by making them dependent on the water it controls.

Syria envisions a scheme in which disputes between the basin states related to sharing an international watercourse must be resolved in international bodies, such as the International Court of Justice, in the framework of dialogue or arbitration governed by such institutions. This is contrary to Turkey's continued efforts to prevent disputes in the basin from becoming internationalized.

Syria and Iraq have argued that the amount of water released by Turkey in both the Tigris and the Euphrates is inadequate. They rely on claims of prior appropriation (usually defined as "first in time, first in right") and seek to enforce the requirement that Turkey not cause "significant harm" to its downstream neighbors. This provision is contained in the United Nations' 1997 Convention on the Law of the Non-navigational Uses of International Watercourses (Watercourses Convention), a treaty that was never signed by Turkey. (See chapter 6 for details on this framework convention.) Turkey refuses to agree with this approach and argues that the quantity of water needed for irrigation should be determined by applying identical criteria to each of the three countries and that this was commonly agreed upon in the Three-Stage Plan. Syria and Iraq believe that each country must be free to choose the criteria it will use to determine its own water needs and that such determinations should not be questioned by the other riparian states. Despite these conflicting positions, all three nations are nevertheless pressing ahead with plans to increase the burden on the rivers. The end result of this approach is that the total amount of planned water utilization by the three riparian countries exceeds the total flow capacity of the Euphrates. For further discussion of projected water demand, see chapter 3.

Syria and Iraq have regularly accused Turkey of not notifying them in advance about planned water installations. Such notification is required by the aforementioned Watercourses Convention. From Turkey's point of view, all necessary data pertaining to its planned water schemes was conveyed to Syria and Iraq during joint technical committee meetings. This committee, envisioned as a forum to discuss regional water matters, was set up with the Protocol of the Joint Economic Committee meetings, held between Turkey and Iraq in 1980. Syria later joined this group meeting in 1983. Since the joint technical committee has not met formally since 1993, a useful regime does not currently exist for sharing information.[21]

Syria's position on the waters of the Euphrates is compromised by its use of the waters of the Orontes River. Emanating from Lebanon, the Orontes passes through Syria and flows into the Mediterranean Sea within the Turkish province of Hatay. In Lebanon, there are two water diversions on the Orontes, and in Syria there are two dams, in addition to smaller water diversions. Both countries, but especially Syria, have been intensively utilizing this river for irrigation purposes. Syria has been making use of 90 percent of the total flow that should reach an annual average of 1.2 BCM at the Turkey-Syria border. Out of this total capacity, only a meager 120 million cubic meters enter into Turkey, after the water has been heavily used by Syria. This amount is expected to further decrease to about 25 million cubic meters when the planned reservoirs in Syria are built. Although Syria accuses Turkey of reducing the amount of water in the Euphrates, it is Syria—as an upstream country—that utilizes almost all the water of the Orontes with little concern for the downstream impacts. Turkey has capitalized on this inconsistency as part of its own public relations efforts.[22]

Currently, Syria is preoccupied with internal conflict, and criticism of Turkey on water issues seems to be officially on hold for the near term.

---

[21] Turkey now maintains that since 1983 there have been "sixteen ministerial and official meetings of the Joint Technical Committee." See the claim of an "emerging institutional framework" on the Ministry of Foreign Affairs Web site: http://www.mfa.gov.tr/data /DISPOLITIKA/WaterASourceofConflictofCoopintheMiddleEast.pdf. For a detailed proposal on a working institutional framework, see Kibaroŭlu's *Building a Regime for the Waters of the Euphrates-Tigris River Basin*, 228. Meetings at the "technocrat" level were suspended in 1983 and although there have been several bilateral "ministerial" level meetings since that time, no significant progress has been reported.

[22] See Turkey Ministry of Foreign Affairs, "Water: A Source of Conflict," under the heading "The River Orontes."

Syria's government seems reluctant to publicly state its difficult water situation because such a statement would make the leadership seem weak for allowing those conditions to occur. Of course the nature of government in Syria is much different than in Turkey, where a higher degree of transparency can be found. Turkey is much more open about its policies and positions, and this might assist any long-term improvement of relations between the countries.

For many years the Syrian government has been focused primarily on regime preservation, which is one explanation for its lack of an easily identifiable water policy. At the time of this writing, the Assad regime is facing the greatest challenge to its rule in more than 40 years. A regime change in Syria will further complicate the geopolitical situation, as well as hydropolitics in the Euphrates-Tigris basin. Nevertheless, it could also provide opportunities for a diplomatic initiative to improve regional cooperation over water.

Iraq's Position on Water Resources

Turkey's reliance on Iraqi oil in the 1970s and 1980s created a long-standing mutual dependency; oil and water will always be important components of their bilateral relations. Iraq's oil potential places it in a strong position to resist Turkish leverage on water resources, although its geographic position as the lowest riparian nation on the Euphrates complicates the issue. This is partially offset by Iraq's control of a number of tributaries of the Tigris, as well as its ability to transfer water from the Tigris to the Euphrates. Iraq was essentially unable to interact on water issues with the other riparian countries between 1991 and 2003 because, under Saddam Hussein, it was preoccupied with war, sanctions, and defiance of the international community.

Similar to Syria, Iraq has maintained its acquired rights relating to ancestral irrigations on the Euphrates and Tigris Rivers. One dimension of this claim stems from its existing irrigation systems and water installations. Iraq has 1.9 million hectares (about 4.5 million acres) of agricultural land in the Euphrates basin, including the ancestral irrigation systems from the Sumerian era. Iraq also has established diversion and irrigation installa-

Flooded village beneath Birecik Lake, Euphrates River, southern Turkey. *Photo by Frederick Lorenz*

tions, although maintenance and efficiency are well below international standards. During the initial filling of the lake behind Ataturk Dam in 1992, Iraq accused Turkey of violating international law by not informing Iraq of its intentions in a timely way and by reducing the amount of flow below the committed level. In addition, Iraq argued that Turkey would cause damage to the downstream riparian states by building new dams and irrigation systems.

After the U.S.-led invasion in 2003, Iraq's government changed, but even now it seems unable to establish a functional policy on water issues. On 16 September 2003, the newly appointed Minister of Water Resources, Abdul Latif Rasheed, stated that Iraq's share of water from the Tigris and Euphrates was insufficient and that it wanted to initiate talks with Turkey and Syria, who also use water from the rivers.[23] "We are intending to hold talks with our neighbors very soon to reach an agreement that divides water among the three of us in a just manner," said Rasheed. "I believe the quantity of water entering to our territory is not enough." He then went on to explain the failure to reach an agreement in the past. "Because of its bad relations with its neighbors, the former [Iraqi] government couldn't reach an agreement on water quotas," Rasheed noted. "Now we have a different strategy. We want to improve our ties with our neighbors."

Iraq's Minister of Municipalities and Public Works at the time, Nasreen Berwari, revealed details of her ministry's plan to provide water during a 24 September 2003 press briefing at the Foreign Press Center in Washington, DC.[24] She claimed that her first priority as minister of public works was to immediately ensure that "appropriate services are available to all Iraqis so that living conditions improve." Her second major challenge, she said, was an "institutional challenge" to build a ministry in which policy was made by "looking at the interests of the people in the context of a democratic, communal effort."

---

[23] Hassan Hafidh, "Iraq Wants to Clinch Water Deal with Syria, Turkey," *Environmental News Network*, 16 September 2003, http://www.enn.com/news/2003-09-16/s_8435.asp.

[24] Embassy of the United States—Italy, "Water Resources Top Agenda for Iraq's Ministry of Public Works, September 24, 2003," public affairs release, www.usembassy.it/file2003_09/alia/a3092403.htm.

Asked about Iraq's historic dispute with Turkey over water from the Euphrates River, Minister Berwari indicated that the Iraqi Governing Council (as the provisional government was known) would be in discussions with Ankara regarding an equitable division of resources. She insisted, however, that Iraq is rich in water resources. The country simply needs to work on conservation and management policies, she said. In her view, the former Baathist regime created a "culture of waste," but she affirmed her commitment to pursuing a more responsible use of resources. Given these seemingly contradictory statements—one claiming the essential concern of trilateral negotiation, the other stressing the wealth of resources at home—the difficulty in establishing a clear position was shown.

On 22 December 2010, Mohanad Salman al-Sady was appointed Minister of Water Resources for Iraq, but no significant change in Iraq's position has been noted since his appointment. Security concerns have continuously overshadowed the development of a forward-thinking water policy. "After years of neglect during the previous regime, Iraq's water managers still lack sufficient technical capability and knowledge to address its growing water crisis," one report stated. "Budget constraints have handicapped the government's ability to implement a long-term water management plan."[25]

Iraq's position on the water issue can be summarized with relative ease: Iraq has historic rights to more water, and action will be required very soon to avoid a major crisis. But achieving any progress on the international stage will require much more than occasional statements of Iraqi officials. International support will be required, and some detailed suggestions will be provided in the final chapters of this book.

Conflict or Cooperation?

The 1975 Incident between Syria and Iraq

There has been a history of incidents between Turkey, Syria, and Iraq

---

[25] Saleem al-Hasani and Basim al-Shara, "Baghdad Urged to Tackle Water Crisis," *Environmental News Service*, 10 June 2010, http://www.ens-newswire.com/ens/jun2010 /2010-06-10-02.html.

driven by water allocation issues.[26] One important incident of note is the 1975 Syria-Iraq dispute. In the mid-1970s, both Turkey and Syria completed several dams on the Euphrates River and began filling their reservoirs. Beginning in late 1973 and reaching maximum fill rates in 1975, the flow of the Euphrates was significantly reduced as it entered Iraq. The filling of the Keban Dam in Turkey and the al-Thawrah (Euphrates) Dam at Tabaqah in Syria occurred during severe drought conditions. While Iraq protested the constriction of river flow, it was not until mid-1974 that Syria agreed to an additional flow of 200 CMS. However, the following year the Iraqi Irrigation Minister (as the Minister of Water Resources was then called) protested that the Euphrates River flow had reached a record low flow rate, at one point reaching 197 CMS. In March 1975, land under cultivation in the basin was only 4 percent of its previous total. The Iraqi News Agency reported that the Iraqi Federation of Peasant Associations and Agricultural Cooperatives sent cables of protest to leaders in Syria and Iraq. Their communication was a call for "swift action" by their country to prevent the death of crops and livestock and hardship for "millions of peasants." The perception was that Syria was withholding additional water from Iraq's allocation.

The Syrian government then refused an Iraqi request for the Arab League to meet to discuss a charge that Syria was withholding this Euphrates water. The Syrians said the water question was technical in nature and did not require discussion by Arab ministers. At this point, Iraq requested Arab League intervention. Syria countered that less than half of its flow was coming from Turkey and pulled out of the committee formed by the league. In response to threats from Iraq, Syria closed the Iraqi consulate in Aleppo and expelled its personnel.

In July 1975, Iraq protested to the Arab League against "continued Syrian encroachments" on the Iraqi border. The government also charged that Syrian border forces ambushed Iraqi traffic and tried to obstruct the build-

---

[26] Portions of this section were taken from Frederick M. Lorenz and Edward J. Erickson, *The Euphrates Triangle: Security Implications of the Southeastern Anatolia Project* (Washington, DC: National Defense University Press, 1999), 22–23.

ing of an Iraqi frontier post. Iraq demanded that the Arab League seek an immediate end to the "Syrian violations of Iraqi territory." Although this could not be directly tied to the water issue, it was all part of an atmosphere of rising tension.

In response to the assassination of Syria's military attaché in July 1975 in Baghdad, Syria expelled Baghdad's military attaché from Damascus and closed down the office, saying the killing was carried out by Iraqi agents. In August, demonstrations were held in Aleppo to protest water shortages, followed by a two-week campaign by Syria that charged Iraq with causing a water shortage in Aleppo by demanding too much water from Syria. Iraq indicated that the Syrian shortage was "part of a political game" and said the real problem in Syria was the buildup of sediment behind the Euphrates Dam. It was asserted that Syria lacked the technology to remove silt from the reservoirs and therefore must compensate by keeping the water level behind dams at a level higher than its agreement with Iraq stipulated.

The Iraqi government issued a protest to Syria charging that Syrian warplanes were violating Iraqi airspace in both August and September 1975. Syria closed its airspace as both countries mobilized troops and equipment to positions near the Syrian-Iraqi border. Only mediation by Saudi Arabia, assisted by the Soviets, prevented armed conflict. The resolution of this incident only addressed river flow amounts between Syria and Iraq during this reservoir-filling episode and did not involve the uppermost riparian state, Turkey. While the tensions were diffused, the management of the Euphrates River system until today has never been formalized and remains, at best, bilateral. The parties have taken diametrically opposed positions, and there is no established forum to discuss the differences.

Asymmetric Power

In terms of negotiation theory,[27] a number of studies have been devoted to the power dynamics of river basins where one party is geographically, po-

---

[27] A leading book on the subject uses the term "mutual gains bargaining"; see Roger Fisher, William Ury, and Bruce Patton, *Getting to Yes: Negotiating Agreement without Giving In* (New York: Penguin, 1991).

litically, and militarily dominant. Although water rights in the Euphrates-Tigris basin are still in the "assertion" phase[28] and few serious negotiations on water allocation have occurred, it is useful to examine the role of power and how it impacts cooperation. Power in negotiations has been defined as one party's ability to get the other party to do something they would not otherwise do.[29] One recent study concludes that traditional elements of power (as in the case of Turkey) are not the only sources of power in the basin.[30] The study also provides an explanation of why the successful interactions between the parties in the Euphrates-Tigris basin have been primarily bilateral.

An example of this bilateralism is Turkey's 1987 agreement with Syria (mentioned earlier in this chapter), in which Turkey agreed to provide 500 CMS (about 16 BCM per year) of the Euphrates at the Turkish-Syrian border. Although there is no agreement on the statistics, reports indicate that Turkey complied with this agreement at an average level of 900 CMS, at least until 2002, but noncompliance could be observed in later years.[31] The weak monitoring capability of the joint technical committee did not provide any useful mechanism to induce Turkey's compliance.

Another instance is from 1989, when Syria and Iraq agreed to share the waters of the Euphrates between them at a scale of 42 percent for Syria and 58 percent for Iraq, based upon the amount released by Turkey to Syria. As these examples make clear, thus far the only water-sharing agreements in the basin are bilateral, which is consistent with the power asymmetry in the region. There is no incentive for Turkey to enter into any multilateral arrangements with Syria and Iraq, and Turkey prides itself on dealing directly with any problems with the concerned countries. It is important to remember that the two bilateral arrangements mentioned above are really not useful water allocation agreements at all, particularly when the parties all refuse to release flow data that might demonstrate a violation. Also, in

---

[28] See Allan, *Middle East Water Question*, 216.

[29] Robert A. Dahl, "The Concepts of Power," *Behavioral Science* 2, no. 3 (1957): 201–2.

[30] Marwa Daoudy, "Asymmetric Power: Negotiating Water in the Euphrates and Tigris," *International Negotiation* 14, no. 2 (2009): 361.

[31] Ibid., 376.

the event of a dispute, there is no effective international mechanism for resolution, a topic that will be discussed in more detail in the next chapter.

Linkage Strategies

Complex interlinkages often underlie the negotiation strategies that might be developed in any river basin. In an earlier publication, the authors outlined the triangular relationship in the Euphrates-Tigris basin and the bilateral relationships between Turkey, Syria, and Iraq.[32] At the time of that study (1999), the principal relationship between Turkey and Iraq was oil versus water; between Iraq and Syria, "regional ascendency" through the Baath Party; and between Syria and Iraq, state response to regional insurgencies. Of these three "linkages," the first is alive, the second is now minimal, and the third still has some play, albeit in a different form.

Complex interlinkages underlie the negotiation strategies that led to the water sharing agreements in 1987 and 1989, and the evolution continues today. Beginning in 1984, Syria's support of the Kurdistan Workers Party (PKK) and its leader Abdullah Ocalan represented an important bargaining chip that enhanced Syria's position in the negotiation process and had an impact on Turkey's security alternatives. The 1987 protocol had an agreement that no party would support violent groups in the other's territory. The expulsion of Ocalan and his later capture in 1999 helped to resolve the issue between Syria and Turkey, and improved economic relations—as well as the opening of the formerly restricted border—have all served as positive steps in Turkish-Syrian relationships. At the same time, improvement in the insurgency linkage to Turkey resulted in a decrease in potential bargaining power for Syria in the water sector.

In the aftermath of the 2003 Iraq War, and before 2011, the relationship between Syria and Turkey consistently improved, and Turkey emphasized the policy of "benefit sharing" rather than focusing on sovereignty

---

[32] Lorenz and Erickson, *The Euphrates Triangle*, 2.

issues.[33] This is a relatively new and ambiguous concept that attempts to borrow some of the standards of "optimal and equitable" allocations contained in the Watercourses Convention (see next chapter) and apply them in a political-economic framework.[34] Turkey has embraced the concept in its foreign policy, mentioning that the benefits can be shared "within the basin."[35] Turkey is essentially offering to provide economic revitalization to its own people in the southeast and to "help bring prosperity to a much wider region, riparian states in particular."[36] Of course the sharing of benefits in terms of increased food production would have to be sold at market value to the other countries in the basin, hardly a substitute for producing food with water that Iraq and Syria view as a historic right. Some reports and conclusions about linkages are overstated or fail to understand the complexities of the situation. In one article, for example, it was claimed that Turkey offered water for an Iraqi crackdown on Kurdish rebels.[37] But it would be nearly impossible to trade water for Iraq's compliance with this type of request, and the lack of transparent flow data is only one of the problems. How to monitor compliance on either side is another unanswered question. The article reveals an important factor, however: at the time 50,000 Turkish workers were believed to be in Iraq, and the economy is much stronger in northern areas of Iraq (the Kurdistan Regional Government) than in the south.

Potential linkages exist today in the basin, and a strong interdependent economy between Turkey and Iraq will provide the best hope for future cooperation. Mohammed al-Zubaidi, a political science professor at Baghdad University, claims that water is already the defining factor in

---

[33] Daoudy, "Asymmetric Power," 381. In 2011 and 2012, the relations between Turkey and Syria took a major turn for the worse in light of the expanding conflict in Syria. Only time will tell if the parties can return to a reasonable discussion of their water issues.

[34] Halla Qaddumi, *Practical Approaches to Transboundary Water Benefit Sharing* (London: Overseas Development Institute, 2008), http://www.odi.org.uk/resources/docs/2576.pdf.

[35] Republic of Turkey Ministry of Foreign Affairs, "Turkey's Policy on Water Issues," section titled "Turkey's Transboundary Water Policy."

[36] Ibid., under the heading "Conclusions."

[37] Jane Arraf, "Turkey Offers Water for Iraqi Crackdown on Kurdish Rebels," *Christian Science Monitor*, 11 August 2009.

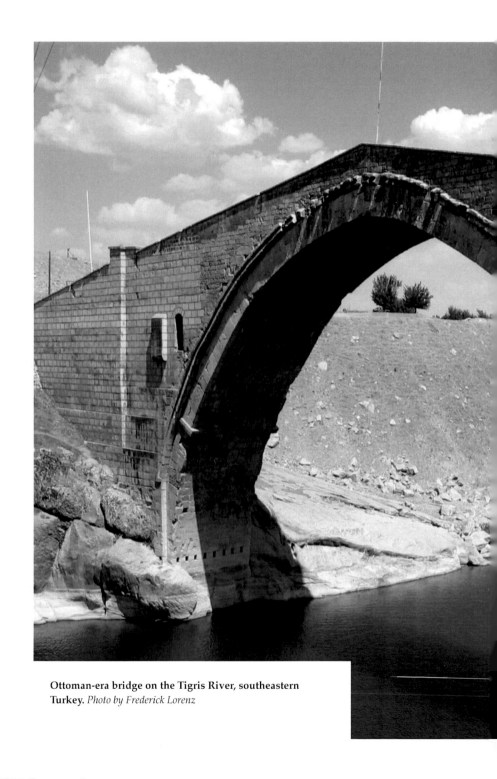

Ottoman-era bridge on the Tigris River, southeastern Turkey. *Photo by Frederick Lorenz*

Iraq's foreign relations.[38] "Let's talk about Turkey and Syria. We have concerns that one day they will ask in return for water, one barrel of water for one barrel of oil," he said. "That day will come soon if Iraq maintains its ignorant strategies of wasteful water management." Although this may be an overstatement, it illustrates the perception of economic reality.

The real linkages in the Euphrates-Tigris basin will not be the direct trading of water for oil, or a crackdown on separatist Kurds. But a rising economic tide in northern Iraq and Southeastern Anatolia will make many things possible. The linkages can only build slowly, as a sharing of economic benefits that bind the countries together and lay the foundation for cooperation in the water sector.

Time as Power

Power in relational terms is usually defined by possession or structure, with the latter being defined as the available economic and military resources.[39] It has already been shown that Turkey has a fundamental power dominance among the three riparians, and geography is an important factor. But power can also be described in temporal terms: Turkey is in a unique position in the basin because the continued development of the GAP can only increase the "facts on the ground" and strengthen its hand in any future negotiations. A 2009 study indicates that the GAP will eventually withdraw as much as 70 percent of the Euphrates natural flow and about 40–50 percent of its observed flow.[40]

The issue of water quality underlies all other water questions, but the first GAP Master Plan in 1989 did not include the water quality impact of the return flows from irrigation.[41] So the risk of salination and waterlogging for downstream countries has never been addressed. This subject was discussed in more detail in chapter 3; the high levels of pollution will pose a greater threat to Syria and Iraq than the declining water quantity,

[38] al-Hasani and al-Shara, "Baghdad Urged."

[39] Daoudy, "Asymmetric Power," 365.

[40] Ibid., 370.

[41] Ibid.

however. Through its Ministry of Foreign Affairs, Turkey makes its position on the pollution issue quite clear:

> Turkey is well aware of the risks involved and will be even more vigilant than it already is in curbing pollution. . . . In point of fact, both Syria and Iraq have a poor environmental record where water is concerned. Both countries use the Euphrates to drain off industrial pollution and sewage, thereby creating an alarming level of pollution in the lower courses of the river and the [Persian] Gulf.[42]

Denial of water quality problems may strengthen Turkey's bargaining position in the short term, but it will eventually lead to a crisis and instability that will require monumental efforts to overcome.

Turkey's refusal to provide detailed information on water quantity and quality, coupled with superficial efforts and commitments at cooperation, could be viewed as a long-term strategy in itself. Time is power for Turkey in the unique environment of the Euphrates-Tigris basin. And perception can also be an important source of power—the belief that Turkey can use water as a strategic weapon may be more important than its actual ability to cut off the water supply.

Can Turkey Use Water as a Strategic Weapon?

Some outside observers assume that Turkey's control of the waters of the Euphrates allows it to manipulate the flow of water, and thus use water as a strategic weapon in any potential conflict with its downstream neighbors.[43] As noted earlier in this chapter, Syria, in large part as political leverage in response to the water policies of Ankara, supported the PKK and its militant activities between 1984 and 1998. The PKK conducted both terror-

---

[42] See Turkey Ministry of Foreign Affairs, "Water: A Source of Conflict," section titled "Water Pollution."

[43] See Mark Adams, *Water and Security Policy: The Case of Turkey* (Washington, DC: National Defense University Press, 2002), http://permanent.access.gpo.gov/websites/nduedu /www.ndu.edu/nesa/docs/marksadams-water.pdf. In this piece, Adams examines previous Turkish responses to crises with Syria and Iraq. He mentions that "turning off the taps" was an option for Turkey without looking at the underlying difficulties in the water faucet approach; see page 59.

ist and military actions in eastern and southeastern Turkey, and according to Ankara, the group has claimed more than 30,000 lives. Although never stated overtly by Syria, it has been speculated that Syria's support of the PKK was the only lever it had against Turkey's overuse of the waters of the Euphrates.[44]

During field visits by one of the coauthors to the region, Turkish officials always took the position that Turkey would *not* have the ability to dramatically alter the flow of the Euphrates.[45] This raises several important factual questions: What is Turkey's real ability to use the GAP as an instrument of foreign policy? Can the flow of water leaving Turkey be manipulated? If so, how quickly and what impact will it have on Turkish hydropower generation and irrigation systems?

To respond to these questions, Turkey has only a limited ability to use the GAP as an instrument of foreign policy, and this will continue in the years ahead. As mentioned in chapter 3, the GAP irrigation scheme is only about 30 percent complete, but it will likely reach completion in the next 10 to 15 years. Because Turkey is short on fuel, it is highly dependent on the electrical power generation of the GAP. In the future, Turkey will increasingly depend on the smooth, regulated, and efficient functioning of the GAP system and would have to disrupt its own economy and electric generation to punish the downstream riparians.[46]

Turkey must maintain a careful balance between hydropower production and delivery of water for irrigation needs. This is particularly true for Ataturk Dam, which generates a large quantity of electricity spread throughout the grid that supports the rest of Turkey. The irrigation water connections are primarily through the Sanliurfa Tunnel to the Harran Plain, and these will be fully developed east to Mardin in the next 10 to

---

[44] Ibid., 55.

[45] Informal interviews with midlevel GAP and Directorate of State Hydraulic Works officials were conducted by coauthor Lorenz in the summer of 1997, and again in 2003 and 2009.

[46] John Kolars, a leading independent expert on scientific issues in the basin, has a number of books and papers on this subject (see references to his work throughout this book). His 1997 paper "Potential for Manipulation of Euphrates River Flow by Turkey," on file with coauthor Lorenz, concludes that Turkey cannot easily manipulate water flow in the Euphrates for the reasons stated in this section.

15 years. Excessive water removed for irrigation is unavailable for power generation at Ataturk Dam; this balance can be observed and studied using the various models that will be mentioned in the following chapter. Also, excessive downstream releases lower the water levels below the Sanliurfa water connections in Ataturk Reservoir. Lowering water levels in reservoirs to increase the ability to "turn off the tap" would essentially shut down the irrigation system in central Turkey. Manipulation of water levels would also have an immediate impact on power production throughout Turkey in a system that is heavily dependent on hydropower.

An essential factor in any Turkish manipulation of water levels or downstream flow would be the requirement to impound water behind the dams within Turkey. This would require a reduced volume in advance; the three major reservoirs on the Euphrates—Keban, Karakaya, and Ataturk—have a total capacity of 88.9 BCM. Two other downstream dams—Birecik and Karkamis—have negligible importance and serve mainly as surge controls for Ataturk Dam. Of the 88.9 BCM available for main storage, 42.1 BCM (47.4 percent) is dead storage—the amount of water stored below the level of the exit channels—and can be ruled out of any regional water manipulation scenario. The remaining 46.8 BCM of live storage (52.6 percent) is not necessarily available for "punishing" downstream users since most of it has to be maintained for power production and irrigation offtakes. Any effort to manipulate water levels would require substantial advance preparation and would have direct internal consequences for Turkey. It is not simply a matter of "turning off the spigot." If there were any attempt to hold back significant amounts of water, there would first have to be a significant drawdown of live storage, and this would be easily detectable by watching water levels within the reservoirs. Such a scenario makes the availability of remote sensing and information technology even more important as a predictor of potential conflict.

The theory that Turkey can simply turn off the tap is not realistic from both engineering and practical standpoints. Even if Turkey could manipulate water levels, under what conditions would it undertake such an action? One scenario would be in response to terrorist activity originating in Syria or Iraq; another would be the threat of an independent Kurdistan. If there were to be a major conflict between Turkey and its southern neighbors, water could theoretically be used as a weapon in response to perceived aggression. Turkey would first have to weigh the use of the "water weapon" against the negative impact on its own economic, irrigation, and power capabilities, however. Nonetheless, the perception that Turkey can use water as an instrument of foreign policy should not be discounted, and perception can be very important in international relations. In interviews in Baghdad and Amman, the authors of this book found a consensus among water professionals that Turkey had the power to manipulate and reduce water levels to punish downstream countries. This makes it increasingly important to find ways to lessen the rhetoric and move toward increased cooperation.

Future Prospects

In the past four years, there have been some promising signs. For instance, the first high-level strategic cooperation council meeting took place between Turkey and Syria in Damascus in December 2009.[47] This was preceded by meetings of the Turkish foreign minister and his Iraqi counterpart in Istanbul. When Prime Minister Erdogan of Turkey visited Baghdad in 2008, a strategic partnership agreement was signed that committed Iraq and Turkey to cooperate in the fields of politics, economy, energy, water, and security. Yet despite high hopes, continued meetings and real progress on water issues have been lacking. The underlying foundation of hydropolitics in the region has not changed: Turkey has no real incentive to change course; water quantity and quality in Syria and Iraq continue to decline; and the parties seem unable or unwilling to deal with it.

The positions of the three primary parties on the water question seem irreconcilable, and an atmosphere of distrust has historically pervaded water relations between them. International law has only limited influence in the Euphrates-Tigris basin, and this topic will be covered in the next chapter. Nevertheless, there may be some opportunities to influence

---

[47] Kıbaroğlu, *Recent Developments and Prospects*, section 7.1.1.

the parties to cooperate using the prior experience from a number of other transboundary water situations around the world. And the most promising opportunities may be in the area of science and diplomacy, another topic that will be covered in the following chapter.

Chapter 6
Law, Science, and Diplomacy

The previous chapter described regional hydropolitics in the Euphrates-Tigris basin and how the three principal riparian countries interact in the face of declining water quantity and quality. This chapter will focus on the next obvious question: how does international law influence the process? Despite many years of development, water law plays only a minor role in the basin.[1]

There is disagreement on all the fundamentals, including the definition of an "international river," the meaning of "equitable and reasonable utilization," and limitations on the obligation not to cause harm (all of which will be explained in this chapter). However, as a counterpoint to this, we will present two successful framework agreements regarding international transboundary waters in the Nile and Mekong basins. Finally, this chapter will describe recent technical developments in earth and water science that are relevant to the Euphrates-Tigris region. Science has the potential to make a major contribution to cooperation, but only with a concerted effort to bridge the gap between the science and diplomacy. Together, science and diplomacy can make a major contribution in advancing the aims of cooperation and stability in the Euphrates-Tigris watershed.

---

[1] This does not prevent the parties from relying on legal theories to support their positions, and law has the potential to support a basinwide water agreement should the parties ever be ready to negotiate one.

International Law

The role of law in international relations has been the subject of debate for more than 200 years. One of the branches of legal theory known as *positivism* holds that normative structures only achieve the status of law when they are issued by a sovereign and backed by sanctions.[2] Since the duties imposed by international law lack a centralized mechanism of accountability, they cannot be called true law, according to this view. Another branch of international relations theory called *realism* recognizes that international law is indeed law, albeit with a very limited role and always circumscribed by prevailing power realities.[3] In contrast to these, other scholars have noted that international law has many functions in today's society and that it can confer legitimacy on state actors and their activities even in the absence of a centralized international authority.[4]

International law was at one time defined as the law that governs relations between states, but today the definition has been expanded to include the rights and obligations of individuals as well.[5] International law functions effectively at many levels, and we often take its operation for granted. International communications, aviation, postal service, and trade are regulated by a web of international rules that are in the interests of all states to observe. International law covers most aspects of international commerce, although questions of whaling and environmental protection have become quite controversial. The issues become more difficult when matters of state sovereignty and the use of military force are at stake.

The primary sources of international law are *international conventions* (treaties), *international custom* (practice), and *general principles of law* recognized

---

[2] John Austin, *The Province of Jurisprudence Determined*, ed. Wilfred E. Rumble (Cambridge: Cambridge University Press, 1995), 22.

[3] Hans J. Morgenthau, *Politics Among Nations: The Struggle for Power and Peace*, 3d ed. (New York: Alfred Knopf, 1965), 285.

[4] David Armstrong, Theo Farrell, and Helene Lambert, *International Law and International Relations* (Cambridge: Cambridge University Press, 2007), 22.

[5] According to one definition, "International law consists of the rules and principles of general application dealing with the conduct of states and of international organizations and their relations *inter se*, as well as with some of their relations with persons, whether natural or judicial." *Black's Law Dictionary*, 8th ed., ed. Bryan A. Garner (Thomson West, 2004).

by civilized nations.[6] The treaty is perhaps the most readily accessible source, while other forms of law have been described as "soft" because of the difficulty of determining the norm or standard to apply. A state may take formal action to express its intent to be bound by a treaty, usually through a signature of a state representative.[7] A state that has signed but not ratified a treaty is obligated to refrain from acts that would defeat the object and purpose of the treaty.[8] A state can formally express its consent to be bound by a treaty in one of the following ways: ratification (usually by the legislature), accession to an existing treaty, or succession (usually for a state that is newly independent or had a major change in status). In the United States, the executive branch typically signs a treaty, but it does not become law until ratified by the Senate.[9]

Treaties apply only between and within the states that have ratified them. The law of treaties is complicated by a state's ability to make reservations, declarations, and objections to a treaty with the intended effect of excluding or modifying certain parts of the treaty in their application to that state. This can make it difficult to determine the obligations of each state, particularly when each state is driven by different and unique national interests.

International Water Law

International water law with respect to rivers is of relatively recent origin.[10] Prior to World War I, the law developed primarily to resolve disputes con-

---

[6] See the statute of the International Court of Justice, article 38, at http://www.icj-cij.org/documents/index.php?p1=4&p2=2&p3=0#CHAPTER_II.

[7] See the Vienna Convention on the Law of Treaties, 1969, article 11.

[8] Ibid., article 18.

[9] Article 2, section 2, of the U.S. Constitution gives the president the power to make treaties subject to ratification in the Senate: "He shall have Power, by and with the Advice and Consent of the Senate, to make Treaties, provided two thirds of the Senators present concur."

[10] Portions of this chapter relating to international water law and the situation in the Euphrates-Tigris basin have been previously published as an article by coauthor Lorenz and are reproduced here with permission. See Frederick M. Lorenz, "Strategic Water For Iraq: The Need for Planning and Action," *American University International Law Review* 24, no. 2 (2008): 275–99, http://www.wcl.american.edu/journal/ilr/24/documents/Lorenz.pdf?rd=1. This section also draws on Erickson and Lorenz, *The Euphrates Triangle*, chapter 7, "International Law," 29–33.

cerning freedom of navigation. Since that time, there have been a number of attempts to provide a framework for increasingly intensive water use, focusing on general guidelines that could be applied to the world's watersheds. The concept of a "drainage basin," for example, was accepted by the International Law Association in the 1966 Helsinki Rules on the Uses of the Waters of International Rivers (Helsinki Rules), which also provide guidelines for the reasonable and equitable sharing of a common waterway. Article IV of the Helsinki Rules describes this principle in the following way:

> Each basin State is entitled, within its territory, to a reasonable and equitable share in the beneficial uses of the waters of an international drainage basin.[11]

Article V of the rules then lists 11 factors that must be taken into account in defining "reasonable and equitable." There is no hierarchy to these components of reasonable utilization, and they are instead to be considered as a whole. One important shift in legal thinking in the Helsinki Rules is that they address the right to beneficial use of water, rather than to water per se. The Helsinki Rules are used only rarely to help define water use. This is consistent with the assertion of Tony Allan that water rights are easy to assert, difficult to recognize, and nearly impossible to attain.[12] One historic example: the Mekong Committee used the definition of "reasonable and equitable use" from the Helsinki Rules in the formulation of its Declaration of Principles in 1975, although no specific allocations were determined.

When the United Nations (UN) reviewed the Helsinki Rules in 1970, some states (Brazil, Belgium, China, and France) objected to the prominence of the drainage basin approach, which might be interpreted as an infringe-

---

[11] UNESCO, "The Helsinki Rules on the Uses of the Waters of International Rivers," http://webworld.unesco.org/water/wwap/pccp/cd/pdf/educational_tools/course_modules/reference_documents/internationalregionconventions/helsinkirules.pdf.

[12] Allan, *Middle East Water Question*, 216. Also see chapter 5, "Hydropolitics," of this book.

ment on a nation's sovereignty.[13] Others, notably Finland and the Netherlands, argued that a watershed was the most rational and scientific unit to be managed. Others contended that, given the complexity and uniqueness of each watershed, general codification should not even be attempted. States were of course determined to promote their own national interest, and each brought a unique history and experience in disputes over water. Some states were heavily reliant on water from outside their own borders, and others—such as China, Canada, and Turkey—were more concerned with sovereignty over water inside their respective countries. On 8 December 1970, the UN General Assembly directed its own legal advisory body, the International Law Commission (ILC), to prepare a draft "Codification of the Law on Water Courses for Purposes other than Navigation."[14]

The ILC, despite an additional call for codification at the 1977 UN water conference in Mar del Plata, Argentina, took 21 years to complete its draft articles. A number of problems, both political and hydrological, slowed the process. For example, in response to a 1974 questionnaire submitted to member states, about half the respondents supported the concept of a drainage basin (e.g., Argentina, Finland, and the Netherlands), while half were strongly negative (e.g., Austria, Brazil, and Spain) or ambivalent. "Watercourse system" referred to a basin, which could be viewed as a threat to national sovereignty. Again, each state was motivated to protect its own special concerns and unique geographical setting. Downstream and upstream states are inherently sceptical of the actions of the other.

In 1994, more than two decades after receiving its charge, the ILC adopted a set of 32 draft articles. The articles were adopted by the UN General Assembly in 1997 as the Convention on the Law of the Non-navigational Uses of International Watercourses, commonly referred to today as the

---

[13] UN, "Other Legal Questions: Progressive Development and Codification of the Rules of International Law Relating to International Watercourses," in *Yearbook of the United Nations* (New York: United Nations, 1970), 817, 819, http://unyearbook.un.org/unyearbook .html?name=1970index.html.

[14] Ibid., 818.

Watercourses (or Framework) Convention.[15] The convention provided that 35 states had to ratify before it would become effective.

The Watercourses Convention includes language very similar to the Helsinki Rules, requiring riparian states along an international watercourse to generally communicate and cooperate.[16] Provisions are included for exchange of data and information, notification of possible adverse effects, protection of ecosystems, and emergency situations. Allocations are dealt with through equally vague language. "Equitable and reasonable use" within each watercourse state, "with a view to attaining optimal and sustainable utilization thereof and benefits therefrom" (article 5) is balanced with an obligation not to cause "significant harm" (article 7).[17] The latter provision is always of greatest concern to the upstream riparian, and it is easy to contemplate a situation where an upstream country would be ordered by an international court to release more water if article 7 had been violated.

Developing broad concepts that apply to all watersheds has been challenging from the start. Even the term "international drainage basin" has proven to be controversial in the Euphrates-Tigris basin, and Turkey has consistently maintained that the two rivers form a single basin.[18] This argument can lead to both practical and political benefits for Turkey. For instance, if Iraq should claim a water shortage in the flow of the Euphrates, Turkey can argue any deficit be made up from the excess flow of the Tigris inside Iraq. Also, Turkey can point to the fact that Iraq has already created a canal to do just that, strengthening its argument on the "one basin" theory.[19]

---

[15] UN, Convention on the Law of the Non-navigational Uses of International Watercourses, adopted by the UN General Assembly on 21 May 1997. UN General Assembly Resolution 51/229, 5–6, www.un.org/documents/ga/res/51/ares51-229.htm (including sections on cooperation and the sharing of information among parties to the treaty). This convention is not yet in force.

[16] See, for example, Stephen C. McCaffrey and Mpazi Sinjela, "The 1997 United Nations Convention on International Watercourses," *American Journal of International Law* 92, no. 1 (1998): 97.

[17] UN, Convention on the Law, 4–5n12 (shows both the obligation to make reasonable use of the waters and to avoid causing significant harm to other watercourse states).

[18] Kîbaroğlu, *Building a Regime*, 241.

[19] Ibid., 241–42.

Water Rights Criteria: Hydrography versus Chronology

Applying general legal guidelines to particular rivers is a daunting task. Certain water law principles have been claimed regularly by riparians in negotiations, often depending on their geographic location in the watershed. Claims for water rights are based either on hydrography (i.e., from where a river or aquifer originates and how much of that territory falls within a certain state) or on chronology (i.e., who has been using the water the longest). National positions are usually extreme, and the *doctrine of absolute sovereignty* is often initially claimed by an upstream riparian. This principle is often referred to as the Harmon Doctrine, named after the U.S. attorney general who suggested this stance in 1895 regarding a dispute with Mexico over the Rio Grande. This theory holds that a state has absolute rights to water flowing through its territory. The doctrine was eventually rejected by the United States, itself a downstream riparian of several rivers originating in Canada. It was never implemented in any water treaty, with the rare exception of administering some internal tributaries of international waters. Nor has it ever been cited as the basis for judgment in any international water case. In fact, it was explicitly rejected by the international tribunal (predecessor to the International Court of Justice [ICJ]) in the Lac Lanoux case in 1957 (described later in this section).

The downstream riparian often asserts the *doctrine of absolute riverain integrity*, which suggests that every riparian is entitled to the natural flow of a river system crossing its borders. This principle has reached acceptance in the international setting as infrequently as the Harmon Doctrine. In an arid or exotic (defined as a humid headwaters region with an arid downstream region) watershed, the downstream riparian frequently has older water infrastructure that must be defended. The principle that rights are acquired through older use is referred to as the *doctrine of prior appropriation*, that is, "first in time, first in right" (also known as the Colorado Doctrine).

These conflicting doctrines of hydrography and chronology clash along many international rivers, with national positions usually defined by relative riparian positions. Downstream riparians, such as Iraq and Egypt, receive less rainfall than their upstream neighbors and have historically depended on river water for the life of their nations. As a consequence, modern "rights-based" disputes often take the form of upstream riparians such as Ethiopia and Turkey arguing in favor of the doctrine of absolute sovereignty, with downstream riparians taking the position of prior appropriation.

The Lac Lanoux case is one of the few international water cases, and it led to the disavowal of the legal principles of absolute sovereignty and absolute riverain integrity. In the early 1950s, France, citing absolute sovereignty, proposed diverting water from the Carol River, which crosses from the French into the Spanish Pyrenees. The diverted water would flow across a divide toward the Font-Vive for hydropower generation, and there was an offer for Spain to be compensated monetarily. Spain objected, citing absolute riverain integrity and the existing irrigation needs on its side of the border. Even when France agreed to first divert back into the river the water needed for Spanish irrigation, through a tunnel between the divide, Spain insisted on absolute riverain integrity, claiming it did not want French hands on its "tap." Both absolute principles were effectively dismissed when a 1957 arbitration tribunal ruled in the case that "territorial sovereignty . . . must bend before all international obligations," effectively negating the doctrine of absolute sovereignty, and also refused the downstream state from the right to veto "reasonable" upstream development, negating the principle of natural flow or absolute riverain integrity. This decision made possible the 1958 Lac Lanoux treaty (revised in 1970), in which it was agreed that water was to be diverted out-of-basin for French hydropower generation, and a similar quantity was to be returned before the stream reached Spanish territory. But, with the Euphrates-Tigris riparians, no case law precedent exists in international law today that will undermine Turkey's fundamental claims of sovereignty over its own water.

One of the major difficulties in managing transboundary water is that much of it is moving underground and is therefore much more difficult to measure and regulate. The term "watercourse" in the Watercourses Convention can include both surface and groundwater, and is based largely on the terms of the Helsinki Rules, but it includes only groundwater that is connected to the surface water. It does not incorporate the broader definition of groundwater contained in the Seoul Rules, which includes transboundary aquifers that are not connected to surface waters of an international drainage basin.[20]

Existing law for transboundary waters has proven easy to argue but very difficult to apply. For example, riparian positions and consequent legal rights shift with changing political boundaries, many of which are still not recognized by the world community. The rules provide what is known in legal terms as a balancing test that is more appropriate for the courtroom than the politically charged atmosphere of international water disputes. Also, a balancing test requires some third party—such as an arbitrator, a watermaster, or a court—to resolve the issues. In water basins without such a regime, balancing tests are not particularly useful.

The uncertainty in international water law is compounded by the fact that cases are generally heard by the ICJ only with the consent of the parties involved, and no practical enforcement mechanism is available.[21] Considering these limitations, it is hardly surprising that the ICJ has decided few cases regarding the law of transboundary rivers.[22] In one case heard by the ICJ the results were mixed, and although the case may have clarified some of the general principles of equitable utilization, it failed to resolve the dispute between the riparian countries.[23] This reveals one of the fundamental problems in transboundary water law: complex standards to be decided by a judge using a "balancing of interests" are of limited value on the international stage.

---

[20] The Seoul Rules were adopted by the International Law Association at its conference in Seoul, South Korea, in 1986. Text for the rules can be found on the International Water Law Project's Web site at http://www.internationalwaterlaw.org/documents/intldocs/seoul_rules .html.

[21] See article 36 of the Statute of the International Court of Justice, available at http://www .icj-cij.org/documents/index.php?p1=4&p2=2&p3=0.

[22] Aaron T. Wolf, "Shared Waters: Conflict and Cooperation," *Annual Review of Environment and Resources* 32 (November 2007): 241–69, http://www.annualreviews.org /doi/abs/10.1146/annurev.energy.32.041006.101434?journalCode=energy.

[23] The 1997 ICJ case related to the Gabcikovo-Nagymaros dam project on the Danube River. See http://www.icj-cij.org/docket/files/92/7375.pdf.

International law plays only a minor role in the Euphrates-Tigris basin, as the Watercourses Convention is not yet in force and Turkey refuses to become a party.[24] In a 2009 report, the Turkish position was stated as such:

> Turkey voted against the Convention, because of her objections to its preamble and to several of its articles. Turkey believes that, as a framework convention, the text should have set forth general principles. Instead, it goes beyond the scope of a framework convention and establishes a detailed mechanism of notification. . . . Moreover, in the 11 years which have followed its signature, the Convention has lost its credibility, given that it has been unable to attract the number of ratifications needed for its entry into force.[25]

All the parties in the basin have legal arguments, but they have more political value than practical effect. Turkey has consistently opposed efforts to "internationalize" the matter, relying on the same legal doctrines that the United States once used in disputes with Mexico concerning the Colorado River.[26] At the time of this writing, only 16 states had ratified the Watercourses Convention and that number includes both Syria and Iraq.

In such regions as North America, with plentiful water resources and good international relations, the record of cooperation between states is excellent. In contrast, Middle Eastern river basins face pressures from growing populations, limited resources, and political turmoil. Unfortunately, international law has often reinforced separate and competitive theories among states that share the same watercourse. The conflicting doctrines that formed the basis of international water law give every state a point to argue, but provide little help in achieving common ground.

---

[24] See Murat Metin Hakki, "Cross-Border Water Conflicts in Mesopotamia: An Analysis According to International Law," *Willamette Journal of International Law and Dispute Resolution* 13, no. 2 (2005): 245, 255.

[25] Republic of Turkey, *Turkey Water Report 2009*, 50.

[26] See Hakki, "Cross-Border Water Conflicts," 261, concerning Turkey's assertion of the Harmon Doctrine, which the United States used in its dealings with Mexico concerning the water of the Colorado River.

It is a fair question to ask, why have so few states supported the Watercourses Convention some 11 years after its opening for signature? The lead counsel for the International Water Resources Association, Salman M. A. Salman, believes that it is due in part to inaccurate perceptions and interpretations of the convention.[27] Salman notes that both upstream riparians (e.g., Turkey and China) and downstream riparians (e.g., Egypt and France) believe that the convention favors the other party. He also points out another area of confusion: it is little understood that upstream riparians can be harmed caused by the prior use and the claiming of rights by downstream riparians.[28] Another reason why the Watercourses Convention has not been adopted, according to Salman, is a "total failure to comprehend the basic rules of contemporary international water law that have long rejected the principle of absolute territorial sovereignty." He argues that it is now generally agreed that the "management of international watercourses should be determined less by the traditional notion of 'restricted sovereignty' than by a positive spirit of cooperation and effective interdependence."[29]

Although he is not a lawyer, Tony Allan provides additional insight on the question of international law and its impact on water rights in the Middle East and North Africa (MENA) countries.[30] He notes that the legal principles are largely developed by "water outsiders" [31] and the introduction of water policy reform (and water law) has been slow. Because water is highly mobile, and monitoring it is difficult, any rules are difficult to enforce. Moreover, "alien legal principles, evolved in alien outsider institutions . . . have little appeal to MENA politicians, professionals and communities when they will disrupt existing practice and are not founded on the cultural and religious conventions of the region."[32]

---

[27] Salman M. A. Salman, "The United Nations Watercourses Convention Ten Years Later: Why Has Its Entry into Force Proven Difficult?" *Water International* 32, no. 1 (2007): 9.

[28] Ibid., 10.

[29] Ibid., 12.

[30] Allan, *Middle East Water Question*. See chapter 7 on international water law in the MENA countries.

[31] Ibid.; see chapter 1 on water pessimists and optimists, and water insiders and outsiders.

[32] Ibid., 288.

Not surprisingly, upstream riparians have advocated that the emphasis between the two competing principles of hydrography and chronology be on equitable utilization, since that gives the needs of the present the same weight as those of the past. Likewise, downstream riparians have pushed for emphasis on no significant harm, effectively the equivalent of the doctrine of prior appropriation in protecting preexisting use. The World Bank, which must follow prevailing principles of international law in its funded projects, recognizes the importance of equitable use in theory but, for practical considerations, gives "no appreciable harm" precedent—it is considered easier to define—and will not finance a project without the approval of all affected riparians. This was the reason Turkey was required to finance and construct the GAP (Southeastern Anatolia Project) using its own resources.

As legal principles for sharing scarce water resources evolve over time, they can eventually reach the status of customary international law. But in the realm of transboundary waters, the general lack of acceptance and the use of a balancing test make the process more difficult. In the absence of a treaty or basinwide agreement, the arguments still emphasize the *rights* of each state and rest on the fundamental dispute between claims based on hydrography and those based on chronology. The parties' positions are driven more by geography, economics, and politics than refined legal principles. Use of the terms "reasonable," "equitable," and "significant" guarantee that each riparian party will have a legal theory to support its position, even when that position may be extreme.

An attorney who has extensively studied the situation in the Euphrates-Tigris basin stated in an article that the Turkish position is "flatly wrong," and he believes that the weight of legal authority supports the Arab downstream riparians.[33] Yet a fair reading of the draft ILC rules supports the Turkish position that the downstream riparians are unable to put the waters to equitable use, at least in comparison to Turkey. Of course the equation could change in the future in the event of a water shortage that

---

[33] Joseph W. Delapenna, "The Two Rivers and the Land Between: Mesopotamia and the International Law of Transboundary Waters," *Brigham Young University Journal of Public Law* 10 (1996): 213.

causes significant harm to the downstream users. In addition, Turkey has recognized in a key document that an upstream riparian may be limited by the concept of significant harm.[34] Whether that represents a change in Turkish policy remains to be seen.

The fact that Turkey has not signed the Watercourses Convention would make no significant difference if the convention reflects customary international law. But the slow progress of ratification seems to indicate that the treaty has not yet reached that status. The failure to sign provides at least one major advantage to Turkey. It reduces the chance that a dispute will become internationalized and that some outside agency will have control over what Turkey considers to be its own natural resource.

International Water Law and Hydropolitics

Political and economic factors will heavily influence the positions of states on important questions of international water law. By July 2012, only a handful of nations had ratified the Watercourses Convention, and Turkey was conspicuously absent. One of Turkey's principal objections was article 7's provision not to "cause significant harm." This is certain to be a concern to Turkey that this provision would be used as a weapon by Syria or Iraq in the event of declining water supply or a deterioration in water quality. Syria signed the convention, but it is much more difficult to determine the official Syrian position on the subject, in view of the tightly controlled and censored Syrian bureaucracy. Water information and policy are treated as a state secret, and the Syrians hold their cards close to their vests. This is true even though there is a strong legal argument to support Syria based on the principles of chronology and historic use.[35] Without the data to support a claim that Turkey is causing a decline in historic flows, the Syrian position would certainly be weakened.

In contrast to Syria, Turkey has a transparent strategy and conducts a public information campaign on the subject. The Turkish Ministry of Foreign Affairs Web site contains a summary of international water law

---

[34] Republic of Turkey, *Turkey Water Report 2009*, 48.
[35] See Dellapenna, "Two Rivers," 244.

and explains why Turkey's position is reasonable under the current state of the law.[36] Although these documents can be subject to criticism regarding their representation of the facts and the law, they do provide a valuable insight into Turkey's position on a matter of national security.

Along with its signature on the Watercourses Convention, Syria filed an "understanding" that "the acceptance by the Syrian Arab Republic of this Convention and its ratification by the Government shall not under any circumstances be taken to imply recognition of Israel and shall not lead to its entering into relations therewith that are governed by its provisions." This is an important issue because Israel occupies the Golan Heights, one of the primary sources for water in Syria. It is clear that the Watercourses Convention is hostage to the same political and security factors that limit co-operation in all the river basins of the Middle East. Turmoil in the Middle East in 2011 and 2012 has not yet provided any more hopeful picture.

Some authors retain a more positive view of the role of international law in transboundary water conflict resolution. If international water law is considered an element of power relations, then it can be viewed as a source of structural or bargaining power.[37] If this is true, then weaker actors should be able to back their claims with "basin hegemons," thus enhancing their bargaining power. However, the differences between Turkey on the one hand and Syria and Iraq on the other are so great that meaningful negotiation between them has never occurred. There is disagreement on all the fundamentals, including the definition of an "international river," the meaning of "equitable and reasonable utilization," and limitations on the obligation not to cause harm.[38] Turkey has little or no incentive to even consider the long-standing legal claims of Syria, and Iraq and has carefully developed and publicized its own legally supportable claims.

---

[36] See Turkey Ministry of Foreign Affairs, "Water: A Source of Conflict," under the heading "International Law and Transboundary Rivers."

[37] Marwa Daoudy, "Hydro-Hegemony and International Water Law: Laying Claims to Water Rights," *Water Policy* 10, supplement no. 2 (2008): 89.

[38] Ibid., 99.

The Fifth World Water Forum in Istanbul in 2009 provided Turkey with the opportunity to showcase all the positive aspects of its water management and demonstrate that Turkey is ready to take its rightful place in Western society. But the unofficial comments made by Turkish officials during the open sessions of the program revealed more than the official pronouncements. During these sessions, there were a number of provocative questions and challenges, mostly by the Turkish delegates, who charged that the panels were biased and gave misleading information. Later in the day in an open session, one Turkish delegate loudly argued that foreign countries were trying to manage Turkey's water resources and meddle in its internal affairs.[39] Another Turkish representative then claimed that a respected international water research organization participating in one of the panels was secretly controlled by Israel.[40]

The frustrating aspect of international water law is that each party can find a theory to support a divergent position. It is unlikely that any court will ever require Turkey to modify its nationalistic interpretation of the law. Furthermore, standards developed by lawyers to be decided by a judge using a balancing of interests are difficult to apply on the international stage. Still, with the right diplomatic and economic incentives, we can look to international law to provide a starting point and a roadmap for some level of cooperation in the Euphrates-Tigris basin. Furthermore, it is helpful to bear in mind that the lack of an international legal framework has not prevented regional mechanisms and initiatives in other basins.

Diplomatic Initiatives and Commissions in Other Basins

A number of working models provide a basis for regional cooperation in the Euphrates-Tigris basin. The Mekong River Commission (MRC) provides one potential model of increased cooperation. Likewise, with international support and improved political will, the affected parties could

---

[39] Coauthor Lorenz was a nongovernmental organization delegate to the 2009 World Water Forum, representing the Public International Law and Policy Group. See www.pilpg.org.

[40] The delegate was referring to the London Water Research Group; see http://lwrg.org/. This group is an internationally renowned and transparent nongovernmental organization based at King's College, London. Dr. Tony Allan is a leading member.

benefit from a diplomatic initiative similar to the one that made progress in the Nile basin.[41] International organizations and the World Bank could be the principal agents for the Euphrates-Tigris, making it a truly international endeavor.

The Mekong Basin

There are a number of other transboundary river organizations that might provide lessons for the Euphrates-Tigris; one possibility is located in the Mekong basin. U.S. involvement in Indochina in the 1950s and 1960s included efforts to develop the lower Mekong basin using a model based on the Tennessee Valley Authority. The history of the Mekong commission dates back to this involvement in Indochina and makes for a fascinating parallel to U.S. involvement in Iraq.

The MRC is an intergovernmental organization for the four riparian countries of Cambodia, Laos, Thailand, and Vietnam. It was first located in Bangkok, Thailand, at the home of the former Mekong Committee, which had been established there in 1957. A new agreement between the member countries in 1995 created the MRC in its present form. The secretariat for the MRC is now located in Pnom Penh, Cambodia, where it has been since 1998.

The MRC consists of three permanent bodies: the council, comprised of a cabinet minister from each member country; the joint committee, comprising senior government officials; and the secretariat, which employs a staff of over 125. It is funded by contributions from member countries and from aid donors, with total yearly operating costs of $12 to 15 million (in U.S. dollars).[42]

Since the 1995 agreement, the MRC has launched a process to ensure reasonable and equitable use of the Mekong River system through a par-

---

[41] See Patrick Rutagwera, "About the NBI," Nile Basin Initiative, http://www.nilebasin.org /newsite/index.php?option=com_content&view=section&id=5&layout=blog&Itemid=68&l ang=en (accessed 17 May 2011). This describes the committee as a partnership developed by the countries of the Nile River and aimed at cooperative development of the Nile.

[42] For updated information, see the MRC's Web site at http://www.mrcmekong.org.

ticipatory process with national Mekong committees in each country to develop rules and procedures for water utilization. The MRC monitors the quality of water resources and is supporting a joint basinwide planning process with the four countries, called the basin development plan. The MRC is also involved in fisheries management, the promotion of safe navigation, agricultural development, flood mitigation, and hydropower planning within an overall framework of renewable resources management. Although the MRC does not have the authority to allocate water among its members, multiple cooperative projects provide a forum to address a variety of important issues. The MRC can provide a structural model for a similar commission in the Euphrates-Tigris basin, if the political will can be mustered by the stakeholders and if some of the current obstacles can be overcome.

There are historical lessons to be drawn from the Mekong River projects, and some parallels with recent events in Iraq. One of the most important factors to consider when conceiving of a similar commission in the Euphrates-Tigris is the unstable and changing definition of "support," both domestic and international, for the construction of water infrastructure projects. By 1968, the Richard M. Nixon administration had abandoned earlier project goals of the John F. Kennedy and Lyndon B. Johnson administrations to fund Mekong construction directly. Like the war in Vietnam, this form of unilateral "New Deal" construction was perceived by the American public as a bottomless pit.

Large infrastructure projects in Vietnam, as with similar projects in Iraq, were often focal points for insurgent activities. Increasing violence around physical construction sites in Vietnam raised the costs of construction tremendously, and American efforts shifted the emphasis from construction to "desk studies" in 1968. These studies have survived and play a guiding role in the contemporary development of the Mekong watershed today. The My Thuan Bridge completed in the Mekong Delta in 2002 is one example of this—it is a project first surveyed as part of the U.S. program in 1963. A wave of water infrastructure construction in the Mekong basin, funded largely by the Asian Development Bank and the World Bank, has frequently been initiated by America's former enemies in the region. This may suggest that a commitment to long-term hydrologic information sharing and surveys may in the end achieve American strategic interests without the direct expenditure of U.S. construction funds.

After the invasion of Iraq in 2003, the United States found itself in a major rebuilding role, including a multibillion dollar effort to restore Iraq's water infrastructure. This was undertaken in an atmosphere of little support from the international community. With increasing levels of insurgency and diversions of funding, large-scale projects became correspondingly difficult to manage, and long-term stability for Iraq—and the region—is still uncertain. There is a fascinating parallel between Vietnam in 1968 and Iraq between 2004 and 2006. As the level of insurgency increased, the ambitious plans for water-related projects were scaled back. As in the Mekong basin, American plans in the Euphrates-Tigris basin never materialized. If these projects are ever completed, they are more likely to be under the auspices of Turkey or Iran.

The MRC model contains some elements that could be applicable to the situation in the Euphrates-Tigris basin. With a focus on a "participatory process" and outside funding from a donor consultative group, the MRC recognizes the common interest in joint management of shared water resources. Lacking the power to allocate water or direct any particular action, the MRC model should not be objectionable to Turkey. Although it is an intergovernmental organization, the day-to-day work of the MRC is completed through a joint committee and a secretariat. There is even a role for "dialogue partners" like China, and this might serve as an example for the participation of Iran in a Euphrates-Tigris initiative.

The Nile Basin

The Nile is one of the world's great rivers, flowing for 6,825 kilometers through much of northeastern Africa, draining approximately 2.9 million square kilometers of territory. Roughly 85 percent of the Nile's water originates in the highlands of Ethiopia, flowing in the Blue Nile to Karthoum, Sudan, where it meets the White Nile. The rivers then join and flow northward to Cairo, Egypt, along the fertile Nile Valley, home to one of the world's most important early civilizations. While there are some major differences between the Nile and the Euphrates-Tigris basins, recent events in the Nile basin may provide some lessons and a possible framework for cooperation.

For much of its length, the Nile is an exotic river, flowing for thousands of kilometers through arid desert lands, providing the lifeblood of early civilizations along its banks. The Euphrates-Tigris is similar, with the lower riparian countries contributing little to the flow but being heavily dependent on the rivers. The major difference between the basins is not geography, though, but rather the political-military balance among countries. The most powerful country in the Nile basin is Egypt, also the country most vulnerable to changes in water availability by upstream countries. In the Euphrates-Tigris, the most powerful country is Turkey, but Turkey also enjoys physical control over most of the basin's freshwater resources.

Like the Euphrates-Tigris, the Nile basin is facing declining water supplies for a growing population. Internal instability and regional conflict have historically prevented any significant cooperation among the Nile's countries. But in the 1970s, with a series of technical initiatives and outside support, the parties began to move toward increased cooperation. Support from the United Nations Development Programme and the World Meteorological Organization helped to produce a series of technical studies aimed at providing a baseline set of measurements for water availability and future needs. Despite the political crises in the region, a treaty was concluded in 1977, creating a basinwide management regime for the Kagera River, which drains Burundi, Rwanda, Tanzania, and Uganda, and is a major upper tributary of the Nile.

An important event in this movement toward cooperation was the creation of the Nile Basin Initiative (NBI) in February 1999 and the official launching of its secretariat in Entebbe, Uganda, in September 1999. The involvement of Ethiopia for the first time made a major difference and provided hope for joint water planning and management along the Nile. The NBI is consciously designed to engage parallel technical and political processes, with regular communication between the two.[43] Using the confidence-building measures of informal exchange among technical experts, the initial dialogue can lead to a greater level of cooperation at the political and economic levels.[44] Also, participation by external funding agencies, including the World Bank, made progress possible, especially given the lack of resources in most of the Nile basin countries.

In 2009 new challenges on the Nile arose when Egypt and Sudan refused to sign the comprehensive framework agreement that had been under consideration for several years. As a result, upstream countries joined to sign an agreement in Entebbe that for the first time would recognize upstream rights and limit the rights of Egypt and Sudan under previous treaties. In May 2011 a spokesman for the NBI reported that "the current political context has slowed the pace of the technical track of the NBI including the progress of activities, the implementation of the NBI programs and projects, as well as the NBI operation."[45] In 2013 the situation remains uncertain, but with a new government in Egypt and a new country recently recognized in the basin (South Sudan became independent in July 2011), we can expect a renewed look at a possible basinwide agreement. Although major obstacles remain, we can look to the NBI for elements that might fit into a framework that could eventually lead to cooperation in the Euphrates-Tigris basin.

Science and Diplomacy: Bridging Technology and Policy

Despite the scale of the threats posed by a deteriorating water situation and poor water management in the Euphrates-Tigris basin, there has been little in terms of cooperation. Water ministers from Iraq, Turkey, and Syria held a joint meeting in September 2009, but continued progress has been

---

[43] For more details, see the NBI's Web site: http://www.nilebasin.org.

[44] Jutta Brunnee and Stephen J. Toope, "The Changing Nile Basin Regime: Does Law Matter?" *Harvard International Law Journal* 43, no. 1 (2002): 139.

[45] NBI, "Nile Council of Ministers Approve[s] NBI Work Plan 2011–2012," http://www.nilebasin.org/newsite/index.php?option=com_content&view=article&id=107%3Anile-council-of-ministers-approve-nbi-work-plan-2011-2012&catid=40%3Alatest-news&Itemid=84&lang=en.

elusive. In 2010 the United States Institute of Peace (USIP) identified a number of obstacles, including a rarely discussed factor:

Lack of open technical data. A crucial roadblock is the lack of agreement on actual flow levels and water quality because of deficient measurement technologies, limited public hydrological data, and insufficient technical expertise to make environmental and agricultural impact assessments based on generally accepted scientific standards.[46]

The USIP made a series of recommendations focusing on an approach based on regional scientific cooperation. Using examples of this type of cooperation from the Nile and Mekong, the USIP argued for a new approach that would provide a strong basis for economic growth and political stability. The remainder of this chapter will attempt to build on the USIP report and describe a number of U.S.-based technical capabilities and programs that should be available for the Euphrates-Tigris basin. This is not a comprehensive list, but it will provide a preliminary inventory of the available science.

Geospatial Intelligence

The U.S. intelligence community is making a major effort to improve the collection of information and make it available to "customers" in a fast-changing world. In *Vision 2015: A Globally Networked and Integrated Intelligence Enterprise*, the Director of National Intelligence recognized "a series of complex and often unpredictable threats and risks that transcend geographic borders and organizational boundaries."[47] With major U.S. security interests at stake in the Euphrates-Tigris basin, it is logical to conclude that this capability could be used effectively in the region, not only to advise U.S. policy makers, but to provide reliable data directly to the

---

[46] Joel Whitaker and Anand Varghese, *The Tigris-Euphrates River Basin: A Science Diplomacy Opportunity*, Peacebrief 20 (Washington, DC: United States Institute of Peace, 2010), http://www.usip.org/files/resources/PB%2020%20Tigris-Euphrates_River_Basin.pdf.

[47] Director of National Intelligence, *Vision 2015: A Globally Networked and Integrated Intelligence Enterprise* (Washington, DC: Director of National Intelligence, 2008), 1, http://www.dni.gov/Vision_2015.pdf.

parties in the basin. One report described this capability in the following manner.

> In a sense, this is the development of strategic intelligence, or the information that is required for forming policy and plans at the national and operational level. Basically, the data flow represents the converting of raw information into a form where expertise can apply, and then out to another form suited for communication.[48]

Information could come from a variety of sources, from publicly available data on the Internet to highly sophisticated satellite imagery. The challenge is to take the raw information, make sense of it, and provide it to right people in the policy-making sector. This could in turn form a foundation for a clearinghouse of information that could ultimately improve regional cooperation. Data collection is relatively easy compared to the crucial steps of evaluation and delivery to the parties as part of a carefully prepared plan.

The U.S. National Geospatial-Intelligence Agency (NGA) has a number of international partnership programs that are designed to assist countries in areas of strategic interest to the United States. One of the countries of strategic interest is Mongolia. Since the NGA first entered into an exchange and cooperative agreement with Mongolia in 2004, its relations with the Mongolian government have grown to include Mongolia's Ministry of Construction and Urban Development, the General Staff of the Armed Forces of Mongolia, the National Emergency Management Agency, and the Border Protection General Board of Mongolia.[49] The NGA program will enable Mongolia to conduct its own improved topographic modeling, and this type of partnership should easily be adapted to other regions, including the Euphrates-Tigris basin.

---

[48] Todd Bacastow, Dennis J. Bellafiore, and Donna M. Bridges, *The Structured Geospatial Analytic Method: Opening the Discussion* (2010), https://www.e-education.psu.edu/drupal6 /files/sgam/SGAMopeningdiscussion_3_15_10.pdf.

[49] Joel Itskowitz, "Creating Partnerships Around the World," *Pathfinder*, July–August 2011, 11, https://www1.nga.mil/MediaRoom/Publications/Documents/Pathfinder%20 Magazines/2011/2011_Jul-Aug.pdf.

Geographic Information Systems

A geographic information system (GIS) is a system of hardware and software used for storage, retrieval, mapping, and analysis of geographic data. The total GIS concept usually includes the operating personnel and the data that go into the system. Spatial features are stored in a coordinate system that includes latitude/longitude or Universal Transverse Mercator (UTM) data, referencing a particular place on the earth. GIS is commonly used for scientific investigations, resource management, and development planning.

In GIS, all spatial data is geographically referenced to a map projection in an earth coordinate system. Spatial data can be realigned from one coordinate system into another, and data from different sources can be brought together into a common database and integrated using GIS software. With the right input data, a user can perform analyses, such as modeling the flow through connecting lines in a network and overlaying different environmental and geographic features.

The U.S. Geological Survey (USGS) has completed a number of projects and studies in the Euphrates-Tigris region, and the satellite images for these are available online.[50] The images document the changes in the region, including the progressive draining of the marshes of southern Iraq (shown in the following satelite images from 1972, 1990, and 1997). In 2003 USGS also completed a modeling survey of surface and underground fluid pathways as part of its World Petroleum Assessment.[51] The technology to support the surveillance and analysis of underground pathways from above is essentially the same for oil and water.[52]

---

[50] Robert Wellman Campbell, ed., "Iraq and Kuwait: 1972, 1990, 1991, 1997" (Earthshots, Satellite Images of Environmental Change: U.S. Geological Survey, 1999), http://earthshots.usgs.gov/Iraq/Iraq.

[51] See a summary of this survey at http://pubs.usgs.gov/of/2003/ofr-03-192/Iraq%20Model_files/v3_document.htm.

[52] Ibid. See the detailed presentation describing the rock and shale underlying the northern part of Iraq.

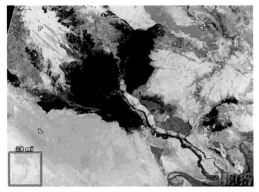

**Landsat 1 satellite image of Iraq, 1–2 August
1972.** *U.S. Geological Survey*

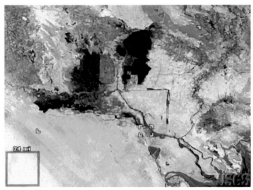

**Landsat satellite image of Iraq, 13–15
August 1990.** *U.S. Geological Survey*

**Resurs 1 satellite image of Iraq, 21 February
1997.** *U.S. Geological Survey*

GIS can be an important tool in watershed analysis; publicly available data such as USGS digital line graphs and digital elevation models, cartographic feature files, and digitized soil surveys can provide a foundation for the analysis. The regional participants can provide agricultural history, land classification, water flow, and other useful data. Current agricultural cover and urban areas can be mapped from satellite photos. The end result product of a watershed analysis is a resource assessment report divided into modules, including hydrology, surface erosion, stream channels, riparian function, and causal mechanisms.

National Aeronautics and Space Administration Programs

The National Aeronautics and Space Administration (NASA), in collaboration with the U.S. Agency for International Development (USAID) and the World Bank, is developing remote-sensing and earth-science data platforms in water critical parts of the world, including the MENA (for water availability, agriculture, and aquifer monitoring). These will address a multitude of issues dealing with water resources, aquifer and stream flow data, agriculture planning, flood management and early warning, and overall water balance. NASA supports a free and open exchange of its earth science and satellite data throughout the world.

In 2009 the USAID Office of Middle East Programs funded a regional effort led by scientists at NASA's Goddard Space Flight Center.[53] The purpose of this project was to provide regional fields of hydrological information relevant for water resources assessments. This is part of the land data assimilation system for the MENA region mentioned below.

The NASA Applied Sciences' SERVIR program is a regional monitoring and visualization system using earth science satellite measurements and other data to support environmental management, development needs, and natural disaster response in developing countries. Jointly supported by NASA and the USAID, SERVIR currently has nodes in Mesoamerica, East Africa, and the Hindu Kush–Himalaya region.

---

[53] See a summary of this program at http://wmp.gsfc.nasa.gov/projects/LinkedProj_Rodell _Bolten_ArabLDAS.pdf.

SERVIR products are used by government agencies, resource managers, researchers, students, news media, and the general public. SERVIR enables scientists, educators, project managers, and policy implementers to better respond to a range of issues, including disaster management, agricultural development, biodiversity conservation, and climate change. Endorsed by governments in Central America and Africa and principally supported by NASA and the USAID, a strong emphasis is placed on partnerships to fortify the availability of searchable and viewable earth observations, measurements, animations, and analysis.

Water Information System Platforms for Water Management

NASA, USAID, and the International Center for Biosaline Agriculture[54] have partnered to provide a regional land data assimilation system for the MENA region using remote sensing to address water management issues. The World Bank, through the Global Environment Facility, and USAID are funding NASA to install water information system platforms throughout the MENA (in Jordan, Tunisia, Morocco, Lebanon, and Egypt) for country and regional (basin) use (map 6.1).

The following are some of the capabilities of these water information platforms:

- regional to local (1 kilometer resolution and better) water availability maps;

- monitoring and predicting drought processes;

- flood warning and inundation mapping;

- climate and land-use change impacts on water resources;

- estimates of crop yield production, irrigation mapping, and land-cover change use;

- satellite data to estimate evapotranspiration and consumptive water loss;

---

[54] Information about this center is available on its Web site at http://www.biosaline.org/.

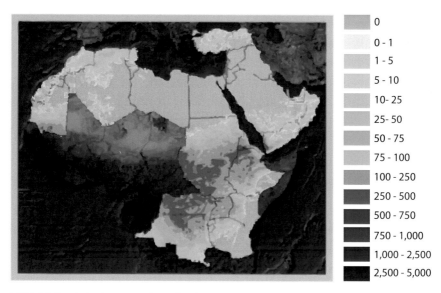

	0
	0 - 1
	1 - 5
	5 - 10
	10- 25
	25- 50
	50 - 75
	75 - 100
	100 - 250
	250 - 500
	500 - 750
	750 - 1,000
	1,000 - 2,500
	2,500 - 5,000

MAP 6.1. **Precipitation map of North Africa and the Middle East (in millimeters).** *NASA*

- generation of maps of evapotranspiration from vegetative covers; and

- estimation of changes to groundwater and terrestrial water storage changes using GRACE (Gravity Recovery and Climate Experiment) satellite data.[55]

This system would have great potential in the Euphrates-Tigris basin and could be integrated into a regional economic and technical development center, a concept that will be further developed later in this chapter.

Collaborative Modeling and Management

Perhaps the most promising technology for use in the Euphrates-Tigris basin is river basin modeling. Scientists at Sandia National Laboratories (SNL) in the United States have developed a collaborative, stakeholder-driven, computer-simulation modeling method to be used for

---

[55] Bradley Doorn, David Toll, and Edwin Engman, "NASA Water Resources Program for Improved Water Management," http://wmp.gsfc.nasa.gov/workshops/5p-Toll_WB2012.pdf.

water-resource management decision support.[56] In this approach, a diverse team of stakeholders (representatives of ministries, universities, nongovernmental organizations, and civic groups) meet periodically with modelers over the course of a year or more. They work with the modelers to develop a computer simulation model of the resources and their relationship to other resources and systems. In Iraq, for example, the model could be used to determine the impact of different Euphrates future flow levels based on various time alternatives (10, 15, or 20 years) for construction of the GAP in Turkey. This will be a critical part of the Strategy for Water and Land Resources in Iraq, a major multisector project recently initiated by the Iraqi government. Basin modeling of this type can aid with questions such as, will there be a water crisis in 10 years that Iraq needs to plan for?

The completed model is designed to allow stakeholders to carefully evaluate the long-term consequences of competing resource management strategies. The collaborative discovery process associated with this work is designed to assist in the development of strong, scientifically derived resource management plans, often with a greater degree of consensus among stakeholders than might otherwise have been achieved. The modeling technology used in this approach, known as system dynamics, also has attributes that should make it especially valuable in the short term. The models are user-friendly, with virtual slider bars and switches that allow users to easily make changes to parameter values, all of which can be carefully annotated for greater understanding by users.[57]

An important feature of the modeling technology is that it has very short run times, usually from under a minute to a few minutes. This allows the use of the model to simulate competing management strategies and view results in real time. For example, stakeholders in Iraq should be able to quickly visualize the relative advantages of supply-side or demand-side management. Direct comparisons could be made between options: either

---

[56] See Howard Passell and others, "Collaborative, Stakeholder-Driven Resource Modeling and Management," in *Handbook of Research on Hydroinformatics: Technologies, Theories and Applications*, ed. Tagelsir Gamelseid (Hershey, PA: IGI Global, 2010), 2.

[57] Ibid., 7.

building more dams or taking water conservation actions such as lining and leveling canals. And the model allows a wide range of comparisons, with a mix of stakeholder-driven inputs. For example, what would be the result of building three dams rather than nine, or lining 30 percent of the canals rather than 70 percent? Time frames can be increased or slowed to clarify results, such as taking 10 years to build a dam instead of 3. In a key aspect of the program, local and regional modelers are trained in the use of the modeling software and approach, and they participate in the development of the model. This allows local and regional modelers to continue improving the model once the initial project is complete, and they can initiate new projects and continuing analysis as part of their long-term strategy.

In 2011, SNL began collaborating with scientists from the Iraqi Ministry of Water Resources (MOWR), the U.S. Department of State, and UNESCO to develop a decision support model for the Euphrates-Tigris basin, including Turkey, Syria, and Iraq. The project began in 2007 and included five modeling workshops between SNL and MOWR modelers. SNL included data and systems previously collected and developed at the U.S. Army Corps of Engineers Hydrologic Engineering Center between 2003 and 2007. The SNL project included an important capacity-building aspect where engineers from the MOWR were to be trained in the use of the modeling approaches and software to become capable of modifying the existing model and building new models of their own. The primary competing uses for water in Iraq include municipal and industrial development, agriculture, power generation, and reestablishing the Mesopotamian Marshes of southern Iraq.

In the following figures, results of a sample model can be seen, but in "real time" the results can be quickly modified as the user inputs new data. Despite the fact that data has been closely held by each country in a basin, enough model input data can be assembled by the users to provide meaningful results. In figure 6.1, for example, a sample is provided that predicts steadily decreasing transboundary river flow.

The model allows an analysis of water quality as well as water quantity. As a major component of water quality, salinization of water and soils presents a challenge for planners. Figure 6.2 shows the change in salinity for water passing across the border between country 1 and country 2.

Graphic representations can also be provided to reveal projected water shortages in multiple sectors under anticipated changes in upstream flow (see figure 6.3). For example, with a buildout of upstream transboundary dams in the next five years, there is a predicted 120-percent shortage of water for agriculture in that year. The model could be recalibrated with a slower buildout of dams, or changes in demand management (lining canals) in the downstream country.

This section indicates the range of scientific capabilities that could potentially lead to improved cooperation in the Euphrates-Tigris basin. The USIP made recommendations for a technical cooperation program with the following elements:

- practices for reliable end-to-end *data collection* about water flow, water quality, salinity, precipitation, irrigation, and consumption rates;

- practices for *data management,* exchange, and public availability according to the most advanced technical standards; and

- *institutional forums* to promote exchange and cooperation among technical experts in the region.[58]

A number of programs developed in the private sector also have the potential for application in the Euphrates-Tigris basin. IBM's advanced water management programs are designed to address the challenges of water efficiency, aging infrastructure, and increased demand for proactive water-related risk management.[59] IBM has programs to deal with the combination of volumes of data, the need for coordination of different and new data types, and the demand for real-time responses. IBM hopes

---

[58] Whitaker and Varghese, *Tigris-Euphrates River Basin*, 4.

[59] For an overview of IBM's advanced water management programs, see http://www-935 .ibm.com/services/us/gbs/bus/html/advanced-water-management.html.

FIGURE 6.1. **Sample inflow from country 1 to country 2: 5-year average**

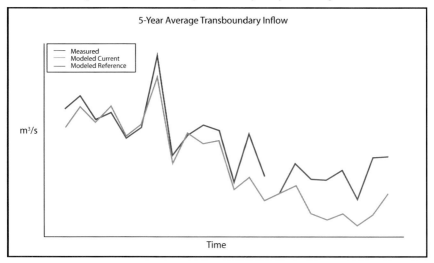

Adapted from Howard Passell, Wael Khairy, Marissa Reno, Jesse Roach, and Vince Tidwell, "Collaborative, Stakeholder-Driven Resource Modeling and Management," T. Gamelseid, ed., *Handbook of Research on Hydroinformatics: Technologies, Theories and Applications* (Hershey, PA: IGI Global Press, 2010), figure 4.

FIGURE 6.2. **Sample river salinity at border between country 1 and country 2: 5-year average**

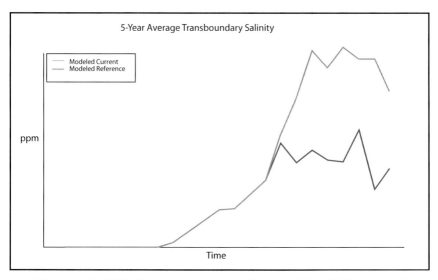

Adapted from Howard Passell, Wael Khairy, Marissa Reno, Jesse Roach, and Vince Tidwell, "Collaborative, Stakeholder-Driven Resource Modeling and Management," T. Gamelseid, ed., *Handbook of Research on Hydroinformatics: Technologies, Theories and Applications* (Hershey, PA: IGI Global Press, 2010), figure 5.

FIGURE 6.3. **Sample average shortages by sector**

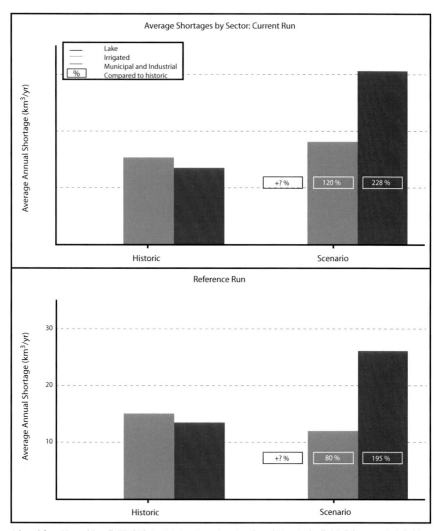

Adapted from Howard Passell, Wael Khairy, Marissa Reno, Jesse Roach, and Vince Tidwell, "Collaborative, Stakeholder-Driven Resource Modeling and Management," T. Gamelseid, Ed., *Handbook of Research on Hydroinformatics: Technologies, Theories and Applications* (Hershey, PA: IGI Global Press, 2010), figure 7.

to develop "next generation water management systems" that are "more flexible while providing more robust real-time analytics, modeling, and decision support capabilities."[60]

The U.S. technical and scientific capabilities described here are now available, but there are major obstacles in moving forward and making a contribution to cooperation in the Euphrates-Tigris basin.

Evaluation and Coordination of U.S. Efforts

There are dozens of programs that have been aimed at improving Iraq's control and management of its own water resources in the past 10 years. In chapter 3 the details of U.S. efforts for Iraq can be reviewed. For one example: in 2003 the U.S. Congress originally appropriated more than $4 billion for water and public works in Iraq, an amount that was subsequently reduced to $2.21 billion. For a variety of reasons, including inefficiency, corruption, and lack of security, little progress was made. Numerous examples can be found of failed and often oversold programs to rebuild Iraq's infrastructure with American dollars and skill.[61]

Some programs have a wider scope, making an attempt to promote basin-wide cooperation. A USAID-sponsored program called "Advancing the Blue Revolution Initiative" (ABRI) that operated between 2007 and 2009 appears to have been poorly managed and did little to achieve its original objectives.[62] One of the goals was to "promote transboundary water cooperation to improve water security." Millions of dollars were spent (it is difficult to tell exactly how much from the publicly available documents) with little return. Efforts to hold an international river basin workshop were cancelled "due to a lack of funds to sufficiently manage an activity of this size." Two ABRI components are described below (from the January

---

[60] For an example of a recent IBM project, see the program to develop real-time monitoring of the Hudson River and Estuary in New York. Project press release: http://www-03.ibm.com/press/us/en/pressrelease/22162.wss. Project Web site: http://www-03.ibm.com/press/us/en/photo/27451.wss.

[61] James Glanz, "Report Finds Iraq Water Treatment Project to Be Late, Faulty and Over Budget," *New York Times*, 27 October 2008.

[62] USAID, *Advancing the Blue Revolution Initiative: Quarterly Report 7; January–March 2009*, http://pdf.usaid.gov/pdf_docs/PDACT089.pdf (accessed 16 July 2012).

to March 2009 ABRI quarterly report), with comments on the apparent effectiveness of the proposed activity immediately following.

> Data Inventory. Data sets and resources are lacking in the TE [Tigris-Euphrates] Region. The effective management of water resources requires current and accurate information recognizing changes in water based studies and linking these trends with their likely causes. This task will create and maintain a data exchange network for the TE Region focusing on water, development, irrigation, soils, socio-economics, health, climate, environment, supplies, and demands information. This task will collect, process, and make available on the Internet a broad range of water and development based on above mentioned data on the TE Region, assemble these data that span the region, and assist in providing training on content and applications of these data through the Internet.[63]

This ABRI project certainly identifies a need and has laudable objectives, not to mention an appealing "revolutionary" name. But the "data inventory" never materialized; there was no meaningful plan for data collection, and no appreciation of the tremendous scope of the proposed project. A plan for a single data exchange network that would span "water, development, irrigation, soils, socio-economics, health, climate, environment, supplies, and demands information" is impossibly broad and would require planning and resources far beyond that contemplated by the ABRI project.

Another component of the program identified in the same ABRI quarterly report was a "clearinghouse":

> Clearinghouse. Our long-range goal is to establish an Internet-accessible clearinghouse of technical information on the TE region, tentatively modeled after the Great Lakes Information Network (GLIN), and to present this information in three languages: Arabic, Turkish, and English. GLIN has been the model for similar efforts, including the Baltic Sea Region On-Line Environmental Information Resources for Internet Access (BALLERINA), which is led by the United Nations Environment Programme (UNEP/GRID-Arendal) and the Stockholm Marine Research Centre,

---

[63] Ibid., 1.

with funding from the European Environment Agency, the ministries of environment in Norway and Sweden, and the Swedish Environmental Protection Agency. GLIN has also been a model for the Gulf of Maine Information Exchange (GOMINFOEX), a hydrological information system for the Upper Paraguay River Basin, and the Border Information and Solutions Network (BISN), a binational regional NGO [nongovernmental organization] that promotes sustainable development of the Mexico-USA border region by enhancing collaboration and communication through the Internet. Completion of this project would have high impact in the TE region by enhancing transboundary collaboration among riparians and by increasing international awareness of technical matters in the TE region.[64]

A clearinghouse is certainly a valid long-term objective, but there are very few parallels between the Euphrates-Tigris and the other basins described in the report. The Gulf of Maine Council on the Marine Environment was established in 1989 by the governments of Nova Scotia, New Brunswick, Maine, New Hampshire, and Massachusetts to foster cooperative actions within the Gulf of Maine watershed. GLIN and GOMINFOEX are located in North America in a heavily regulated, technically sophisticated, and politically cooperative environment.[65] The border information network is mentioned above as a possible model for collaboration and communication, but the organization and its Web site seem to have devolved primarily into a promotion site for Texas tourism and no river data could be found in a May 2011 search.

Based upon the authors' observation, there is minimum coordination and evaluation of the many U.S. scientific capabilities,[66] and each agency naturally promotes its own programs. The Web sites cited previously in this chapter tend to overstate the capability and provide little in the way of documentation of results achieved. There is always competition for visibility and resources; this will be even more intense in a time of a declining U.S. federal budget. Water-related programs funded by USAID have few

---

[64] Ibid., 1.

[65] Details on the Gulf of Maine Council are available at http://www.gulfofmaine.org/.

[66] The authors conducted research and interviewed officials at the U.S. State Department and USAID in the spring of 2011.

measures to evaluate and prioritize between programs. Moreover, multiple organizations have provided technical aid to Iraq, with no overarching vision or strategic plan. This was only one of the reasons that U.S. efforts in Iraq since 2003 have yielded little in the way of positive results.

The U.S. Department of State takes the lead in coordinating federal activities that provide support to the region, but the department is organized along lines that do not reflect the cross-boundary nature of the Twin Rivers. For instance, its Bureau of Near Eastern Affairs includes Syria, Iraq, and Iran but not Turkey, which is within the boundaries of the Bureau of European and Eurasian Affairs. A few individuals have a portfolio that includes the entire Euphrates-Tigris basin, but they are woefully understaffed and lack adequate resources to fully evaluate and coordinate all the technical programs.[67] The problem is not the technology, but evaluating it and coordinating federal efforts to be effective and have a lasting impact in the region.

In her remarks on World Water Day 2011, Secretary of State Hillary R. Clinton recognized the importance of water:

> Access to reliable supplies of clean water is a matter of human security. It's also a matter of national security. And that's why President Obama and I recognize that water issues are integral to the success of many of our major foreign policy initiatives.[68]

The proposed "five streams" of U.S. focus provide a framework to approach the critical themes covered in this book:

> First, we need to build capacity at the local, national, and regional levels. . . . We need to strengthen regional cooperative mechanisms for managing water resources that transcend national boundaries.

---

[67] Authors' conclusions are based on a series of phone calls and meetings in February and March 2011 with State Department and U.S. Army Corps of Engineers officials in Washington, DC. These officials preferred not to be quoted directly on the issue of coordination of federal efforts.

[68] Hillary R. Clinton, "World Water Day [2010]" (speech, National Geographic Society, Washington, DC, 22 March 2010), http://www.state.gov/secretary/rm/2010/03/138737.htm.

Second, we need to elevate our diplomatic efforts and we need to better coordinate them.

The third element of our water strategy is mobilizing financial support.

Fourth, we must harness the power of science and technology. . . . In cooperation with nearby countries, USAID and NASA are developing a system that will provide a clearer picture of water supply and demand for the region and facilitate efforts to adapt to climate change.

The final aspect of our water efforts is broadening the scope of our partnerships. By focusing on our strengths and leveraging our efforts against the work of others, we can deliver results that are greater than the sum of the parts.[69]

In a time of declining U.S. influence with Turkey, Syria, and Iraq, the most promising approach seems to be in the field of science and technology. For a comparatively low investment, the United States can provide the capabilities described in this chapter to the people of the Euphrates-Tigris basin. This type of support can increase understanding and improve relations in ways that military involvement and diplomatic pressure cannot. The real challenge is to properly coordinate the activities and to bridge the gap between science and diplomacy in delivering the support.

Coordinating International Efforts

In April 2011, there were signs of increasing international recognition that freshwater scarcity can be a threat to international peace and stability. "We think that water is an issue that would be appropriate for the U.N. Security Council," Zafar Adeel, chair of UN-Water, told the press prior to a meeting of experts in Toronto, Canada, on 21 March 2011, the day before World Water Day.[70] Adeel said the UN should try to promote past tradi-

---

[69] Ibid.

[70] Alister Doyle, "'Hydro-Diplomacy' Needed to Avert Arab Water Wars," Reuters, 20 March 2011, found at http://www.trust.org/alertnet/news/hydro-diplomacy-needed-to-avert -arab-water-wars/. UN-Water coordinates water-related activities of all UN agencies. The UN designated 22 March as World Water Day in 1993. See the UN-Water Web site for further information at http://www.unwater.org/.

tions of rivals cooperating over supplies in a form of "hydro-diplomacy." Yet renewed interest will not necessarily yield results, and much more needs to be done. Additionally, each country providing funds for international development has its own interests in the region it chooses for development aid and promotes the use of its own private companies to conduct the work.

In April 2010, Iraq signed an agreement for a strategic study of its water and land resources with two Italian companies at a cost of $35.8 million. "The contract will be implemented within 42 months," said the statement received by Aswat al-Iraq news agency. "The long term study represents the future policy of the water situation in Iraq, as it includes a comprehensive plan to develop water resources in Iraq until 2035 through the integrated management of the water resources." [71] Although a strategic plan is vitally important, the government of Iraq is certain to face major challenges in absorbing the contents of the plan and putting it into practice. Also, there seems to be no effort to coordinate the plan with any of the support and studies previously provided and funded by the U.S. government.

Thus, the fundamental problem remains: international organizations and various states provide assistance to Iraq with no overarching vision or strategic plan. Without better coordination, little hope for advancement can be expected.

The Challenge for Scientists and Engineers

Scientists are regularly generating more data on world water and developing more sophisticated software to manage it. An evolution in science has been described in a UNESCO report that should improve the sharing of knowledge, know-how, and techniques to respond to the challenges of the twenty-first century.

> Several major factors have transformed and will continue to affect the relationships between science and society as they have developed over the past

---

[71] *Iraq Business News*, "Iraq Signs Contract to Implement Water Strategy with Italian Companies," 30 April 2010, http://www.iraq-businessnews.com/2010/05/03/iraq-signs-contract-to-implement-water-strategy-with-italian-companies/.

fifty years. Great changes have been taking place in science itself, in terms of scale and the nature of inquiry. Boundaries between disciplines are breaking down, as are interfaces between science, technology, industry, university, etc.[72]

Scientists and engineers face a special challenge because they rarely have to deal with the politics and information outside their own field of knowledge. In traditional logic, water data should be shared by everyone; in the United States water flow and quality data are transparent and ubiquitous.

In Washington State, for instance, anyone can go to a computer and read the real-time flow data for every river and creek in the state when planning a kayak trip. Likewise, the Washington State Department of Ecology maintains detailed monitoring records of water quality, both for in-stream uses and drinking water.[73] From a U.S. perspective, it would seem natural and logical that water data could only lead to cooperation if developed and provided to all parties by a neutral third party. But Americans will always be viewed as outsiders in the Euphrates-Tigris basin, and as detailed in chapter 3, a very different insider discourse on the value and management of water is maintained in each of the basin countries.[74]

In the view of the authors of this book, a new breed of scientifically astute diplomats will be necessary to bridge the gap between science and diplomacy. Only this type of effort will yield a functioning system of data sharing in water basins such as the Euphrates-Tigris. There is one organization that might be able to assist, at least to help the U.S. diplomats charged with developing and implementing foreign policy. The American Association for the Advancement of Science has a Center for Science Diplomacy whose stated goal is "using science and scientific cooperation to promote international understanding and prosperity." The center "provides a forum for scientists, policy analysts, and policy-makers through which they can share information and explore collaborative opportuni-

---

[72] UNESCO Office of Public Information, "Science Agenda—Framework for Action," UNESCO, http://www.unesco.org/bpi/science/vf/content/press/franco/16.htm.

[73] See http://www.ecy.wa.gov/programs/eap/flow/shu_main.html for access to real-time data.

[74] Allan, *Middle East Water Question*, 8.

ties." It is "interested in identifying opportunities for science diplomacy to serve as a catalyst between societies where official relations might be limited, and to strengthen civil society interactions through partnerships in science and technology."[75]

Unique Challenges and Opportunities in the Euphrates-Tigris Basin

International relations concerning transboundary water can only achieve positive outcomes if the political will exists. The parties in the Euphrates-Tigris basin interact on water issues regularly, but on different levels— some public and some private. One important question is, how can the historic resistance of the basin countries to exchange data be changed? More importantly, how can Turkey be persuaded to participate in a new technical initiative in view of the traditional concern about "internationalizing" an issue that is firmly under Turkey's control?

The development of a program like the collaborative modeling and management discussed earlier and its implementation in the region could have unintended consequences. For example, the release of new developed data might show that salinity levels as the Euphrates flows from Turkey to Syria and Iraq are already high, and projected to be much higher in the next 10 years as the GAP develops. This would confirm the data already provided concerning high salinity levels, mentioned previously in chapter 3.[76] Would Turkey "accept" that data, or reject it and continue to keep control of its own information? As another example, the model provided by an outside agency to Iraq might show that its dam building plans were misguided, and Iraq needs to invest in smaller infrastructure improvements, such as lining canals, to avoid a water shortage. This could essentially prove the point that Turkey has made for years: there is plenty of water if Syria and Iraq use it more efficiently. Would Iraq participate in a program that would release this information to Turkey? This presents the diplomats' challenge, and innovative ways need to be developed if improved cooperation is sought. It calls for a renewed U.S.

---

[75] American Association for the Advancement of Science, "About the Center," American Association for the Advancement of Science, http://diplomacy.aaas.org/.

[76] See Trondalen, *Water and Peace*, and accompanying technical report.

science-diplomacy effort, training the right people in the U.S. Foreign Service and providing the resources and political will to be successful.

Diplomacy is always a matter of finding the right opportunities, and the dynamics in the Euphrates-Tigris basin are certainly entering a new phase. The Arab Spring has threatened the Assads' 40-year hold on power in Syria, and the outcome in that country is still to be seen. If there is a new Syrian government in the next few years, there could be a much more aggressive stance on the use of Euphrates water by Turkey. With a more stable and effective government, Iraq will be able to take a greater control of its own foreign policy regarding water. And the international community needs to be ready to respond effectively to whatever conditions prevail in the basin. The next two sections examine a unique opportunity for collaboration in the Euphrates-Tigris basin that could expand this new phase even further: the creation of an international center for the riparian nations modeled after one serving the Hindu Kush–Himalayan nations.

ICIMOD: A Model for the Euphrates-Tigris Basin?

Located in Kathmandu, Nepal, the International Centre for Integrated Mountain Development (ICIMOD) is a knowledge development and learning facility serving the eight member countries of the Hindu Kush–Himalaya region: Afghanistan, Bangladesh, Bhutan, China, India, Myanmar, Nepal, and Pakistan. The developers of ICIMOD recognize that globalization and climate change have an increasing influence on the stability of fragile mountain ecosystems and the livelihoods of mountain people. They "support regional transboundary programs through partnership with regional partner institutions, facilitate the exchange of experience, and serve as a regional knowledge hub."[77] ICIMOD is based on economic development and sharing of knowledge, with no powers to regulate water quantity or quality. This model could be more effective, and less threatening to Turkey, than the Nile and Mekong regimes that have been previously described.

---

[77] See ICIMOD (International Centre for Integrated Mountain Development), "About ICIMOD," http://www.icimod.org/?page=abt.

Proposal: The International Centre for Integrated Basin Development

At this point in the chapter, the authors would like to propose the creation of a development center for the riparian nations in the Euphrates-Tigris basin. A suggested name: the International Centre for Integrated Basin Development (ICIBAD; figure 6.4). All three riparian countries would be asked to participate; Turkey would be the natural host and should be pleased to take a leadership role, displaying the expertise shown at the Fifth World Water Forum in Istanbul in 2009. This might help overcome Turkey's traditional concern about "internationalizing" the issue. Turkey has already indicated a willingness, at least on the surface, to cooperate.[78]

A memorandum of understanding would carefully set out the responsibilities of the parties, and there could be multiple levels of data sharing and a regular series of training programs. Ideally, there would be a full-time staff, and facilities could be based in Turkey, probably in Urfa, a fast-developing city at the center of the GAP region. As with ICIMOD, the center's mission statement would be grounded in economic development and include the latest developments in dealing with climate change and the effects of globalization. At a time of increased political and military turmoil in the region, the economic model of the ICIBAD could prove to be the most effective approach. Coordinated action to mitigate the impact of climate change would be a theme to garner international support and attention.

A Science-Diplomacy Opportunity

Science and diplomacy can make a major contribution in advancing the aims of cooperation and stability in the Euphrates-Tigris basin, but only with a careful prioritization of programs, better coordination, and an increase in the training of U.S. diplomats will it be possible. Another point was emphasized in the 2012 report of the National Intelligence Council that "US expertise on water resource management in both the public and

---

[78] See, for instance, Republic of Turkey Ministry of Foreign Affairs, "Turkey's Policy on Water Issues," section titled "Turkey's Transboundary Water Policy": "Turkey is eager to find ways of reaching a basis for cooperation, which will improve the quality of life of the peoples of the three countries."

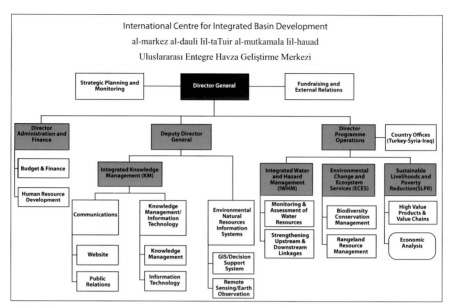

FIGURE 6.4. **Proposed International Centre for Integrated Basin Development (ICIBAD) organizational chart**

private sectors is highly regarded and will be sought after worldwide."[79] The wealth of resources that can be applied to the problem has been summarized in this chapter and is noted in a new program called the Water Partnership, and the need for careful coordination is emphasized.

> The United States has much to contribute to solving the global water challenge. For instance, we have a huge wealth of water information and resources spread throughout the federal government, state and local government agencies, the private sector, NGOs and academic research institutions, but there is no single mechanism or platform for uniting and mobilizing this rich profusion to share with those most in need. Individual solutions are being scaled up (more wells, more hydropower dams, etc.) and it is imperative that we consider such solutions from an integrative trans-sector perspective so as not to cause other larger problems.[80]

[79] Director of National Intelligence, *Global Water Security* (2012), vi, http://www.dni.gov/files/documents/Special%20Report_ICA%20Global%20Water%20Security.pdf.

[80] U.S. Department of State, Bureau of Oceans and International Environmental Scientific Affairs, *U.S. Water Partnership* (Washington, DC: Department of State, 2012), http://www.state.gov/e/oes/rls/fs/2012/186581.htm.

Judging from the statements of Secretary Clinton, we can be hopeful that the U.S. government has identified the problem and is developing the political will to move ahead. She pointed out that "it actually is our duty and responsibility to make sure that this water issue stays at the very top of America's foreign policy and national security agenda."[81] There lies the challenge. The final chapter of this book will take a look at the nature of the coming crisis and make some specific recommendations for the United States and the international community.

---

[81] Hillary R. Clinton, "Remarks in Honor of World Water Day [2012]" (speech, George C. Marshall Auditorium, Washington, DC, 22 March 2012), http://www.state.gov/secretary/rm/2012/03/186640.htm.

CHAPTER 7

THE APPROACHING CRISIS AND A FRAMEWORK FOR ACTION

The previous chapters of this book reviewed the current research and explored how water scarcity might cause instability in a volatile region of the world—the Euphrates-Tigris basin. This book is written from the perspective of the year 2013 with the understanding that the political landscape and natural environment may change dramatically in the space of a few short years. Although the subject is complex and conditions in the region seem to be shifting daily, some basic conclusions can be drawn:

1. History should inform any study of water issues in the Euphrates-Tigris basin. Water scarcity is compounded by serious environmental problems that have grown out of the ancient cycle of deforestation, desertification, soil erosion, salination, and the contamination of water supplies. But today we are in much better position than the Sumerians to understand the nature of the problem and to find effective ways to deal with it.

2. The geopolitical landscape in the Euphrates-Tigris basin is fragile but promising. The political entities of the riparian nations have much in common historically, economically, and

socially. Dramatic political changes that began in the Arab Spring could provide new opportunities for cooperation on water resources.

3. Although the level of regional water scarcity in the next 10 to 15 years is difficult to measure precisely, Syria and Iraq can be expected to experience crisis conditions as available freshwater declines. Based on available research, climate change will have a significant impact, and the nature of this impending crisis will be explored later in this chapter.

4. Turkey will have little or no capability to "turn off the tap" and use water as a strategic weapon. But the perception in Syria and Iraq of Turkey's control over the waters of the Euphrates will continue to be a major factor in their relationship.

5. Even more important than water quantity, the issue of increasing salinity is of vital concern to Iraq. Recent studies have documented the dangerous levels for the first time, and this will further complicate water management in the region.

6. Despite the continued emphasis in the region on new dams and infrastructure by all the riparian nations, more can be achieved by demand management and increased efficiency of existing facilities, particularly in Syria and Iraq.

7. A strong central government is essential to effectively managing the water resources of any country, and increasing Kurdish autonomy and development of the Tigris basin will have a negative impact on Iraq's overall policies and positions.

8. Hydropolitics is a multilayered and complex game; Iraq and Syria are at a serious disadvantage. Instability and inefficiency in water management will provide additional obstacles to both countries.

9. Despite many years of development, international water law plays only a minor role in the Euphrates-Tigris basin. With many divergent theories and no effective enforcement mechanism, the law will not provide meaningful redress to Syria and Iraq as they face increasing water scarcity.

10. Science and diplomacy can make a major contribution in advancing the aims of cooperation and stability in the Euphrates-Tigris basin, but only with a careful prioritization of programs, better coordination, and the necessary political will.

11. Although Turkey has few incentives or imperatives to cooperate based on its geographic, political, economic, and military superiority, opportunities should still be attainable when national interests coincide.

The Approaching Crisis: Potential Threats and Possible Outcomes

The term "crisis" may seem alarmist, but it is used here with a caveat. Will there be a water war in the Euphrates-Tigris basin in the next 10 to 20 years, when the GAP (Southeastern Anatolia Project) in Turkey significantly impacts the natural flow of the rivers? Rather than a classic shooting war, we are more likely to see rising tensions, exacerbated relations, population displacement, human suffering, and localized violence.

What might an approaching water crisis in the basin actually look like, and how would it affect the three nations most directly involved? What are the broader implications of such a crisis, and how would it affect international peace and security? As mentioned in the introduction, this is not a book of predictions, but a look at potential situations that should be of concern to those inside and outside the region. In this chapter, we will attempt to look ahead to the next 10–15 years (to approximately 2023–28) and identify possible outcomes.

With additional demands being made on the Tigris and Euphrates by uncooperative parties, water quantity and quality will be an important factor in regional instability, leading to a decline in economic and public health conditions. This decline, in turn, will make the region's peoples more susceptible to fundamentalism and extremism, thereby undermining recent security gains, particularly in Iraq. In 2012 the National Intelligence Council confirmed this concern.

However, we judge that as water shortages become more acute beyond the next 10 years, water in shared basins will increasingly be used as leverage; the use of water as a weapon or to further terrorist objectives also will become more likely beyond 10 years.[1]

In his article "Waterworld," Robert Kaplan looks at the potential consequences of climate change and rising sea levels in Bangladesh.[2] He describes how the explosive mix of environmental degradation, human misery, and religious extremism is at work to destabilize the government. Water shortages can provoke the same results as people find it more difficult to live their daily lives. This can in turn cause the people to resort to extremism and violence as their only recourse against an unresponsive government.

Iraq is already faced with the major challenges of factionalism and a lack of public respect for the government and security forces. Some scholars are warning that large numbers of environmental refugees could be among the most significant of all upheavals caused by global warming and climate change.[3] Movement of "climate refugees" from Iraq to neighboring countries would be certain to heighten tensions and make cooperation in other areas more difficult. Already there are reports of major displacements within Iraq as rural people "fleeing in droves from the increasingly arid provinces" show up in the cities.[4] As mentioned in chapter 3, the precise impact of climate change in the Euphrates-Tigris basin is uncertain, but it is sure to complicate an already dangerous situation.

---

[1] Director of National Intelligence, *Global Water Security*, 3.

[2] Robert D. Kaplan, "Waterworld," *Atlantic*, January–February 2008, 60.

[3] Norman Myers, "Environmental Refugees in a Globally Warmed World," *BioScience* 43, no. 11 (1993): 752–61. Also see Thomas L. Friedman, "Without Water, Revolution," *New York Times*, 18 May 2013.

[4] Martin Chulov, "Iraq: Water Nowhere," *World Policy Journal* 26 (December 2009): 38.

In 2011 there were disturbing signs of instability based on regional food shortages; riots over food prices can even affect governments with a good record of keeping order.[5] This unrest could be a prelude to a greater threat when water supplies and water quality decline. Recent events in Darfur, Sudan, and southwestern Somalia, for example, provide a glimpse of a situation where water scarcity contributes to a volatile combination of political, economic, and military problems that seem all but impossible to solve. But history teaches that there are things that can be done to avoid such problems, or at least to limit the negative consequences. And there is increasing concern that the turbulence of the Arab Spring can be tied to water issues.[6]

An international economic risk analysis group recently released a report that classifies countries on a "water security risk list." Iraq and Syria rank in the top 10 countries in terms of risk as numbers 7 and 10, respectively. The list was developed to "enable business and investors to identify the countries where water supply will be limited or interrupted in the future." Water security was measured for each country by looking at water stress; population rates; reliance on external water supplies; sustainability of water use; intensity of water use in the economy; government effectiveness; and virtual water use, the assessment of the water intensity of imported goods such as food and oil. This is just another indication that water stress is closely bound with issues of economics, stability, and food security. It has broad implications for the international community and the development of a strategically vital part of the world.[7]

Following the research of Tony Allan mentioned in earlier chapters, one of the themes of this book concerns water pessimism and optimism. The pessimists may be wrong in the long term, but their views can help generate

---

[5] Josh Kron, "Protests in Uganda Over Rising Prices Grow Violent," *New York Times*, 21 April 2011. Uganda is one of the most stable and prosperous countries in Sub-Saharan Africa, but opposition political elements can use food prices and popular dissatisfaction as a powerful tool to induce violence there.

[6] Friedman, "Without Water."

[7] Maplecroft, "Oil Producing Middle East and North African Countries Dominate Maplecroft Water Security Risk List," Maplecroft news, 22 March 2011, http://www.maplecroft.com/about/news/water_security.html.

initiatives to deal with the problems. Below are some possible outcomes that look ahead 10 to 15 years.

The positive outcome. A stable Iraq with a developing economy has the ability to successfully manage its own foreign affairs. In the water sector, Iraq has developed and properly implemented a long-range plan to manage its own water resources. Cooperation with Turkey and Syria on water issues has increased, leading to an active "sharing of benefits" in terms of technical expertise and trade in food and oil. The Kurdish Regional Government has resolved most of the issues related to Kirkuk and oil and has relegated control of water issues to the central Iraqi government. International efforts to aid security and the developing economy in the region have been successful. Although its available water has not increased, Iraq has learned to use water more efficiently and overcome the serious threat posed by high salinity levels.

The negative outcome. Continued instability in Iraq makes the development of an effective foreign policy, and coordinated water management, impossible. The fall of the Assad regime in Syria leads to factional strife and continued unrest within the country. Cooperation with Turkey and Syria on water issues has declined, leading to a general breakdown in technical exchanges and trade in food and oil. International efforts to aid security and the developing economy have not been successful. Iraq continues down the path of water inefficiency and fails to overcome the serious threat posed by high salinity levels. Extremist elements in Iraq and Syria take advantage of increasing public unrest, the central government collapses, and countries break down into a perpetual state of civil war with the potential of becoming failed states. Water is not the primary causal factor, but a significant contributing element.

The likely outcome. An increasingly stable Iraq has a growing economy and improved relations with its neighbors. In the water sector, Iraq still has challenges in managing its own water resources. Cooperation with Turkey and Syria on water issues is stable but only on the technical level, despite increasing pressure from declining water quantity and quality. The Kurdish Regional Government is operating autonomously and now controls and manages its own water issues. International efforts to aid security and the developing economy in the region have had some success but still face challenges. The water crisis in Iraq ultimately reaches a level that increases tensions and human suffering, leading to localized violence and preventing the Iraqi government and its people from realizing their full potential. In the authors' view, this is still an optimistic scenario.[8]

What, if anything, can be done to avoid negative consequences? There may now be a historic opportunity for a number of initiatives that can benefit the people of the region and promote regional security. Science and diplomacy may provide some of the most promising options, and the time for action is upon us. Despite the current turmoil in Syria and Iraq, the parties have demonstrated the ability to meet and discuss confidence-building measures that could lay the groundwork for further cooperation. Despite Turkey's views of outside interference, the momentum should be carried to the next level. Even if the government of Syria undergoes a major transition, there could be room for innovative diplomatic initiatives on the water issue.

At this point, it is clear there are multiple obstacles to prosperity and stability in the Euphrates-Tigris basin. Nevertheless, there are a number of relevant options, and years of experience in other basins, that can provide a framework for action.

Some Possible Solutions

Better Management

Integrated Water Resources Management (IWRM) is a relatively new concept that promotes the linking of land-use hydrological models with economics and ecology as a framework for integrated management.[9] In many developing countries, rapid changes are taking place in land use

---

[8] In the remaining parts of the chapter, the authors will use the "estimative language" contained in Director of National Intelligence, *Global Water Security*, "Annex," 13. The term "likely" generally means a greater than even chance. The authors reach this conclusion with a "moderate" degree of confidence.

[9] Ian R. Calder, *The Blue Revolution: Land Use and Integrated Water Resources Management* (London: Earthscan, 1999), 2.

and water resource impacts without a clear plan or effective management techniques. International organizations, including the United Nations (UN) and the World Water Council, are developing tools and models to prevent the long-term degradation of land and water resources.

A series of international conferences and forums have played a key role in the development of the IWRM concept, starting with the UN's conference on the human environment in Stockholm in 1972. The first UN water conference at Mar del Plata, Argentina, in 1977 was a key meeting that promoted the importance of water and water management to world governments. In 1992, the International Conference on Water and the Environment in Dublin, Ireland, was an opportunity for water experts from governmental and nongovernmental organizations (NGOs) to develop proposals to be presented at the UN Conference on Environment and Development in Rio de Janeiro, Brazil, later that year.

At the Rio conference (also known as the Rio Summit or the Earth Summit), the UN adopted the *Dublin Statement on Water and Sustainable Development*, first presented at the earlier Dublin conference, and the conference report, which recognized that the problems of water scarcity and management were not purely speculative but that "the future survival of many millions of people demands immediate and effective action."[10] The conference called for fundamental new approaches to the assessment, development, and management of freshwater resources and changes that could only be brought about by political commitment and involvement from the highest levels of government to the smallest communities.

The Fifth World Water Forum, held in Istanbul in 2009, brought together experts concerned about the world's dwindling supply of freshwater. The purpose was to create an action agenda as a follow-up to a number of prior meetings on water issues. It included the goals set forth at the UN's Millennium Summit in New York (2000); the International Freshwater Conference in Bonn, Germany (2001); and the World Summit on

---

[10] See International Conference on Water and the Environment, *The Dublin Statement on Water and Sustainable Development* (Dublin, 1992), http://www.wmo.int/pages/prog/hwrp /documents/english/icwedece.html.

Sustainable Development in Johannesburg, South Africa (2002). The 2000 ministerial declaration of the Second World Water Forum at The Hague identified meeting basic water needs, securing food supply, protecting ecosystems, sharing water resources, managing risks, valuing water, and governing water wisely as the key challenges for our direct future.[11] A number of this forum's sessions were devoted to IWRM issues, as well as to efforts to promote peace and cooperation in international river basins. The 2009 World Water Forum also provided Turkey with an opportunity to showcase its own progress in managing water resources. Declarations and national posturing at international water conferences often result in grand statements that prove very difficult to implement, but they still can provide the groundwork for planning at the regional and local levels.

There are three essential principles of IWRM: the basics of river basin management, full recovery of cost and appropriate pricing of water, and public participation in basin management decisions. River basin management implies a reallocation of power among administrative bodies and definitions of new and competent authorities for each basin.[12] Over the past 10 years, many of Turkey's environmental reforms have been driven by a desire for European Union (EU) membership and have been guided and funded in large part by the EU. The EU's water quality and management standards have played a significant role in water resources development, but Turkish prospects for EU membership are clouded by numerous issues ranging from Cyprus to human rights and political reforms, as well as by questions of how "European" Turkey really is.

While Turkey remains an EU candidate, the EU's standards may have a beneficial impact on water quality and management issues for Turkey. If Turkey gains EU admission, there will be continued progress and positive reinforcement for cooperation with Syria and Iraq on water issues. In the

---

[11] See Ministerial Declaration of The Hague, *Second World Water Forum: Ministerial Declaration of The Hague on Water Security in the 21st Century*, http://www.idhc.org/esp /documents/Agua/Second_World_Water_Forum%5B1%5D.pdf (accessed 17 July 2012).

[12] See Carlos Gonzales-Anton and Carlos Arias, "The Incorporation of Integrated Management in European Water Policy," in *Integrated Water Resources Management*, eds. Miguel A. Marino and Slobodan P. Simonovic (Wallingford, UK: International Association of Hydrological Sciences, 2001), 69.

long term, the question of benefit is more difficult to calculate, particularly if Turkey turns away from the EU. Because of Turkey's dominant geographic, military, and political position in the Euphrates-Tigris basin, EU standards could have a basinwide impact. Prospects for Turkey and the EU have dimmed in recent years, however, and Turkish reforms will likely be driven by interests other than EU membership.[13]

The real challenge to IWRM in the Euphrates-Tigris basin is the fractured nature of the political boundaries. The foundations for the current difficulties were laid during the colonial period when water management was a relatively low priority (see chapter 1). Today Turkey clearly has the superior water management practices in the region, but only as it relates to its own resources. Even with the "positive outcome" mentioned previously in this chapter, an effective basinwide management plan will be unlikely in the short or long term. Nevertheless, the IWRM principles can strengthen basin planning for all the parties, particularly Iraq as it moves to develop its own strategic water resources plan.

Building Confidence

Emerging during the Cold War, confidence-building measures (CBMs) are an important component of arms control methodology. They help to cement ties and build mutual interdependence. CBMs have direct application to water disputes and are relevant to current conditions in the Euphrates-Tigris basin. In a 2003 article, James Kraska described six basic advantages to CBMs:

1. They tend to restrain nations in exchange for restraint from other nations.

2. They encourage rational behavior by building certainty and dispelling uncertainty.

3. They buy time to prevent surprise.

4. They provide "rules of the road" for crisis management.

---

[13] The authors have high confidence in this conclusion.

5. They provide assurances and reassurances by reflecting the belief that increasing familiarity at all levels makes conflict less likely.

6. They diffuse coercion directed against member states.[14]

CBMs have no universally accepted definition; they provide a basket of concepts rather than a particular tool. The Henry L. Stimson Center in Washington, DC, which has been engaged for over a decade in studying the application of CBMs, describes them as "diverse national security tools, such as hot lines, people-to-people exchange, prior notification of exercises and cross-border economic projects that can help defuse tension, resolve misunderstanding, and promote cooperation to address security concerns."[15] The concept of CBMs began in Europe during the Cold War, and by using them substantial progress was made in improving the polarized relationship between the United States and NATO on the one side, and the Soviet Union and the Communist bloc on the other.

The Conference on Security and Cooperation in Europe grew out of an informal mechanism to begin dialogue based on the Helsinki Final Act of 1975. It has since matured into the Organization for Security and Cooperation in Europe (OSCE) with 55 member states, including Russia and the United States. The OSCE had success with a number of measures designed to promote mutual trust and dispel concern about military activities by encouraging openness and transparency.[16] OSCE efforts resulted in a number of arms control agreements, including the Intermediate-Range Nuclear Forces Treaty that was ratified by the U.S. Senate in 1988. As illustrated below, there are a number of parallels between arms control agreements and international water agreements, with common elements of diplomacy, pragmatism, and national interest.

---

[14] James Kraska, "Sustainable Development Is Security: The Role of Transboundary River Agreements as a Confidence Building Measure (CBM) in South Asia," *Yale Journal of International Law* 28 (Summer 2003): 465.

[15] Benjamin L. Self and Ranjeet K. Singh, "Introduction," in *Investigating Confidence-Building Measures in the Asia–Pacific Region*, ed. Ranjeet K. Singh (Washington, DC: Henry L. Stimson Center, 1999), ix, http://www.stimson.org/images/uploads/research-pdfs/cbmapintro.pdf.

[16] See Kraska, "Sustainable Development," 470.

In the case of India, Pakistan, and Bangladesh, the introduction and management of transboundary river agreements has helped to build confidence and reduce the risk of military confrontation between the parties. The Indus and Ganges basins in South Asia create a contentious area of political instability and recurring threats. With both India and Pakistan as members of the "nuclear club," perhaps nowhere else in the world presents a greater threat for neighboring states to come to the brink of nuclear war. But even during the crisis between Pakistan and India in 2002, following the 2001 attack on the Indian parliament, the annual meeting of the Permanent Indus Commission to discuss water issues between the two countries was not cancelled.[17]

Between Bangladesh and India, the Ganges Treaty (1996) helped transform the relationship between the countries for the better, despite the fact that water issues have historically aggravated nationalist tensions. This treaty sets out a schedule of river flows with several assurances that an equitable division of the river is the target. There is a verification regime embedded in the treaty and a commitment to "the principles of equity, fairness and no harm to either party." Although the agreement has been heavily criticized by nationalist factions in each country, it remains in force and provides a baseline for cooperation.

Experience in the Indus and Ganges basins shows that there can be a collective benefit for nations that share water resources, starting with nonbinding agreements that provide for the simple exchange of data and moving toward more formal regimes. Finally, agreements on water issues can positively impact the broader context of international relations and regional security. Turkey has favorably endorsed the concept of CBMs,[18] and this could help develop initiatives that will lead to further cooperation in the Euphrates-Tigris basin. Examples of such initiatives might include expanded technical cooperation, as discussed later in this chapter.

Better Training

In recent years, the plight of Arab countries in dealing with water issues

---

[17] Ibid., 492.

[18] Republic of Turkey, *Turkey Water Report 2009*, 48.

has received increased attention. It has been demonstrated in this book that Syria and Iraq will soon be unable to meet current water demand. Indeed, they will likely face full-blown crises in the future, and the situation is likely to get worse. Per capita water availability will fall by half by 2050, with serious consequences for the region's already stressed aquifers and natural hydrological systems. As the region's economies and population structures change over the next few decades, demands for water supply and irrigation services will change accordingly, as will the need to address industrial and urban pollution. Throughout the Arab world, some 60 percent of the region's water flows across international borders, further complicating the resource management challenge. Finally, rainfall and evaporation patterns are predicted to shift as a result of climate change.

A number of questions are now at the forefront of discussion, and the Arab countries are beginning to look at their own practices in the water sector. Are countries in the Arab region able to adapt their current water management practices to meet these combined challenges? If they cannot, the social, economic, and budgetary consequences could be enormous. Potable water services will probably become more erratic than they already are, and as a result cities will have to rely more and more on expensive desalination and during droughts will be forced to rely more frequently on emergency supplies brought by tanker or barge. Service outages will stress expensive network and distribution infrastructure. For irrigated agriculture, unreliable water services will depress farmers' incomes. The economic and physical dislocation associated with the depletion of aquifers or unreliability of supplies will increase, and local conflicts could intensify. All of this will exacerbate social tensions within and between communities and put increasing pressure on public budgets.

In response to these concerns, the Arab Water Academy was established in July 2008 in Abu Dhabi under the patronage of Sheikh Hamdan bin Zayed al-Nahyan, deputy prime minister of the United Arab Emirates and chairman of the Environment Agency–Abu Dhabi. Hosted by the Islamic Development Bank's Dubai-based International Center for Biosaline Agriculture, in partnership with the Environment Agency–Abu Dhabi, the water academy is a groundbreaking, regional-capacity development program targeting decision makers and industry executives.[19] The academy is closely associated with the Cairo-based Arab Water Council and is supported by the Environment Agency, the Islamic Development Bank, and the World Bank. Its mission is to transform the governance and management of water in the Arab region. Its overall aim is to encourage and support the emergence of new ways of thinking and acting about water that will allow decision makers to successfully meet the growing challenges of water scarcity in the region. In combination with other initiatives, this effort has the potential to make real progress in avoiding a regional crisis over water.

Some Reports and Proposals to Deal with the Problem

The Academic and Scientific Literature: A Summary

There is no shortage of academic studies that identify a host of problems in the Middle East water sector and provide some suggested solutions. The work of Tony Allan has been groundbreaking, providing an economic and political framework to understand the nature of the problem.[20] The leading Turkish scholar on the subject, Ayşegül Kıbaroğlu, recognizes that the three riparians continue to carry out uncoordinated water development projects coupled with inefficient water use and management practices.[21] She concludes that progress is likely dependent on strong trade relations between Turkey and Iraq. The leading American scholar on the Euphrates-Tigris, John Kolars, suggests the development of a "river ethic" for the basin that would view the rivers as a vulnerable whole and recognize the mutual dependency of the parties.[22] Other authors have made valuable contributions to the discussion, providing insight on how to make progress in possible negotiations between powerful parties (Turkey) and downstream riparians (Syria and Iraq).[23]

---

[19] For more information, visit the academy's Web site at http://www.awacademy.ae/.

[20] In particular, see Allan's *The Middle East Water Question: Hydropolitics and the Global Economy*.

[21] Kıbaroğlu, *Building a Regime*, 269.

[22] Kolars, "Defining the Political/Ecological Threshold," 107.

[23] Daoudy, "Asymmetric Power," 382.

In *Managing and Transforming Water Conflicts*, a comprehensive and thoughtful study of worldwide water conflicts, Aaron Wolf and Jerome Delli Priscoli observe that the debate is frequently heavy on problems and light on solutions.[24] To remedy this, Wolf and Delli Priscoli suggest a "retrospective balance of benefits and costs," but this would be difficult in the Euphrates-Tigris basin. There has been very little progress in terms of projects and programs with respect to water, and "developments in the basin have been made unilaterally without the cooperation of other riparian countries."[25] Nevertheless, we will attempt to provide a preliminary cost-benefit analysis for the final recommendations at the end of this chapter. This will also include some estimates of likelihood that the proposals could eventually be implemented.[26]

Three significant reports and studies deserve special mention at this point in our discussion.

The Trondalen Study (2008)

The most significant study for the Euphrates-Tigris basin was conducted by Jon Martin Trondalen and published as part of the United Nations Educational, Scientific and Cultural Organization's (UNESCO's) Water and Conflict Resolution Series.[27] The study focuses primarily on the Euphrates principally due to the availability of historic data and opportunities for sampling; it is discussed in more detail in chapter 3. Its technical annex provides important data on the nature of the threat to Iraq from increased pollution from agricultural return flow in the near term.

Trondalen's study goes further than other reports in providing detailed recommendations and models designed for increased cooperation. He first provides two alternative models for a trilateral water agreement

---

[24] Delli Priscoli and Wolf, *Managing and Transforming Water Conflicts*, xxiv.

[25] Ibid., 245.

[26] For these estimates, the authors use the terminology in the "Annex" to *Global Water Security* by the Director of National Intelligence.

[27] See Trondalen, *Water and Peace for the People: Possible Solutions to Water Disputes in the Middle East* (2008).

between the parties.[28] Two models are necessary, in his view, based on the fact that Turkey argues a "single basin" and Iraq argues a "separate basin" theory. In any event, he concludes that without a trilateral agreement, "irreversible damage" will soon occur to Iraq as irrigation volumes increase. He sets a proposed "absolute minimum flow level" for the Euphrates as it enters Iraq at 450 cubic meters per second. This rate would presumably be set by a trilateral agency and would be a monumental step forward from the existing bilateral arrangements.[29]

A unique aspect of the Trondalen study is a proposal for mitigating cross-border pollution (including high salinity) through a third-party compensation mechanism.[30] This is built on the assumption, now well documented, that irrigation return flows are the root of the problem. Trondalen proposes that the international community, including the World Bank and the United Nations Development Programme (UNDP) Global Environmental Facility,[31] cover the incremental costs of a scheme to achieve minimum water quality standards. He recognizes that the amount of funds required would be so large that only a "multi-donor effort" would be able to meet the requirements.

Another innovative aspect of Trondalen's study is his proposal for the establishment of a desalination plant[32] on the Euphrates River on the Syrian side of the border that would treat river water before it enters Iraq. In support of this, he describes a mechanism in the United States that is designed to maintain water quality in the Colorado River as part of an agreement between the United States and Mexico. Although an interesting comparison and proposal, the Colorado River facility in Arizona is

---

[28] Ibid., 195.

[29] Ibid. Based upon the analysis in the previous chapters, the authors believe (with moderate confidence) that such a proposal is very unlikely to be implemented in the short or long term.

[30] Ibid., 199.

[31] See UNDP, "International Waters," http://web.undp.org/gef/do_iwaters.shtml: "This includes developing capacity in integrated water resources management, and water supply and sanitation."

[32] Desalination is discussed in more detail in chapter 3, including its high costs, risks, and benefits in developing countries.

only functioning at a minimal level 38 years after it was authorized by the U.S. Congress.[33] In fact, the plant has sat idle for most of the 20 years since its completion in 1992. The high cost, changing technology, and availability of other options have all played a part in the plant's history.

In 2010 the Arizona desalination plant geared up for a test run at a cost of $23 million, but it is unlikely that the plant will ever reach its design potential. One news report described the situation in 2009:

> The desalination plant, here in Yuma, about 30 miles north of the Cienega [de Santa Clara, a wetland in Mexico], is a $256 million federal facility that although completed 17 years ago, has never run beyond two brief trial periods. It has been long maligned as among the federal government's biggest white elephants, a plant essentially mothballed from the start by budget and technical difficulties and the vagaries of the Colorado River supply.[34]

Other measures, such as local water conservation and proper water pricing to farmers, might be less expensive in the long run for the Colorado River. Although the Arizona example of in-stream desalination may not provide a model for the Euphrates, there may be some applicable lessons learned from the Colorado River experience. For instance, it could provide support for the development of more training programs and make U.S. technical expertise available to water professionals in the Euphrates-Tigris basin.

Another major difference between the situation on the Colorado and on the Euphrates-Tigris is the relationship between the United States and Mexico. The Arizona facility was funded by the United States in compliance with a treaty that required it to provide a minimum flow to Mexico. But no legally binding allocation agreement is likely between Turkey, Syria, and Iraq, and a huge investment will not be made based entirely on goodwill. In-stream desalination (that is, a plant located in

---

[33] Tony Davis, "Yuma Desalination Plant to Start Flowing," *Arizona Daily Star*, 1 May 2010, http://azstarnet.com/news/science/health-med-fit/article_8e4f368f-1779-50cc-b084 -3f265e1912a4.html#ixzz1S6M2UwwQ.

[34] Randal C. Archibold, "Eyes Turn to Mexico as Drought Drags On," *New York Times*, 14 September 2009.

the Euphrates River) is not a feasible solution to the problem.[35] Although many of Trondalen's proposals may seem impractical, he should be credited for his groundbreaking work and his vision for the future of the Euphrates-Tigris basin.

The Geopolicity Report (2010)

In a report commissioned by the UNDP,[36] Geopolicity—an international management consultancy group—focused on the challenges facing Iraq in its management of the Euphrates-Tigris watershed. This report recognizes that if the Iraqi constitution of 2005 were to be fully implemented, and new regional entities evolved within Iraq, then the complexity of managing the utilization of water resources will increase immeasurably. The Geopolicity authors note that "each upstream administrative division enhances the risk that they divert water in an unsustainable way, to the eventual detriment of downstream users."[37] This supports the comments in chapter 4 of this book relative to the impact of an autonomous Kurdistan on the waters of the Twin Rivers.

The Geopolicity report is available online, unlike the Trondalen and *The Blue Peace* reports cited in this section. It also provides a detailed look at internal Iraqi governmental structures and advances made in the planning process. Yet in spite of gains in strategic planning, the report concludes there is no "sector wide approach, and no integrated riparian framework" to bind the various sectors of the Iraqi government together.[38]

The report concludes with an ambitious 12-step action plan with the goal of strengthening strategic water resource management across the Euphrates-Tigris watershed. The first key element includes a "permanent trilateral commission tasked with monitoring and oversight" that would include Iran.[39] Although this proposal does not go quite as far as the tri-

---

[35] The authors have high confidence in this conclusion.

[36] See Geopolicity, *Managing the Tigris Euphrates Watershed: The Challenge Facing Iraq* (2010), http://www.geopolicity.com/upload/content/pub_1293090043_regular.pdf.

[37] Ibid., 41.

[38] Ibid., 40.

[39] Ibid., 57.

lateral agency with allocation powers proposed by Trondalen, it clearly goes beyond the current regime that is built primarily on bilateral relationships. Additional parts of the action plan call for the creation of an Iraqi National Water Authority and the development of a strategic water resources master plan. The recommendations are primarily directed to the Iraqi government; at the time of this writing, it is not clear if any of the recommendations have been absorbed or implemented.

The Blue Peace Report (2011)

The Strategic Foresight Group recently completed a report titled *The Blue Peace: Rethinking Middle East Water* that was designed to provide a "comprehensive, long-term regional framework for thinking about water in the Middle East."[40] Funded by the governments of Sweden and Switzerland as well as other donors, this study covers the riparian countries of the Jordan basin as well as the Euphrates-Tigris. It includes useful data, cited earlier in chapter 3 of this book, with separate sections on Turkey, Syria, and Iraq. The report summarizes available water resources as well as anticipated changes in supply and demand. Although the data is incomplete, it also provides some predictions for the impact of climate change and the anticipated water deficit for each country in coming years.

The basinwide initiative for cooperation is a recurring theme in all three of the reports and studies mentioned in this section. Recommendations in *The Blue Peace* include a "Cooperation Council" with all three riparian countries working to promote research; create regional protocols; develop principles of cooperation; and prepare the ground for basinwide, integrated water management. There is also mention of joint desalination plants, with the recognition that the current technology is energy intensive and financially beyond the reach of most nations in the Middle East.[41]

---

[40] Strategic Foresight Group, *The Blue Peace*, i.

[41] Desalination has been successful primarily in the Gulf States (Saudi Arabia and the United Arab Emirates), where oil revenue and effective government planning and management have made it successful. The authors have a high degree of confidence that desalination is unlikely to provide meaningful assistance to Syria or Iraq, even in the long term.

Another recommendation in *The Blue Peace* concerns mitigation and control of the growing regional water demand. Despite the continued emphasis in the region on new dams and infrastructure, more can be achieved by demand management and increased efficiency of existing facilities, particularly in Syria and Iraq. This can be implemented in the short term, with a relatively low capital expenditure, compared to the cost of new infrastructure. *The Blue Peace* gains additional credibility because it uses local country experts for each country covered, helping to avoid the common criticism that "outsiders" are telling the locals how to manage their own resources.

A Proposed Framework for Action

A Transboundary Water Initiative?

All three of the studies propose various forms of a trilateral agency with the power to make decisions on the waters of the Euphrates-Tigris, and there are at least three river basin initiatives that can provide possible examples of programs with some degree of success. The Nile Basin Initiative and the Mekong River Commission were described in the previous chapter, and the Permanent Indus Commission is mentioned earlier in this chapter. But every basin is unique, with its own geopolitical relationships. Any Euphrates-Tigris initiative that results only in improved exchange of technical information could provide a basis for a more effective organization at a later date. As detailed above, CBMs can slowly improve the level of cooperation with relatively small-scale and nonthreatening projects.

Since 2003, the United States has been a principal supporter of the Iraqi government and has provided senior advisors to the Iraqi water ministry. Still, U.S. efforts have fallen short of expectations despite its multimillion dollar investment. The Advancing the Blue Revolution Initiative mentioned in chapter 6 was poorly managed and wasteful, and did little to achieve its original objectives. After the end of formal U.S. troop presence in Iraq, it will certainly face declining influence in the next few years. This has been reflected in the major drawdown at the vast U.S. embassy in Baghdad, which reached a peak of 16,000 people by the end of 2011. In

2012, Americans were "largely confined to the embassy because of security concerns, unable to interact enough with ordinary Iraqis to justify the $6 billion annual price tag."[42]

The best hope to advance regional cooperation can be found in an analysis of the complementary policies and interests of the three riparian countries, as discussed in detail at the end of chapter 2. All three riparian nations have complementary economic interests and a shared interest in continuing to develop strong trade relationships. Furthermore, all three nations (for now) have governments based on secular ideas and are moving, albeit at different rates, toward modernity and westernization.

Turkey has long resisted the "internationalization" of water issues and, in light of its increasing influence in the region, will not be persuaded to compromise on this issue. As stated in its 2009 water report:

> Turkey believes that transboundary waters have their own specific characteristics and peculiarities. Each case of a transboundary water has its own social, economic, developmental, cultural and historic aspects. *For this reason, the involvement of third parties cannot be fruitful for the settlement of any disputes.* . . . The best approach is therefore to seek a solution among riparian countries. Mediation is not considered a workable option either, as each country has its own priorities, which could only complicate the situation. (italics added)[43]

For the short term (the next five years), there is only a remote chance that a basinwide trilateral agency could be created with even minimal powers to allocate waters between the parties.[44] Nonetheless, if a proposed Euphrates-Tigris transboundary river initiative can be portrayed as a positive exchange of views and technical expertise, it is more likely to be successful. The theme of the proposed first meeting should be "sharing the benefits" rather than "regulating the rivers." Any new regime must be

---

[42] Tim Arango, "U.S. Planning to Slash Iraq Embassy Staff by as Much as Half," *New York Times*, 7 February 2012.

[43] Republic of Turkey, *Turkey Water Report 2009*, 47.

[44] The authors have a high degree of confidence in this judgment.

based on shared economic interests and present a minimal threat to national sovereignty.

In the previous chapter, the International Centre for Integrated Mountain Development (ICIMOD) was mentioned as a possible model for the riparian nations of the Euphrates-Tigris basin.[45] The developers of this center recognize that globalization and climate change have an increasing influence on the stability of fragile ecosystems and the livelihoods of the people. They hope to "improve understanding of the impacts that climate change may have on the hydrological regimes of river basins and support policy decisions to address those impacts."[46] Such a model should be more effective, and less threatening to Turkey, than the Nile and Mekong initiatives that have been previously described. As discussed in chapter 6, the authors of this book propose the creation of a center for the riparian nations of the Euphrates-Tigris basin—the International Centre for Integrated Basin Development (ICIBAD), a proposal that appears as one of our final recommendations.

Technical Assistance

Much has been mentioned in this book about the challenges facing Iraq in terms of water management and internal coordination; the Geopolicity report mentioned previously provides a thorough analysis of these difficulties. Technical assistance to Iraq can help develop the "sector wide approach" to bind the various sectors of the Iraqi government together. The United States and other countries have been providing support, but much more needs to be done. This can strengthen Iraq in the water sector and help resolve its internal issues over water.

A report published by the United States Institute of Peace identified a number of obstacles to progress, including this key factor:

> *Intragovernmental relationships.* Water management in Iraq is not centrally administered. The Ministry of Water Resources takes the lead on water

---

[45] See ICIMOD's Web site for further details at http://www.icimod.org/?page=abt.

[46] See ICIMOD, "Strengthening Upstream-Downstream Linkages," http://www.icimod.org/?q=245.

related issues, but its purview is limited. The ministry decides water distribution between regions, but it has little to do with ensuring water quality, proper agricultural use, and the supply of safe drinking water to urban populations. Iraq's Ministry of Agriculture, Ministry of Planning and Development Cooperation, Ministry of Environment and various local bodies deal with these issues jointly. These internal dynamics add another stratum of political interests that inhibit coordinated problem-solving.[47]

This observation is consistent with the comments made in the Geopolicity report and should be the subject of additional training programs and diplomatic efforts initiated by the United States. The U.S. Bureau of Reclamation, the U.S. Army Corps of Engineers, and other U.S. agencies have the technical expertise to assist, and U.S. efforts could provide major returns in environmental security. This type of foreign aid should be fundamentally nonthreatening and can help lay the foundation for a more significant initiative at a later date.

Development of an Early Warning Mechanism

Water will certainly play an important role in future conflict, but is it possible to develop an early warning system to alert those concerned? This has been the subject of a number of studies, and there is much that can be done.[48] Although the technology exists to monitor water levels, and even predict water flow through a basin model, the resources have not been effectively used to predict conflict. There has been little coordination among the organizations, both public and private, responsible for monitoring. A 2004 report issued by the United Nations Environment Programme described some success in developing an environment-conflict early warning

---

[47] Whitaker and Varghese, *Tigris-Euphrates River Basin*, 2–3.

[48] On 2 December 2004, a UN panel issued a report on threats to international stability and peace, including environmental degradation. See UN, *A More Secure World: Our Shared Responsibility* (New York: United Nations Department of Public Information, 2004), 26: "Rarely are environmental concerns factored into security, development and humanitarian strategies." Available online at http://www.un.org/secureworld/report2.pdf. Also see the Director of National Intelligence, *Global Water Security*.

system.[49] This report used an example from the Horn of Africa and the use of a Conflict Early Warning and Response Mechanism (CEWARN)[50] to monitor and prevent conflict across border areas. The authors of this study argue that there is a need to integrate environmental variables into planning and warning systems more effectively.

There are few incentives to coordinate the efforts of agencies that benefit from the early prediction of conflict over water. Relief organizations, the UN, the U.S. State Department, NATO, and U.S. military planners all must plan for conflict and contingency operations, but each agency pursues its own interests and must compete for increasingly scarce funding. In 2009 the Central Intelligence Agency announced a plan to launch a center on climate change to help identify conditions (including water availability) that could impact national security, but that initiative has been controversial and may not survive federal budget cuts.[51] Today there is little experimentation, testing, and innovation to develop new methodologies for early warning of environmental security threats. But there is no reason why such a project could not be based on open-source information and the results available in the public sector.

Receiving input from other interested organizations and agencies, a single agency should take the initiative and develop an early warning mechanism. A U.S. federal agency is unlikely to step forward to take this responsibility—each has its own standards, strengths, and limitations, and each uses classified data that cannot be publicly shared. An institution such as the Woodrow Wilson International Center and its Environmental Change and Security Program[52] could be provided the necessary re-

---

[49] Marc A. Levy and Patrick Philippe Meier, "Early Warning and Assessment of Environment, Conflict, and Cooperation," in *Understanding Environment, Conflict, and Cooperation* (Nairobi: United Nations Environmental Programme, 2004), 38.

[50] See CEWARN's Web site for more information at http://www.cewarn.org/index.php.

[51] Jeff Stein, "CIA's Unit on Climate Change Faces Uncertain Future," *Washington Post*, 11 January 2011, http://voices.washingtonpost.com/spy-talk/2011/01/cias_climate-change_unit_faces.html.

[52] For details about the Environmental Change and Security Program, see the Wilson Center's Web site at http://www.wilsoncenter.org/index.cfm?fuseaction=topics.home&topic_id=1413.

sources, however. The Wilson Center is nonpartisan, supported by public and private funds, and engaged in the study of national and world affairs. Its status as nongovernmental entity would also make it easier to obtain the necessary cooperation from similar entities, academia, and concerned states.

Science and Diplomacy

There is a serious deficiency in terms of reliable data on water supplies in the Euphrates-Tigris basin. Without reliable data that can be shared by the affected parties, prospects for real cooperation will remain out of reach. There is a growing consensus among water experts, the World Bank, and the UNDP that a real-time hydrometeorological data system is essential.[53] There is also a new understanding of the connection between water quality and quantity and that decreasing flow levels will have a serious negative impact on the remaining water.[54] If the Euphrates-Tigris nations could be persuaded to share streamflow, precipitation, groundwater level, and selected water quality measurements—basic hydrometrics—enormous collective benefits would accrue. But without some impetus from outside the region, the climate of mistrust in the region is likely to hamper such an effort in the near term. Chapter 6 of this book sets out the challenges and opportunities for science and diplomacy in greater detail.

A simulation model for dams, diversions, and other storage and major conveyance systems in the Tigris and Euphrates River systems in Iraq will help analyze alternative decision scenarios in the timing of retention and distribution of water for various operational goals. Although water

---

[53] An example of the program currently in use in the United States is available on the National Oceanographic and Atmospheric Administration's Web site at http://www.nws.noaa.gov/oh/hads/.

[54] In the United States, individual states have the right to place conditions on water quality certificates issued pursuant to the Clean Water Act that are designed to protect the biological integrity of a body of water. In a decision on 31 May 1994, the U.S. Supreme Court ruled in a case involving the City of Tacoma and the State of Washington Department of Ecology. Tacoma proposed to construct a hydroelectric dam, and the state issued a "water quality certification" for the project that required Tacoma to maintain a minimum instream flow in the Dosewallips River. In the western United States, minimum streamflow levels are regularly set by administrative agencies as a means of protecting water quality.

management information systems in Iraq are outdated and in disarray, a preliminary analysis of information suggests that a reservoir simulation model can be constructed to simulate all important reservoirs and delivery systems. Such a model can provide water managers with a situational understanding of the state and transitory aspects of what is a complex system of reservoirs and water delivery facilities. It will allow the water managers to better plan water deliveries and appropriately anticipate shortage and overabundance situations within the system. In the long term, such a study will contribute to long-range planning for the basin and provide a reliable basis for cooperation between the parties.

Sandia National Laboratories is now collaborating with scientists in the Iraqi Ministry of Water Resources (MOWR), the U.S. Department of State, and UNESCO to develop a decision support model for the Euphrates-Tigris basin, including Turkey, Syria, and Iraq (see chapter 6). The Sandia project includes an important capacity-building aspect in which engineers from the MOWR are being trained in the use of modeling approaches and software and are becoming capable of modifying the existing model and building new models of their own. In a time of declining U.S. influence with Turkey, Syria, and Iraq, the most promising approach seems to be in the field of science and technology. For a comparatively low investment, the United States can provide significant capabilities.[55] This type of support can build bridges and improve relations in ways that military involvement and diplomatic pressure cannot. The real challenge is to properly coordinate the activities and to bridge the gap between science and diplomacy in delivering the support.

Informal Cooperative Ventures: "Track Two" Approaches

Nongovernmental voluntary entities can play a role in developing an improved atmosphere for cooperation in the basin. These are "track two" approaches to diplomacy that that are outside official government channels. In May 2012, a conference titled "Advancing Cooperation in the Euphrates-Tigris Region: Institutional Development and Multidisciplinary Perspectives" was organized in cooperation with the Euphrates

---

[55] The authors have a high degree of confidence in this judgment.

Tigris Initiative for Cooperation (ETIC). It was held at Okan University in Istanbul, Turkey, and more than 20 renowned researchers and scientists (most of whom were from the region) presented on technical and scientific issues, as well as legal frameworks, and discussed conflicting opinions and problems.[56]

The leading personality in the development of ETIC was Olcay Unver, formerly the head of the GAP in Turkey and later a visiting professor at Kent State University. Under his leadership, ETIC developed an ambitious agenda with a number of outreach programs.[57] In 2008 Unver left Kent State to take a position as head of UNESCO's World Water Assessment Programme.[58] Since his departure, ETIC has a lower profile but is still active; an informal meeting was held with representatives of all three basin countries at the World Water Forum in Istanbul in March 2009.

ETIC has had some success with joint training and capacity-building programs,[59] as well as with research and projects with an aim to respond to the common needs and concerns of the people in the region. In conducting these activities, ETIC has built partnerships with international organizations such as UNESCO, the Food and Agriculture Organization of the UN, and the UNDP, as well as with NGOs such as the Stockholm International Water Institute and universities such as Kent State University, the University of New Mexico, and the American University in Beirut.

ETIC received some funding from the United States Agency for International Development in 2008 and 2009, but more financial support is needed

---

[56] Max Planck Institute for Comparative Public Law and International Law, "Advancing Cooperation in the Euphrates Tigris Region: Institutional Development and Multidisciplinary Perspectives" (conference report, conference held in Istanbul, Turkey, 2–4 May 2012), http://www.mpil.de/shared/data/pdf/mpil_istanbul_conference_report_may_2012_(online_version).pdf.

[57] See http://webapps01.un.org/dsd/partnerships/public/partnerships/1479.html.

[58] For more information about this program, go to http://www.unesco.org/water/wwap/.

[59] For instance, ETIC, in collaboration with UNESCO, organized a training program on dam safety in 2006 for professionals from Iran, Iraq, Syria, and Turkey. ETIC also organized a workshop on knowledge technology in March 2009 in Gaziantep, Turkey, for participants from Iraq, Syria, and Turkey. Likewise, a training workshop was organized by ETIC in Aleppo in January 2010 on geographic information systems and their implementation in natural resources management.

to ensure meaningful results. Today ETIC exists only as an informal volunteer network of academics and water professionals from Turkey, Syria, and Iraq. A functioning Web site and a small paid staff would provide the groundwork for improvement and could support the establishment of a more formal intergovernmental network, such as the proposal for ICIBAD mentioned earlier in this chapter.

Better Coordination

Each country providing funds and programs for international development has its own interests in the region and promotes the use of its own private companies to conduct the work. For instance, an Italian company recently received the funding for the first strategic water resources plan for Iraq. Norway, too, has a significant interest in the region, and a Norwegian NGO, the Center for Environmental Studies and Resource Management (CESAR), supported the work of Jon Martin Trondalen mentioned earlier in this chapter.[60] Yet there are entities that will provide support despite the fact that they have no clear national strategic interest in the region. The Netherlands, for example, provided support for Turkey's development of its water resources under EU auspices and should be invited to participate. Finally, NGOs such as the International Center for Agriculture Research in Dry Areas in Aleppo, Syria, should be included because of their ability to provide special technical support and expertise. The center's mission is to "contribute to the improvement of livelihoods of the resource-poor in dry areas by enhancing food security and alleviating poverty through research and partnerships to achieve sustainable increases in agricultural productivity and income, while ensuring the efficient and more equitable use and conservation of natural resources."[61]

Hence, the fundamental problem remains: international organizations and various states have many capabilities to provide assistance to Iraq and the other riparians in the basin with no overarching vision or strategic plan. Without better coordination, little hope for advancement can be expected.

---

[60] See Trondalen, *Water and Peace*.

[61] International Center for Agriculture Research in Dry Areas (ICARDA), "Mission," http://www.icarda.org/icarda-today.

The Way Ahead: Final Conclusions and Recommendations

The following conclusions and recommendations are provided with the proviso that some have a higher *likelihood* of success. Some can provide a higher impact if implemented. "Short term" is defined as less than 5 years, "long term" as 10–15 years or more. Each recommendation can be independently evaluated to help identify a suggested priority in a time of decreasing budgets. "Success" will be separately defined for each recommendation, with a brief cost-benefit analysis if possible.

1. **A transboundary water initiative.** Success would be a trilateral agency that has the power to allocate or make binding decisions about water in the basin. But trilateral initiatives similar to those for the Nile or Mekong have a low likelihood in both the short and long term. Turkey will continue to resist any "internationalization" of the issues and will increasingly dominate the basin. Bilateral agreements may be a short-term substitute, but only when perceived to be in Turkey's national interest. *Potential impact of this option is high, but the likelihood of success is extremely low in the short term and only slightly higher in the long term.*

2. **Continued assistance to the Iraqi government in developing effective water management and a long-term water management plan.** Success would be an energized and capable Iraqi MOWR that can coordinate and plan its actions both internally and internationally. Action needs to be taken in the short term to have any long-term impact.[62] *Potential impact is high and the likelihood of success moderate.* Detailed recommendations for this can be found in the Geopolicity report cited previously in this chapter. Because of the relatively low cost of technical assistance for this option, it should be a high priority.

3. **Development of an early warning mechanism to identify conflict and instability related to water.** Water will play an

---

[62] Authors have a high degree of confidence in this judgment.

important role in future conflict, and it is technically feasible to develop an open source early warning system to alert those concerned. Success would be a single NGO, such as the Wilson Center, that takes the initiative to develop a functioning early warning mechanism while receiving input from other interested organizations and agencies. *Potential impact is moderate and the likelihood of success moderate.* Cost would be moderate, but this avenue should still be pursued.

4. **Science and diplomacy: the potential for the game-changing role of innovation.** Success would be a breakthrough in developing a trilateral technical and development center for the Euphrates-Tigris region. There is great promise in the science and technology initiatives mentioned in chapter 6, and the ICIBAD is provided as a possible model for the riparian nations to share information and technology. However, the technology needs to be carefully evaluated, prioritized, and delivered as part of a comprehensive diplomatic strategy. *Potential impact is high for this recommendation, and the likelihood of success is high if political will can be mustered and the efforts can be properly coordinated.*[63] Cost would be moderate but well worth the effort.

5. **Track two approaches such as ETIC and informal "confidence-building" initiatives.** These efforts are having some impact but should not be considered a substitute for governmental action. Success would be an improved track two system that meets regularly and shares important information and expertise at the nongovernmental level. *The impact would be moderate but could lead to more significant cooperation. There is moderate likelihood of achieving some success, slightly higher in the long term.* This is a relatively low-cost approach that should be pursued.

6. **Improved coordination of U.S. efforts.** There are many federal agencies (20 in all) that have critical support capabilities, but

---

[63] Authors have a high degree of confidence in this judgment.

more effort needs to be devoted to their coordination. The needs have been identified in the statements of Secretary of State Clinton in 2011 and 2012, previously mentioned in chapter 6. Success would be an improved U.S. federal capability that can successfully evaluate and prioritize programs. This should involve a whole-of-government approach with increased staffing and training within the State Department and the United States Agency for International Development as well as technical assistance and advice from the Department of Defense (from Sandia National Laboratories and the U.S. Army Corps of Engineers, for example). *Potential impact is high, and the likelihood of success (better coordination) is high at a relatively low cost with little additional investment.*

7. **Improved coordination of international efforts.** Success would be an improved international coordination mechanism for supporting the countries in the Euphrates-Tigris basin. There are many countries and international agencies working in the field, but U.S. diplomacy needs to be "elevated" to coordinate and focus more on the basin. *Potential impact is high, and the likelihood of success (better coordination) is moderate due to challenges from competing agencies and diverse national interests.* This initiative would be low cost, involving only diplomatic initiatives and should be pursued.

The conclusions and recommendations provided here all have their own strengths and limitations. Initiatives with a high impact and a reasonably high probability of success should be the priority. Initiative 4 (science and diplomacy) and initiative 6 (improved coordination of U.S. efforts) are directly related and can be initiated in the short term (within five years) at a relatively low cost and with the greatest potential return. Focusing U.S. and international efforts in these particular areas offers a realistic and affordable path toward assisting the riparians maintain and improve regional stabilization as we approach 2025.

The Future

Water and security issues in the Euphrates-Tigris basin have received little publicity as the world watches each new crisis unfold in the Middle East. Despite the current volatility and uncertainty in the region, the international community cannot wait to take action on water and security matters in the basin. Such actions will not detract from immediate priorities but will in fact serve to support broader initiatives, including regional cooperation and a stable government in Iraq.

Today, the reports of water deficits and human suffering are carrying wake-up calls for the future and also "hope for creativity and opportunities for community building."[64] The failure to deal with these long-term issues will become apparent in 10 to 15 years when water quantity and quality deteriorate beyond acceptable levels. Iraq has the most to lose if the water situation in the Euphrates-Tigris basin deteriorates as now predicted.

In spite of the difficult and dangerous regional security environment, there is still much that can be accomplished. The United States and the international community can support the initiatives mentioned in the "Final Conclusions and Recommendations" section with little additional capital investment. The benefits of these initiatives will go far beyond the mere availability of water—action now manages the problem rather than merely responding to the crisis, and it also supports U.S. strategic interests to maintain peace and stability in the region.

---

[64] Delli Priscoli and Wolf, *Managing and Transforming Water Conflicts*, xxiv.

ACRONYMS AND ABBREVIATIONS

ABRI   Advancing the Blue Revolution Initiative

AKP   Justice and Development Party (Turkey)

AOR   area of responsibility

BCM   billion cubic meters

CBM   confidence-building measure

CESAR   Centre for Environmental Studies and Resource Management

CEWARN   Conflict Early Warning and Response Mechanism

CFS   cubic feet per second

CIA   Central Intelligence Agency

CM   cubic meter

CMS   cubic meters per second

D-8	the Developing 8
DAT	Dam Assessment Team
DSI	Directorate of State Hydraulic Works (Turkey)
ETIC	Euphrates Tigris Initiative for Cooperation
FAO	Food and Agriculture Organization
FAOSTAT	Food and Agriculture Organization of the United Nations Corporate Statistical Database
GAP	Guneydogu Anadolu Projesi (in Turkish); Southeastern Anatolia Project (in English)
GDP	gross domestic product
GIS	geographic information system
GRACE	Gravity Recovery and Climate Experiment
Helsinki Rules	1966 Helsinki Rules on the Uses of the Waters of International Rivers
ICARDA	International Center for Agriculture Research in Dry Areas
ICIBAD	International Centre for Integrated Basin Development
ICIMOD	International Centre for Integrated Mountain Development
ICJ	International Court of Justice
ILC	International Law Commission
IMF	International Monetary Fund
IWRM	Integrated Water Resources Management

KDP	Kurdistan Democratic Party
km	kilometer
km²	square kilometer
KRG	Kurdistan Regional Government
kWh	kilowatt hour
MAF	million acre-feet
MENA	Middle East and North Africa
mg/L	milligrams per liter
MoD	Iraqi Ministry of Defense
MOWR	Iraqi Ministry of Water Resources
MRC	Mekong River Commission
MW	megawatt
NASA	National Aeronautics and Space Administration
NATO	North Atlantic Treaty Organization
NBI	Nile Basin Initiative
NGA	U.S. National Geospatial-Intelligence Agency
NGO	nongovernmental organization
OECD	Organisation for Economic Co-operation and Development
OIC	Organization of the Islamic Conference
OPEC	Organization of the Petroleum Exporting Countries

OSCE	Organization for Security and Cooperation in Europe
PKK	Kurdistan Workers Party
PUK	Patriotic Union of Kurdistan
SIIC	Supreme Iraqi Islamic Council (also called the Sadr movement)
SNL	Sandia National Laboratories
TDS	total dissolved solids
UN	United Nations
UNDP	United Nations Development Programme
UNESCO	United Nations Educational, Scientific, and Cultural Organization
USAID	U.S. Agency for International Development
USDA	U.S. Department of Agriculture
USGS	U.S. Geological Survey
USIP	United States Institute of Peace
USSR	Union of Soviet Socialist Republics
UTM	Universal Transverse Mercator
Watercourses Convention	1997 Convention on the Law of the Non-navigational Uses of International Watercourses
WTO	World Trade Organization

BIBLIOGRAPHY

Ackerman, Robert K. "Turkey's Defense Industry Matures." *Signal*, September 2010, 27–29.

Adams, Mark. *Water and Security Policy: The Case of Turkey*. Washington, DC: National Defense University Press, 2002. http://permanent .access.gpo.gov/websites/nduedu/www.ndu.edu/nesa/docs/marks adams-water.pdf.

Allan, [J. A.] Tony. "'Virtual Water': A Long Term Solution for Water Short Middle Eastern Economies?" Paper presented at the 1997 British Association Festival of Science, Water and Development Session, University of Leeds, England, 9 September 1997. http://www.soas.ac.uk/water /publications/papers/file38347.pdf.

———. *The Middle East Water Question: Hydropolitics and the Global Economy*. London: I.B. Tauris, 2002.

Al-Muqdadi, Sameh Wisam. "Groundwater Investigation and Modeling in the Western Desert of Iraq." PhD thesis, Freiberg [Germany] Technical University, 2012. http://www.qucosa.de/fileadmin/data/qucosa /documents/8747/Sameh%20Al-Muqdadi%20May%202012.pdf.

American Association for the Advancement of Science (AAAS). "About the Center." American Association for the Advancement of Science. http://diplomacy.aaas.org/.

Ansaray, Tamim. *Destiny Disrupted: A History of the World through Islamic Eyes*. New York: PublicAffairs, 2009.

Arango, Tim. "U.S. Planning to Slash Iraq Embassy Staff by as Much as Half." *New York Times*, 7 February 2012.

Archibold, Randal C. "Eyes Turn to Mexico as Drought Drags On." *New York Times*, 14 September 2009.

Armstrong, David, Theo Farrell, and Helene Lambert. *International Law and International Relations*. Cambridge: Cambridge University Press, 2007.

Arraf, Jane. "Turkey Offers Water for Iraqi Crackdown on Kurdish Rebels." *Christian Science Monitor*, 11 August 2009.

Austin, John. *The Province of Jurisprudence Determined*. Edited by Wilfred E. Rumble. Cambridge: Cambridge University Press, 1995.

Bacastow, Todd, Dennis J. Bellafiore, and Donna M. Bridges. *The Structured Geospatial Analytic Method: Opening the Discussion*. 2010. https://www.e-education.psu.edu/drupal6/files/sgam/SGAMopeningdiscussion_3_15_10.pdf.

Bakour, Yahia, and John Kolars. "The Arab Mashrek: Hydrologic History, Problems and Perspectives." In *Water in the Arab World: Perspectives and Progress,* edited by Peter Rogers and Peter Lydon, 121–46. Cambridge, MA: Harvard University Press, 1994.

Barnes, Julian E. "$100 Million Down the Drain in Iraq." *Los Angeles Times*, 27 October 2008.

Billington, David P., and Donald C. Jackson. *Big Dams of the New Deal Era: A Confluence of Engineering and Politics*. Norman: University of Oklahoma Press, 2006.

Brabeck-Letmathe, Peter. "A Water Warning." In "The World in 2009," special issue, *Economist* (2008): 112.

Brunnee, Jutta, and Stephen J. Toope. "The Changing Nile Basin Regime: Does Law Matter." *Harvard International Law Journal* 43, no. 1 (2002): 105–59.

Busch, Briton C. *Mudros to Lausanne: Britain's Frontier in West Asia, 1918–1923*. Albany: State University of New York Press, 1976.

Calder, Ian R. *The Blue Revolution: Land Use and Integrated Water Resources Management*. London: Earthscan, 1999.

Campbell, Robert Wellman, ed. "Iraq and Kuwait: 1972, 1990, 1991, 1997." Earthshots, Satellite Images of Environmental Change: U.S. Geological Survey, 1999. http://earthshots.usgs.gov/Iraq/Iraq.

Carkoglu, Ali, and Mine Eder. "Domestic Concerns and the Water Conflict over the Euphrates-Tigris River Basin." *Middle Eastern Studies* 37 (January 2001): 41–71.

Carnegie Endowment for International Peace. *The Treaties of Peace 1919–1923*. Vol. 2. New York: Carnegie Endowment for International Peace, 1924.

Center for Emerging Threats and Opportunities. *2011 Edition of Flashpoints*. Quantico, VA: Center for Emerging Threats and Opportunities, 2011.

Central Intelligence Agency (CIA). "Syria." In *The World Factbook*. Washington, DC: Central Intelligence Agency, 2009. https://www.cia.gov/library/publications/the-world-factbook/geos/sy.html.

Centre for Environmental Studies and Resource Management (CESAR). *The Euphrates River and the Tigris River Water Resources Management: Water Resources Analysis Methodology*. 2006. Second reference document in Jon Martin Trondalen, *Water and Peace for the People: Possible Solutions to Water Disputes in the Middle East*. Paris: United Nations Educational, Scientific, and Cultural Organization (UNESCO), 2008.

Chesnoff, Richard Z. "When Water Feeds Flames." *U.S. News and World Report*, 21 November 1988.

Chulov, Martin. "Iraq: Water Nowhere." *World Policy Journal* 26 (December 2009): 33–41.

Clinton, Hillary R. "World Water Day [2010]." Speech, National Geographic Society, Washington, DC, 22 March 2010. http://www.state.gov/secretary/rm/2010/03/138737.htm.

———. "Remarks in Honor of World Water Day [2012]." Speech, George C. Marshall Auditorium, Washington, DC, 22 March 2012. http://www.state.gov/secretary/rm/2012/03/186640.htm.

Cook, Steven A. "How Do You Say 'Frenemy' in Turkish? Meet America's New Rival in the Middle East." *Foreign Policy*, 1 June 2010.

———. Lecture, Marine Corps University, Quantico, VA, 2 March 2011.

Dahl, Robert A. "The Concepts of Power." *Behavioral Science* 2, no. 3 (1957): 201–15.

Daoudy, Marwa. "Hydro-Hegemony and International Water Law: Laying Claims to Water Rights." *Water Policy* 10, supplement no. 2 (2008): 89–102.

———. "Asymmetric Power: Negotiating Water in the Euphrates and Tigris." *International Negotiation* 14, no. 2 (2009): 361–91.

Davis, Tony. "Yuma Desalination Plant to Start Flowing." *Arizona Daily Star*, 1 May 2010. http://azstarnet.com/news/science/health-med-fit/article_8e4f368f-1779-50cc-b084-3f265e1912a4.html#ixzz1S6M2UwwQ.

Davutoğlu, Ahmet. "The Turkish-American Relationship." Lecture, Georgetown University, Washington, DC, 16 November 2010.

Delapenna, Joseph W. "The Two Rivers and the Land Between: Mesopotamia and the International Law of Transboundary Waters." *Brigham Young University Journal of Public Law* 10 (1996): 213–61.

Delli Priscoli, Jerome, and Aaron T. Wolf. *Managing and Transforming Water Conflicts*. International Hydrology Series. Cambridge: Cambridge University Press, 2009.

Director of National Intelligence. *Vision 2015: A Globally Networked and Integrated Intelligence Enterprise*. Washington, DC: Director of National Intelligence, 2008. http://www.dni.gov/Vision_2015.pdf.

———. *Global Water Security*. Intelligence Community Assessment. 2 February 2012. http://www.dni.gov/files/documents/Special%20Report_ICA%20Global%20Water%20Security.pdf.

———. "Assessment on Global Water Security." News release, 22 March 2012.

Dolatyar, Mostafa, and Tim S. Gray. *Water Politics in the Middle East: A Context for Conflict or Co-operation?* London: Macmillan, 2000.

Doorn, Bradley, David Toll, and Edwin Engman. "NASA Water Resources Program for Improved Water Management." http://wmp.gsfc.nasa.gov /workshops/5p-Toll_WB2012.pdf.

Economist Intelligence Unit. *Country Report—Iran.* London: Economist Intelligence Unit, 2011.

———. *Country Report—Iraq.* London: Economist Intelligence Unit, 2011.

———. *Country Report—Syria.* London: Economist Intelligence Unit, 2011.

———. *Country Report—Turkey.* London: Economist Intelligence Unit, 2011.

Economist. "The Marsh Arabs of Iraq: Do They Want to Go Back in Time?" 5 June 2003. http://www.economist.com/node/1827561.

———. "The Worrying Tayyip Erdogan." 5 December 2008.

———. "For Want of a Drink: Special Report on Water." 22 May 2010 http://www.economist.com/specialreports?page=2&year[value][year]= 2010&category=All.

———. "A Fading European Dream." In "Anchors Aweigh: A Special Report on Turkey," special issue, 23 October 2010.

———. "The Davutoglu Effect." In "Anchors Aweigh: A Special Report on Turkey," special issue, 23 October 2010.

———. "Survival in the Sahel: It's Getting Harder All the Time." 2 December 2010.

———. "Iran's Battered Opposition: A Leadership Neutered." 10 March 2011.

———. "The Battle for Libya: The Colonel Fights Back." 10 March 2011.

Elhadj, Elie. "Dry Aquifers in Arab Countries and the Looming Food Crisis." *Middle East Review of International Affairs* 12, no. 4 (December 2008).

Elhance, Arun P. *Hydropolitics in the Third World: Conflict and Cooperation in International River Basins*. Washington, DC: United States Institute of Peace Press, 1999.

Embassy of the United States—Italy. "Water Resources Top Agenda for Iraq's Ministry of Public Works, September 24, 2003." Public affairs release. www.usembassy.it/file2003_09/alia/a3092403.htm.

Erickson, Edward J. *Ordered To Die: A History of the Ottoman Army in the First World War*. Westport, CT: Greenwood Press, 2001.

———. *Defeat in Detail: The Ottoman Army in the Balkans, 1912–1913*. Westport, CT: Praeger, 2003.

———. "Turkey as Regional Hegemon—2014: Strategic Implications for the United States." *Turkish Studies* 5, no. 3 (Autumn 2004): 25–45.

Eyal, Zisser. "Where is Bashar al-Assad heading?" *Middle East Quarterly* 15, no. 1 (Winter 2008): 35–40.

Food and Agriculture Organization of the United Nations (FAO) Aquastat Database. "Iraq." http://www.fao.org/nr/water/aquastat/countries/iraq/index.stm.

———. "Turkey." http://www.fao.org/nr/water/aquastat/countries/turkey/index.stm.

Food and Agriculture Organization of the United Nations Corporate Statistical Database (FAOSTAT). "Preliminary 2009 Data, Top Agricultural Production—Turkey." http://faostat.fao.org/site/339/default.aspx.

———. "Preliminary 2009 Data, Top Agricultural Production—Syria." http://faostat.fao.org/site/339/default.aspx.

Ford, Roger. *Eden to Armageddon: World War I in the Middle East*. New York: Pegasus Books, 2010.

Freudenheim, Milt. "The Ancients Had Water Politics, Too." *New York Times*, 13 September 1981.

Friedman, George. "Geopolitical Journey, Part 5: Turkey." Stratfor, 23 November 2010. http://www.stratfor.com/weekly/20101122_geopolitical_journey_part_5_turkey.

Friedman, Thomas L. "Without Water, Revolution." *New York Times*, 18 May 2013.

Fromkin, David. *A Peace to End All Peace: The Fall of the Ottoman Empire and the Creation of the Modern Middle East*. New York: Henry Holt, 1989.

Fulco, Ludwig, Pavel Kabat, Henk van Shaik, and Michael van der Valk, eds. *Climate Change Adaptation in the Water Sector*. London: Earthscan Publishing, 2009.

Gelvin, James L. *The Modern Middle East: A History*. Oxford: Oxford University Press, 2008.

Geopolicity. *Managing the Tigris Euphrates Watershed: The Challenge Facing Iraq*. Dubai: Geopolicity, 2010. http://www.geopolicity.com/upload/content/pub_1293090043_regular.pdf.

German Marshall Fund of the United States and Compagnia di San Paolo. "Turkey and the West—Drifting Away." Section 5 in *Transatlantic Trends: Key Findings 2010*. [Washington, DC?]: German Marshall Fund of the United States and Compagnia di San Paolo, 2010.

Glanz, James. "Iraqis Warn U.S. Plan to Divert Billions to Security Could Cut Off Crucial Services." *New York Times*, 21 September 2004.

———. "Report Finds Iraq Water Treatment Project to Be Late, Faulty and Over Budget," *New York Times*, 27 October 2008.

Gonzales-Anton, Carlos, and Charles Arias. "The Incorporation of Integrated Management in European Water Policy." In *Integrated Water Resources Management*, edited by Miguel A. Marino and Slobodan P. Simonovic, 69–75. Wallingford, UK: International Association of Hydrological Sciences, 2001.

Grossman, Marc. *What Next for Energy and Environmental Diplomacy?* Policy Brief: Climate and Energy Program. Washington, DC: German Marshall Fund of the United States, 2010.

Haaretz Service. "Turkey Policy Paper: Israel's Actions Threaten Mideast." *Haaretz* (Israel), 1 November 2010.

Hafidh, Hassan. "Iraq Wants to Clinch Water Deal with Syria, Turkey." *Environmental News Network*, 16 September 2003. http://www.enn.com/news/2003-09-16/s_8435.asp.

Hakki, Murat Metin. "Cross-Border Water Conflicts in Mesopotamia: An Analysis According to International Law." *Willamette Journal of International Law and Dispute Resolution* 13, no. 2 (2005): 245–69.

Hammad, Waleed-Abdel. Interview by Frederick Lorenz, 1 August 2004, Baghdad.

Hasani, Saleem al-, and Basim al-Shara. "Baghdad Urged to Tackle Water Crisis." *Environmental News Service*, 10 June 2010. http://www.ens-newswire.com/ens/jun2010/2010-06-10-02.html.

Hillel, Daniel. *Rivers of Eden: The Struggle of Water and the Quest for Peace in the Middle East*. Oxford: Oxford University Press, 1994.

Hnoush, Ali Aziz. *Water Security and Environmental Security of States of the Euphrates and Tigris Basins: Towards a Strategy of Sustainable Development* (on file with authors).

Howe, Carol, Joel B. Smith, and Jim Henderson, eds. *Climate Change and Water: International Perspectives on Mitigation and Adaptation*. London: IWA Publishing and American Water Works Association, 2009.

Hürriyet (Turkey). "Turks See US as Biggest External Threat, Poll Results." 5 January 2011.

ICIMOD (International Centre for Integrated Mountain Development). "About ICIMOD." http://www.icimod.org/?page=abt.

Inter-Agency Information and Analysis Unit. *Water in Iraq Factsheet*, October 2010. http://www.iauiraq.org/documents/1138/Water%20in%20Iraq%20 Factsheet-Final.pdf.

International Center for Agriculture Research in Dry Areas (ICARDA). "ICARDA Today: Mission." http://www.icarda.org/icarda-today.

International Conference on Water and the Environment. *The Dublin Statement on Water and Sustainable Development*. Dublin, 1992. http://www .wmo.int/pages/prog/hwrp/documents/english/icwedece.html.

International Crisis Group. *Turkey and the Iraqi Kurds: Conflict or Cooperation?* Middle East Report no. 81-13. November 2008.

International Institute for Strategic Studies. "Turkey's Bid to Raise Influence in Middle East." *Strategic Comments* 16, no. 38 (October 2010).

———. "Dashed Hopes for Turkish-Armenian Rapprochement." *Strategic Comments* 16, no. 43 (November 2010).

Invest in Turkey. Ankara: Republic of Turkey Prime Ministry Investment Support and Promotion Agency, 2011.

Iraq Business News. "Iraq Signs Contract to Implement Water Strategy with Italian Companies." 30 April 2010. http://www.iraq-businessnews .com/2010/05/03/iraq-signs-contract-to-implement-water-strategy -with-italian-companies/.

———. "Tenders Soon for Repairs of Mosul Dam." 4 September 2010. http:// www.iraq-businessnews.com/2010/09/04/tenders-soon-for-repair -of-mosul-dam/.

———. "Half of Iraq's Water Is Wasted." 22 March 2011. http://www .iraq-businessnews.com/2011/03/22/half-of-iraqs-water-is-wasted/.

Iraq Directory. "Iraq Demanding the Guarantee of Water Rights." 19 September 2009. http://www.iraqdirectory.com/DisplayNews.aspx?id=10404.

Iraqi Ministry of Foreign Affairs. *Foreign Policy*. Baghdad: Iraqi Ministry of Foreign Affairs, 2011. http://www.mofa.gov.iq/english/foreignpolicy/.

Itskowitz, Joel. "Creating Partnerships Around the World." *Pathfinder*, July–August 2011: 10–11. https://www1.nga.mil/MediaRoom/Publications/Documents/Pathfinder%20Magazines/2011/2011_Jul-Aug.pdf.

Jawad, Sadik B. "Integrated Water Resources Management of Diyala River Basin in Central Iraq Using System Dynamics Modeling." Research proposal, 2005. https://waterportal.sandia.gov/iraq/documents/W03%20full%20proposal%2C%20Diyala%20modeling.doc/view.

Kaplan, Robert D. "Waterworld." *Atlantic*, January–February 2008.

Kïbaroğlu, Ayşegül. *Building a Regime for the Waters of the Euphrates-Tigris River Basin*. The Hague: Kluwer Law International, 2002.

———. *Recent Developments and Prospects for Cooperation in the Euphrates Tigris Basin*. Ankara: Middle East Technical University, 2011.

Kitchener, Lord Horatio. Memorandum for the Committee of Imperial Defence, 16 March 1915. The National Archives, Kew, United Kingdom, Cabinet Records (CAB 24/1/12).

Kliot, Nurit. *Water Resources and Conflict in the Middle East*. New York: Routledge, 1994.

Kolars, John. "Defining the Political/Ecological Threshold for the Euphrates and Tigris Rivers." *Arab Studies Quarterly* 22, no. 2 (Spring 2000): 101–12.

Kolars, John F., and William A. Mitchell. *The Euphrates River and the Southeast Anatolia Development Project*. Carbondale: Southern Illinois University Press, 1991.

Kraska, James. "Sustainable Development Is Security: The Role of Transboundary River Agreements as a Confidence Building Measure (CBM) in South Asia." *Yale Journal of International Law* 28 (Summer 2003): 465–503.

Kron, Josh. "Protests in Uganda Over Rising Prices Grow Violent." *New York Times*, 21 April 2011.

Kurdish Globe. "Iran Adds to Drought Misery." 14 May 2008. http://www
.kurdishglobe.net/display-article.html?id=6F241EA0928DCF7898746DC
9703AF8DB.

———. "Protests in Mosul over Annexing Parts of City to Kurdistan." 4
July 2009. https://www.kurdishglobe.net/display-article.html?id=89AD
4FF14A94095FCA0504885F8AFDA7.

Kurdistan Regional Government. "Invitation to Tender Deadline Extended: Feasibility Study for Three Hydropower Plants." Press release,
21 October 2008. Kurdistan Regional Government. http://www.krg.org
/articles/detail.asp?smap=02010100&lngnr=12&anr=25710&rnr=223.

———. "France's Trade Minister Opens Agriculture and Environment
House in Erbil." Press release, 2 November 2010. Kurdistan Regional
Government. http://krg.org/a/d.aspx?l=12&s=02010100&r=223&a=375
76&s=010000.

———. "Ministry of Agriculture and Irrigation." Kurdistan Regional
Government. http://old.krg.org/about/ministries/moai/index.asp (accessed 19 March 2011).

———. "About KRG: Structure and Mission." Kurdistan Regional Government. http://old.krg.org/about/background.asp.

———. "About Kurdistan Region." Kurdistan Regional Government.
http://www.krg.org/articles/?lngnr=12&rnr=140&smap=03010300.

Levy, Marc A., and Patrick Philippe Meier. "Early Warning and Assessment of Environment, Conflict, and Cooperation." In *Understanding
Environment, Conflict, and Cooperation*, 38–47. Nairobi: United Nations Environmental Programme, 2004.

Lev-Yadun, Simcha, Avi Gopher, and Shahal Abbo. "The Cradle of Agriculture." *Science* 288, no. 5471 (2 June 2000): 1602–3.

Lorenz, Frederick M. "Strategic Water for Iraq: The Need for Planning
and Action." *American University Law School Journal of International Law*
24, no. 2 (2008): 275–99. http://www.wcl.american.edu/journal/ilr/24
/documents/Lorenz.pdf?rd=1.

Lorenz, Frederick M., and Edward J. Erickson. *The Euphrates Triangle: Security Implications of the Southeastern Anatolia Project*. Washington, DC: National Defense University Press, 1999.

———. *The Thread of Life: A Survey of Hydropolitics in the Tigris-Euphrates Basin*. 2d ed. Tacoma: International Research Associates, 2004.

Lowi, Miriam R. *Water and Power: The Politics of a Scarce Resource in the Jordan River Basin*. Cambridge: Cambridge University Press, 1993.

MacMillian, Margaret. *Paris 1919: Six Months that Changed the World*. New York: Random House, 2003.

Mango, Andrew. *Atatürk: The Biography of the Founder of Modern Turkey*. New York: Overlook Press, 1991.

Maplecroft. "Oil Producing Middle East and North African Countries Dominate Maplecroft Water Security Risk List." Maplecroft news, 22 March 2011. http://www.maplecroft.com/about/news/water_security.html.

Masters, Gilbert M., and Wendell P. Ela, *Introduction to Environmental Engineering and Science*. 3d ed. Upper Saddle River, NJ: Prentice Hall, 2007.

Mawloodi, Ayob. "Vegetable Imports Banned." *Kurdish Globe*, 26 April 2010. http://www.kurdishglobe.net/displayArticle.jsp?id=B9AA82BED53BEA9E3F47F97DC7A3337A (accessed 19 March 2011).

Max Planck Institute for Comparative Public Law and International Law. "Advancing Cooperation in the Euphrates Tigris Region: Institutional Development and Multidisciplinary Perspectives." Conference report, conference held in Istanbul, Turkey, 2–4 May 2012. http://www.mpil.de/shared/data/pdf/mpil_istanbul_conference_report_may_2012_(online_version).pdf.

McCaffrey, Stephen C., and Mpazi Sinjela. "The 1997 United Nations Convention on International Watercourses." *American Journal of International Law* 92, no. 1 (1998): 97–107.

McDowall, David. *A Modern History of the Kurds*. London: I.B. Tauris, 1997.

Mearsheimer, John J., and Stephen M. Walt. *The Israel Lobby and U.S. Foreign Policy*. New York: Farrar, Straus and Giroux, 2007.

Ministerial Declaration of The Hague. *Second World Water Forum: Ministerial Declaration of The Hague on Water Security in the 21st Century*. http://www.idhc.org/esp/documents/Agua/Second_World_Water _Forum%5B1%5D.pdf (accessed 17 July 2012).

Mitrany, David. *The Functional Theory of Politics*. New York: St. Martin's Press, 1975.

Morgenthau, Hans J. *Politics Among Nations: The Struggle for Power and Peace*. 3d ed. New York: Alfred Knopf, 1965.

Morissette, Jason J., and Douglas A. Borer. "Where Oil and Water Do Mix: Environmental Scarcity and Future Conflict in the Middle East and North Africa." *Parameters* 34, no. 4 (Winter 2004–5): 86–101.

Muqdadi, Sameh Wisam al-. "Groundwater Investigation and Modeling in the Western Desert of Iraq." PhD thesis at Freiberg [Germany] Technical University, 2012. http://www.qucosa.de/fileadmin/data/qucosa /documents/8747/Sameh%20Al-Muqdadi%20May%202012.pdf.

Myers, Norman. "Environmental Refugees in a Globally Warmed World." *BioScience* 43, no. 11 (1993): 752–61.

National Intelligence Council. *Global Trends 2025: A Transformed World*. Washington, DC: U.S. Government Printing Office, 2008. http://www .dni.gov/nic/PDF_2025/2025_Global_Trends_Final_Report.pdf.

OECD (Organisation for Economic Co-operation and Development). "Turkey." In *Agricultural Policies in OECD Countries: At a Glance 2010*, 66–67. Paris: Organisation for Economic Co-operation and Development, 2010.

Pacific Institute. "Water Conflict Chronology." Pacific Institute. http:// worldwater.org/conflict.html.

Parthemore, Christine, and Will Rogers. *Promoting the Dialogue: Climate Change and the Quadrennial Defense Review*. Working Paper. Washington, DC: Center for a New American Security, 2010.

Partow, Hassan. *The Mesopotamian Marshlands: Demise of an Ecosystem*. Nairobi: United Nations Environmental Programme, 2001.

Passell, Howard, Marissa Reno, Jesse Roach, Vince Tidwell, and Wael Khairy. "Collaborative, Stakeholder-Driven Resource Modeling and Management." In *Handbook of Research on Hydroinformatics: Technologies, Theories and Applications*, edited by Tagelsir Gamelseid, 36–53. Hershey, PA: IGI Global Press, 2010.

Postel, Sandra L., and Aaron T. Wolf. "Dehydrating Conflict." *Foreign Policy*, September–October 2001, 60–67.

President of the United States. *National Security Strategy*. Washington, DC: the White House, 2010. http://www.whitehouse.gov/sites/default/files/rss_viewer/national_security_strategy.pdf.

Qaddumi, Halla. *Practical Approaches to Transboundary Water Benefit Sharing*. London: Overseas Development Institute, 2008. http://www.odi.org.uk/resources/docs/2576.pdf.

Rafaat, Aram. "U.S.-Kurdish Relations in Post-Invasion Iraq." *MERIA* (*Middle East Review of International Affairs*) 11, no. 4 (December 2007): 79–89.

Republic of Iraq Cabinet and National Security Council. *Iraq First: Iraqi National Security Strategy, 2007–2010*. Baghdad: Republic of Iraq, 2007.

Republic of Iraq. Iraqi Constitution (English version). 2005.

Republic of Iraq Ministry of Water Resources. *2003 Strategic Plan* (on file with authors). 2003.

Republic of Turkey. *Turkey Water Report 2009*. Ankara: General Directorate of State Hydraulic Works, 2009. http://www.dsi.gov.tr/english/pdf_files/TurkeyWaterReport.pdf.

Republic of Turkey Ministry of Foreign Affairs. "Turkey's Policy on Water Issues." Republic of Turkey Ministry of Foreign Affairs. http://www.mfa .gov.tr/turkey_s-policy-on-water-issues.en.mfa.

———. "Water: A Source of Conflict of Coopeariton [or Cooperation] in the Middle East?" Republic of Turkey Ministry of Foreign Affairs. http://www .mfa.gov.tr/data/DISPOLITIKA/WaterASourceofConflictofCoopinthe MiddleEast.pdf.

Republic of Turkey Ministry of National Defence. *White Paper—Defence 1998*. Ankara: Ministry of National Defence, 1998.

———. *Turkey's National Defense Policy Part Four*. White paper. Ankara: Ministry of National Defence, 1998.

———. *Turkey's National Defense Policy, Part Four, Section One*. White paper. Ankara: Ministry of National Defence, 2000.

Robertson, Campbell. "Iraq Suffers as the Euphrates Dwindles." *New York Times*, 13 July 2009. http://www.nytimes.com/2009/07/14/world /middleeast/14euphrates.html.

Roskin, Michael G., and James J. Coyle. *Politics of the Middle East: Cultures and Conflicts*. 2d ed. Upper Saddle River, NJ: Pearson/Prentice Hall, 2008.

Rutagwera, Patrick. "About the NBI." Nile Basin Initiative. http://www .nilebasin.org/newsite/index.php?option=com_content&view=section& id=5&layout=blog&Itemid=68&lang=en.

Salman, Salman M. A. "The Helsinki Rules, the UN Watercourses Convention and the Berlin Rules: Perspectives on International Water Law." *Water Resources Development* 23, no. 4 (2007): 625–40.

Salman, Salman M. A. "The United Nations Watercourses Convention Ten Years Later: Why Has Its Entry into Force Proven Difficult?" *Water International* 32, no. 1 (2007): 1–15.

Salt, Jeremy. *The Unmaking of the Middle East: A History of Western Disorder in Arab Lands*. Berkeley: University of California Press, 2008.

Samman, Nabil. "Syrian Water Resources: Strategic Issues" (on file with authors).

Self, Benjamin L., and Ranjeet K. Singh. "Introduction." In *Investigating Confidence-Building Measures in the Asia–Pacific Region,* edited by Ranjeet K. Singh, ix–xi. Washington, DC: Henry L. Stimson Center, 1999. http://www.stimson.org/images/uploads/research-pdfs/cbmapintro.pdf.

Shaw, Stanford J., and Ezel K. Shaw. *History of the Ottoman Empire and Modern Turkey.* Vol. 2, *Reform, Revolution and Republic: The Rise of Modern Turkey, 1808–1975.* Cambridge: Cambridge University Press, 1977.

Smiley, Xan. "Iraq Wants Its Sovereignty Back." In "The World in 2009," special issue, *Economist,* 19 November 2008, 120.

Soffer, Arnon. *Rivers of Fire: The Conflict over Water in the Middle East.* Translated by Murray Rosovesky and Nina Kopaken. Lanham, MD: Rowman and Littlefield Publishers, 1999.

Stakhiv, Eugene Z. "Fact Sheet." Iraqi Ministry of Irrigation, 4 July 2003.

Stein, Jeff. "CIA's Unit on Climate Change Faces Uncertain Future." *Washington Post,* 11 January 2011. http://voices.washingtonpost.com/spy-talk/2011/01/cias_climate-change_unit_faces.html.

Stevanovic, Zoran, and Miroslav Markovic. *Hydrogeology of Northern Iraq.* Vol. 1, *Climate, Hydrology, Geomorphology and Geology.* Rome: Food and Agriculture Organization, 2004.

Strategic Foresight Group. *The Blue Peace: Rethinking Middle East Water.* Mumbai: Strategic Foresight Group, 2011.

Streusand, Douglas E. *Islamic Gunpowder Empires: Ottomans, Safavids, and Mughals.* Boulder, CO: Westview, 2010.

Syrian Arab Republic Ministry of Agriculture and Agrarian Reform, National Agricultural Policy Center. *National Programme for Food Security in the Syrian Arab Republic.* Damascus: National Agricultural Policy Center, 2010.

Traub, James. "Turkey's Rules." *New York Times Magazine*, 23 January 2011.

Travaglia, Carlo, and Niccolo Dainelli. *Groundwater Search by Remote Sensing: A Methodological Approach*. Rome: Food and Agriculture Organization of the United Nations, 2003.

Trondalen, Jon Martin. *Water and Peace for the People: Possible Solutions to Water Disputes in the Middle East*. Paris: United Nations Educational, Scientific, and Cultural Organization (UNESCO), 2008.

Turkish Embassy. *Foreign Policy—Synopsis*. Washington, DC: Turkish Embassy, 2011. http://www.washington.emb.mfa.gov.tr/MFA.aspx.

U.S. Department of Agriculture (USDA). *USDA at Work for Agriculture in Iraq*. Fact sheet. November 2009.

U.S. Department of Defense. *Quadrennial Defense Review Report*. Washington, DC: U.S. Department of Defense, 2010. http://www.defense.gov/qdr/images/QDR_as_of_12Feb10_1000.pdf.

———. *The National Military Strategy of the United States of America 2011: Redefining America's Military Leadership*. Washington, DC: U.S. Department of Defense, 2011.

———. *Defense Budget Priorities and Choices*. Washington, DC: U.S. Department of Defense, 2012.

———. *Sustaining Global Leadership: Priorities for 21st Century Defense*. Washington, DC: U.S. Department of Defense, 2012.

U.S. Department of State, Bureau of Oceans and International Environmental Scientific Affairs. *U.S. Water Partnership*. Washington, DC: Department of State, 2012. http://www.state.gov/e/ocs/rls/fs/2012/186581.htm.

U.S. Energy Information Administration. "How Dependent Are We on Foreign Oil?" U.S. Energy Information Administration. http://tonto.eia.doe.gov/energy_in_brief/foreign_oil_dependence.cfm.

U.S. Marine Corps. *Marine Corps Vision and Strategy 2025*. Washington, DC: Headquarters United States Marine Corps, [2008?]. http://www.marines .mil/news/publications/Documents/Vision%20Strat%20lo%20res.pdf.

UNESCO (United Nations Educational, Scientific and Cultural Organization) Office of Public Information. "Science Agenda—Framework for Action." United Nations Educational, Scientific and Cultural Organization. http://www.unesco.org/bpi/science/vf/content/press/franco/16.htm.

United Nations (UN). "Other Legal Questions: Progressive Development and Codification of the Rules of International Law Relating to International Watercourses." In *Yearbook of the United Nations*, 817–19. New York: United Nations, 1970. http://unyearbook.un.org/unyearbook .html?name=1970index.html.

———. Convention on the Law of the Non-Navigational Uses of International Watercourses. Adopted by the UN General Assembly on 21 May 1997. UN General Assembly Resolution 51/229. www.un.org/documents/ga /res/51/ares51-229.htm.

———. *A More Secure World: Our Shared Responsibility*. New York: United Nations Department of Public Information, 2004. http://www.un.org /secureworld/report2.pdf.

United States Agency for International Development (USAID). *The Role of Agriculture in Achieving Strategic Development Objectives in Iraq*. Agricultural Policy Dialogue Series #1. 2010.

———. *Advancing the Blue Revolution Initiative: Quarterly Report 7; January–March 2009*. http://pdf.usaid.gov/pdf_docs/PDACT089.pdf (accessed 16 July 2012).

Wada, Yoshihide, Ludovicus P. H. van Beek, Cheryl M. van Kempen, Josef W. T. M. Reckman, Slavek Vasak, and Marc F. P. Bierkens. "Global Depletion of Groundwater Resources." *Geophysical Research Letters* 37, L20402 (2010). doi:10.1029/2010GL044571.

Washington Times. "Iraqi Kurds Demand OK for Oil Deals Made in Self-Ruled Areas." 29 December 2010.

Water Encyclopedia. "Hydropolitics." Advameg. http://www.water encyclopedia.com/Hy-La/Hydropolitics.html.

Whittaker, Joel, and Anand Varghese. *The Tigris-Euphrates River Basin: A Science Diplomacy Opportunity*. Peacebrief 20. Washington, DC: United States Institute of Peace, 2010. http://www.usip.org/files/resources /PB%2020%20Tigris-Euphrates_River_Basin.pdf.

Wolf, Aaron T. "Conflict and Cooperation Along International Waterway." *Water Policy* 1, no. 2 (1998): 251–65.

———. "Criteria for Equitable Allocations: The Heart of International Water Conflict." *Natural Resources Forum* 23, no. 1 (1999): 3–30.

———. "Shared Waters: Conflict and Cooperation." *Annual Review of Environment and Resources* 32 (November 2007): 241–69. http://www.ann ualreviews.org/doi/abs/10.1146/annurev.energy.32.041006.101434?jour nalCode=energy.

World Water Council, ed. *E-Conference Synthesis: Virtual Water Trade — Conscious Choices*. 2004. http://www.waterfootprint.org/Reports virtual _water_final_synthesis.pdf.

Yinanç, Barçin. "Turkish Ties with N Iraq to Continue despite Cable Revelations, Official Says." *Hürriyet Daily News* (Turkey), 9 December 2010.

Zanotti, Jim. *Turkey-U.S. Defense Cooperation: Prospects and Challenges*. Washington, DC: Congressional Research Service, 2011.

Zimmer, Daniel, and Daniel Renault. "Virtual Water in Food Production and Global Trade Review of Methodological Issues and Preliminary Results." http://www.fao.org/nr/water/docs/VirtualWater_article_DZDR.pdf.

Zisser, Eyal. "Where Is Bashar al-Assad Heading?" *Middle East Quarterly* 15, no. 1 (Winter 2008), 35–40.

INDEX

al-Thawrah Dam (Tabaqah Dam), 38, 105, 108

al-Zubaidi, Mohammed, 183, 186

Ahmedinejad, President Mahmoud, 76–77

American Association for the Advancement of Science Center for Science Diplomacy, 231–32

Anglo-Persian Oil Company, 28

Arab Spring, 59, 69

Arabs, 20–21, 33

    Abdallah, 33

    Faisal, 33

    Ibn Saud, 33

Arab Water Academy, 249–50

Arab Water Council, 250

Armenians (people), 30–32

Ataturk Dam, 95, 100, 168

Ataturk, Mustafa Kemal, 30, 34, 54

asymmetric power, 180–82

Babylon, 19–20

    Cyrus the Great, 23

    Hammurabi, 20

    Hanging Gardens, 23

    Nebuchadnezzar II, 23

    Nahrawan Canal, 23

    Nimrod Dam, 23

Baghdad, 25, 26, 29, 56

Balfour Declaration, 29

Barzani, President Massoud, 51, 76

Berwari, Minister of Municipalities and Public Works Nasreen, 177–78

Blue Peace: Rethinking Middle East Water, The (Strategic Foresight Group), 255–56

Brabeck-Letmathe, Peter, 9

Bush, President George W., 66–67

Centre for Environmental Studies and Resource Management in Norway (CESAR), 102–3, 264

Chesnoff, Richard Z., 10

Clinton, Secretary of State Hillary R., 228–29, 236

Clinton, President William J. "Bill," 66

climate change, 129–33

collaborative modeling and management, 262

Colorado River, 89, 252–53

confidence-building measures (CBMs), 246–48

Conflict Early Warning and Response Mechanism (CEWARN), 260, 265

Convention of Friendship and Good Neighbourly Relations, 37

Convention on the Law of Non-navigational Uses of International Watercourses (UN Watercourses Convention), 173, 183, 197–98

Fertile Crescent, 18–20

    Mesopotamia, 22–23

First World War, 28–31

France, 29–30, 57, 153, 200

Fromkin, David, 27

Ganges Treaty, 248

GAP (Guneydogu Anadolu Projesi). *See* Southeastern Anatolia Project

Gaza Flotilla Incident (*Mavi Marmara*), 56

Geographic information system (GIS), 215, 217

Geopolicity report (*Managing the Tigris Euphrates Watershed: The Challenge Facing Iraq*), 254–55

Gleick, Peter H., 6

global warming, U.S. Defense Department position, 3

Goodman, Robert (U.S. pilot), 60

Great Zab (river), 144–47

Greece, 30–31

Gul, President Abdullhah, 42–43

Gulf of Maine Information Exchange (GOMINFOEX), 227

Habbaniyah Lake, 38

Harmon Doctrine, 165, 199

Harran Plain, 91

Helsinki Rules on the Uses of the Waters of International Rivers (Helskini Rules), 196

High-Level Strategic Cooperation Councils, 57–58

Hindiyah Barrage, 26–27

Hizballah, 56, 59, 78, 79

Hussein, Saddam, 12, 35–36, 137

Hussein-McMahon letters, 29

Hydropolitics, 157–63

    riparian positions, 163–78

Integrated Water Resources Management (IWRM), 243–46

International Center for Agricultural Research in Dry Areas, 264

International Center for Biosaline Agriculture, 218, 249

International Centre for Integrated Mountain Development, 233

International Centre for Integrated Basin Development (proposed), 234–36, 258

international custom, 194

international law, 194

International Law Commission, 197

International Monetary Fund (IMF), 59

international rivers, 193

international water law and hydropolitics, 205–7

International Water Resources Association, 203

Iran (Islamic Republic of Iran), 50

Iraq (*continued*)

    surface water resources and infrastructure, 115–19, 124

    water and security, 64–65

    water usage and management, 115, 123–24, 230

Israel, 56, 78–80

    invasion of Lebanon 2006, 79

    Operation Cast Lead (Gaza 2008), 79

Joint Technical Committee on Regional Waters, 12, 174

Joint Trilateral Committee, 13

Kaplan, Robert, 240

Karakaya Dam, 39

Karkamis Dam, 166–67

Keban Dam, 38

Khabur (Bassel al-Assad) Dam, 108–9

Kĭbaroğlu, Ayşegül, 250

Kirkuk, 151

Kitchener, Lord Horatio, 28–29

Kolars, John F., 103, 134–35, 188, 250

Koran, 21

Kraska, James, 246–47

Kurdish Democratic Party (KDP), 51, 150

Peace Pipeline Proposal (Ceyhan and Seyhan Rivers), 172–73

Petraeus, General David H., 52, 75–76

PKK. *See* Kurdistan Workers Party

potential threats and outcomes, 239–43

Qaddafi, Colonel Muammar, 59, 69, 70

Ramsar Convention for Wetlands, 112–13

Rasheed, Minister of Water Resources Abdul Latif, 177

Reagan, President Ronald W., 35

Rumsfeld, Secretary of Defense Donald H., 67

salination (salinity), 21–22

Salman, M. A. Salman, 203

Sanliurfa Tunnel, 188–89

science and diplomacy, 212–25, 234, 261–62, 266

Seljuk Turks, 25

Shatt al-Arab, 18, 28

Sistani, Grand Ayatollah Ali, 51

Southeastern Anatolia Project (GAP), 11–12, 44, 95–96
    master plan and potential, 38–39, 96–101

Strategic Foresight Group, 136

strategic water, 2, 5, 16

U.S. Marine Corps

> Center for Emerging Threats and Opportunities, 73
>
> *2011 Edition of Flashpoints*, 73
>
> *Marine Corps Vision and Strategy 2025*, 4

Union of Soviet Socialist Republics (USSR), 35, 105, 110

Unver, Olcay, 263

virtual water, 9–10, 138. *See also* Allan, J. A. (Tony)

Washington State Department of Ecology, 231

water

> agricultural return flow, 90, 91
>
> desalination, 252–54
>
> freshwater availability, 133–39
>
> groundwater, 90–91
>
> salination (salinity), 21–22, 125–29, 222–23
>
> supply versus demand, 39, 87, 139–41
>
> total dissolved solids, 125–27
>
> waterlogging, 22
>
> water basin (water systems) 196–98, 219–21
>
> water deficit, 87, 140–41
>
> water-food trade, 10

About the Authors

Colonel Frederick M. Lorenz, USMC (Ret.), is a senior lecturer at the Jackson School of International Studies, University of Washington, where he currently teaches International Humanitarian Law and Water and Security in the Middle East. He served in the U.S. Marine Corps for 27 years as a judge advocate, including a tour as an infantry company commander. In 1992 and 1993, he was the Staff Judge Advocate for Operation Restore Hope in Somalia, and he returned there as Staff Judge Advocate to General Anthony Zinni for the UN evacuation in 1995. Before his retirement from the Marine Corps in 1998, he taught political science at National Defense University as well as the first course in environmental security at this institution. As a consultant to the World Water Assessment Program of UNESCO, he published the current online report *The Protection of Water Facilities under International Law.* He traveled regularly to Turkey, Syria, Iraq, and Jordan between 1997 and 2004, researching water and security issues in the Euphrates-Tigris basin. His email address is lorenz@uw.edu.

Lieutenant Colonel Edward J. Erickson, USA (Ret.), is a professor of military history at Marine Corps University in Quantico, Virginia. He is a field artilleryman and Turkish specialist with 16 years of overseas service in Europe and the Middle East. He served in Operations Desert Shield/ Desert Storm with the 3d Armored Division, Joint Endeavor in Bosnia with the NATO Implementation Force, and Operation Iraqi Freedom with the 4th Infantry Division. After retiring from active duty, Dr. Erickson worked as a high school teacher and school administrator in his hometown of Norwich, New York. He returned to Baghdad, Iraq, in 2007 for a year to teach as professor of political science at the Ministry of Defense Training and Development College. Since 2009, he has taught at the Marine Corps Command and Staff College. He is the author of 11 books about the Ottoman Army and modern Turkey, the most recent of which is *Gallipoli: The Ottoman Campaign*, as well as numerous articles on similar topics. Professor Erickson holds a doctorate in history from the University of Leeds in the United Kingdom. He can be contacted at ederickson100@gmail.com.